XML Elements of Style

XML Elements of Style

Simon St.Laurent

McGraw-Hill

New York San Francisco Washington, D.C.
Auckland Bogotá Caracas Lisbon London
Madrid Mexico City Milan Montreal New Delhi
San Juan Singapore Sydney Tokyo Toronto

McGraw-Hill

A Division of The ***McGraw-Hill*** *Companies*

1 2 3 4 5 6 7 8 9 0 AGM/AGM 9 0 4 3 2 1 0 9

ISBN 0-07-212220-X

The sponsoring editor for this book was Regina Brooks and the production supervisor was Clare Stanley. It was set in Stone Serif by Patricia Wallenburg.

Printed and bound by Quebecor Martinsburg.

This book is printed on recycled, acid-free paper containing a minimum of 50% recycled, de-inked fiber.

For Tracey, magic

Contents

Part 1 Elementary Rules of Usage

Acknowledgments

I owe Tracey Cranston St.Laurent infinite thanks for putting up with me throughout the writing of this book, and Spring, our dog, made certain that I got enough walking breaks.

Regina Brooks of McGraw-Hill got this book rolling and Jennifer Perillo helped it through production. Patricia Wallenburg did an excellent job on layout, as always.

Finally, I'd like to thank the XML community, especially the members of the xml-dev mailing list, for its tradition of active and thorough discussions, even on (perhaps especially on) the minutiae of the spec. Without that community and its constant striving to make XML great, this book would never have been written.

PART ONE

Elementary Rules of Usage

CHAPTER 1

XML Documents: An Overview

XML documents are containers for information. Within the primary container may be information and more containers, which themselves may contain information and more containers. These named containers form neatly hierarchical structures, creating an incredibly flexible and remarkably powerful framework for storing and exchanging information of all kinds, from memos to database tables to poetry to program structures to invoices. XML documents may also include or reference sets of rules describing their structures, which applications may use to validate that documents conform to those rules.

XML's main strength is its ability to store labeled information, and the ease with which new labels can be created to represent different kinds of information. A set of labels is often called a *vocabulary*. When large groups of people can accept a common vocabulary, or even declare it a standard of some sort, applications of many different kinds on many different kinds of computers and networks can share an understanding of the contents of XML documents using that vocabulary. Information that might previously have been stored in a single vendor's proprietary format is now exposed, using a cleanly structured format that labels its contents in plain text. Although understanding and agreeing on the labels and structures is still very much a challenge, XML provides a solid foundation that lets such work get started.

Unicode Text as the Foundation

All information within an XML document is stored as text, and is processed as a series of Unicode characters. Unicode is a character encoding defined by the Unicode Consortium. XML references both Unicode and ISO 10646, a standard from the International Organization for Standardization, which are supposed to stay in sync. More details of Unicode and ISO 10646 will be explored in Chapter 21, but for now it's enough to know that Unicode makes it possible to mix languages from all over the world much more easily than encodings like US-ASCII (which is pretty much limited to English), ISO-8859-1 or its siblings (which encode European languages), or Shift_JIS (which is one encoding for Japanese).

Within this series of characters, XML uses certain key characters (notably <, >, and &) to separate markup—labels and other information needing special processing—from the rest of the content. The information within the markup is used to build labeled structures containing the content and in some cases to build the content itself.

Although text isn't always the most efficient way to store information, it is easily processed, readily examined and edited, and more easily understood than binary formats. XML's origins in the document management and processing world of SGML give it an original bias toward textual representation, but this doesn't prohibit the use of XML for the storage of numeric information. On the other hand, it probably isn't the best idea to use XML to represent bitmapped graphics, sound, and video, where file size is critical given current limitations on transmission speeds.

Although all XML is text, and can be edited with ordinary text editors if desired, it is highly structured text that comes with a set of strict rules. These rules must be obeyed—deviations, according to the XML spec, should result in the XML processor that reads the document reporting an error and refusing to continue. XML is case-sensitive, requiring that all names match in case as well as letters precisely. (There are exceptions for language and character encoding codes that come from outside the XML recommendation, but otherwise this rule holds absolutely.)

Conformance: Well-formed and Valid Documents

The XML 1.0 recommendation describes two levels of conformance to these rules. Well-formed documents (and documents must be well-formed to deserve the name "XML document") must obey the basic syntax rules precisely. If a document violates any of the well-formedness constraints laid out in the XML 1.0 recommendation, document processing stops and the processor sends an error message to the application. Valid documents are well-formed documents that meet an additional set of strictures (the Document Type Definition, or DTD), most of which are actually created by a document designer, not the XML 1.0 recommendation itself. The validation process is optional, but can be very useful for making certain that documents contain all the parts they should.

Well-formedness is (generally) a property of the document itself. (Chapter 27 explores various complexities that sometimes cause problems with that description.) Validity involves comparing the contents of the Document Type Declaration presented in the prolog (and any external resources it may reference) and the document to determine if the document conforms to those descriptions. Validation is more about checking the structure of the document than about checking its content, though some limited content checking is available in XML 1.0.

Inside XML Documents

XML documents have three parts: the optional prolog, required root element, and optional miscellaneous material following the root element. The prolog usually contains material describing the root element that follows it, which holds the primary content of the XML document. The "miscellaneous" material at the end of the document is typically used for documentation, if it appears at all. The root element is the only part of an XML document that must appear.

The prolog may include the XML declaration, white space, comments, processing instructions, and the document type declaration. It usually contains information describing how to process the rest of the document, or comments describing the contents or versioning of the document. Chapter 2 describes the prolog in more detail. All of the contents of the prolog are optional.

The body of an XML document is a single ("root") element, which may hold content including attributes, text, and other elements. The *root element* is the core of the XML document, the real "payload." It's reasonable to say that the rest of the XML document is just information about how to process the document body. Chapter 3 (and much of the rest of the book) will explore the document body in greater detail. The root element begins, and the prolog ends, with the start tag of the root element, and the root element ends with its end tag.

Comments, processing instructions, and white space may follow the root element. This space could be used for extra documentation or processing instructions, although documents often end with the closing tag of the root element. Chapter 10 will note some possibilities for using these tools after the root element.

A Sample XML Document

The example below shows a nonsensical (though valid) XML document and the overall structure it contains.

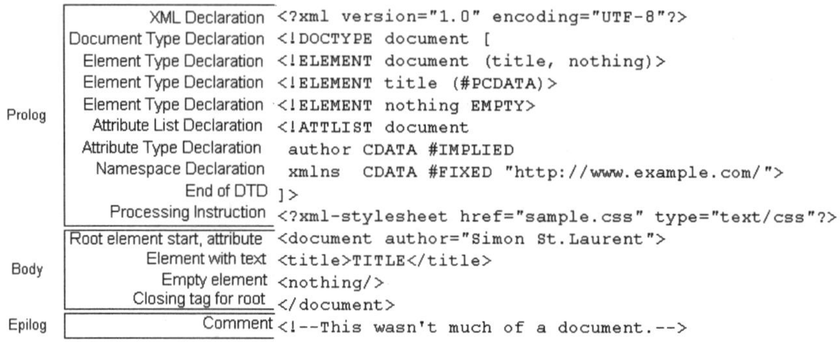

Prolog	XML Declaration	`<?xml version="1.0" encoding="UTF-8"?>`
	Document Type Declaration	`<!DOCTYPE document [`
	Element Type Declaration	`<!ELEMENT document (title, nothing)>`
	Element Type Declaration	`<!ELEMENT title (#PCDATA)>`
	Element Type Declaration	`<!ELEMENT nothing EMPTY>`
	Attribute List Declaration	`<!ATTLIST document`
	Attribute Type Declaration	`author CDATA #IMPLIED`
	Namespace Declaration	`xmlns CDATA #FIXED "http://www.example.com/">`
	End of DTD	`]>`
	Processing Instruction	`<?xml-stylesheet href="sample.css" type="text/css"?>`
Body	Root element start, attribute	`<document author="Simon St.Laurent">`
	Element with text	`<title>TITLE</title>`
	Empty element	`<nothing/>`
	Closing tag for root	`</document>`
Epilog	Comment	`<!--This wasn't much of a document.-->`

Figure 1.1 The structure of a simple valid (and nonsensical) XML document.

Most documents use some combination of the features shown here, though some documents may use additional features and many others will use fewer features. The prolog (which includes the DTD) provides information the parser or the application can use to process the document. The body consists of a single root element (document, in this case), and its contents. The epilog contains a comment in this case. Over the next two sections, we'll explore all of these parts in detail.

CHAPTER 2

Starting the Document: The Prolog

The prolog provides information about what is to follow in the root element. The prolog can identify the version of XML used and the character encoding, as well as connect the document to the document type definition describing its structure and potentially providing some of its content. The prolog may include the XML declaration, the document type declaration, white space, comments, and processing instructions. All the contents of the prolog are optional, although documents must have a document type declaration in order to be valid.

The XML declaration and document type declaration are discussed below. Comments and processing instructions are discussed in Chapter 9, and white space is discussed in Chapter 10.

The XML Declaration

The XML declaration must appear, if it is used, at the very beginning of a document. No white space or markup may come before the XML declaration, which may supply additional information useful for processing. In its simplest form, the XML declaration can look like:

```
<?xml?>
```

Although the XML declaration looks very much like a processing instruction (which also would begin with <? and end with ?>), it is its own type with its own strict rules.

Three parameters may be defined in the XML declaration, although all of them are optional. If the parameters are used, they must appear in the order described here. The first parameter is `version`. Documents based on XML 1.0 should identify their version as "1.0" as shown below.

```
<?xml version="1.0"?>
```

The next parameter is the `encoding` declaration, which identifies the character encoding used in this document. Chapter 21 will describe the use of this declaration in much more detail. All the XML documents presented in this book can be represented with an 8-bit Unicode transformation, called UTF-8, which all XML processors are required to recognize. An XML declaration for a document using this encoding might read:

```
<?xml version="1.0" encoding="UTF-8"?>
```

Unlike the rest of the XML declarations, character encoding identifiers are not case-sensitive. The declaration above could use `"utf-8"` in place of `"UTF-8"`.

In general, it is always a good idea to include an XML declaration identifying both the version and the encoding of the document. The `encoding` declaration makes it easier for parsers to process your documents correctly, and the version number ensures that applications built for possible future versions of XML will have some way of dealing with your "legacy" documents.

The final parameter is the `standalone` declaration, which can be used to tell a parser that a document contains no references to external declarations, which may be encountered in the DTD, described below. If the value of `standalone` is "yes" and the document refers to an external declaration, an error will be raised. If the value of `standalone` is "no" (or the `standalone` declaration was omitted), no error will be raised. Typically, the `standalone` declaration is omitted. However, if a document made no references to external declarations, the XML declaration could look like:

```
<?xml version="1.0" encoding="UTF-8" standalone="yes"?>
```

The `standalone` declaration cannot be used to tell a processor that it needs to retrieve external declarations, a problem discussed in detail in Chapter 27. All it can do is raise an error if `standalone` is set to yes and a reference to an external resource is encountered by a validating parser.

Two more things about the declarations above are important. First, XML 1.0 *does* let you choose whether to use single or double quotes around the values you specify. (They have to match, however—you can't use "1.0" as a version number, for instance.) Second, the order is important. You can leave out any given piece, but you can't put the standalone declaration before the encoding declaration or the version declaration at the end, for example. This declaration is legal:

```
<?xml encoding="UTF-8" standalone="yes"?>
```

but this declaration is not legal:

```
<?xml encoding="UTF-8" version="1.0"?>
```

The rest of the prolog or (if there isn't any more prolog) the root element may follow the XML declaration.

The Document Type Declaration

The document type declaration connects information describing your document structure and its content, called a *grammar,* to your document. This information may be included directly within the document type declaration or included by reference to an external resource containing declarations, or both. All the declarations contained within or referenced by the document type declaration form the document type definition, or DTD, for a given document. For a document to be valid, it must contain a document type declaration that identifies a grammar that describes the structure and possibly the content of the document.

The document type declaration (sometimes called the *DOCTYPE declaration*) uses slightly different syntax, depending on where the declarations that form the grammar are actually kept—inside this document type declaration, in a separate document, or both. If the declarations appear only within the document type declaration, the document type declaration will look like:

```
<!DOCTYPE rootElement [...declarations...]>
```

The name of the root element of the document is always the first thing included in the document type declaration. For the document to be valid, its root element must be the one declared in this declaration. Within the braces following the root element, declarations, parameter entity references (see Chapter 14), processing instructions, and comments may appear.

The declarations included directly within the document type declaration are called the *internal DTD subset.* A complete DTD for a given document is the combination of the internal and external DTD subsets, if either or both are declared. The external subset includes declarations stored in external *resources*. These resources are typically files, but they could be generated on the fly or retrieved from a system with no concept of "file," so it is often better to call them resources. The resources referenced by document type declarations may only contain declarations, parameter entity references, comments, and processing instructions, using proper XML syntax but containing no elements, attributes, or free-floating text. XML allows the document type declaration to reference these resources through two different mechanisms, which may be combined if desired. The simpler mechanism uses a system identifier—a Uniform Resource Identifier (URI). URIs include the familiar URLs that make it easy to point to a file on a Web server, for instance. The syntax for a document type declaration that uses a system identifier looks like either:

```
<!DOCTYPE rootElement SYSTEM "uri" [...declarations...]>
```

or, if there are no declarations:

```
<!DOCTYPE rootElement SYSTEM "uri">
```

For example, if a document needed to reference the DTD for XML Processing Description Language (a project of the author's, not an "official" W3C project), the document type declaration might look like:

```
<!DOCTYPE xpd SYSTEM "http://www.simonstl.com/projects/xpdl/v1/xpd.dtd">
```

The external DTD subset will consist of the declarations in the resource referenced by the URI, while the internal DTD subset will include the declarations made between the braces ([ ]) of the document type declaration itself. There are slightly different rules for the two subsets' contents.

XML offers another approach to referencing external resources, using *public identifiers*. Public identifiers are a convention often used in the SGML world from which XML was created, but never standardized or supported with widely implemented infrastructure. As a result, XML allows the use of public identifiers, but requires that they be followed by URIs in case there is no way to resolve the public identifier. Applications need to provide their own mechanisms for resolving public identifiers, and no generic directory service has appeared. URIs typically rest on the foundations of the TCP/IP networking system at the core of the Internet and the Domain Name Service, or DNS, which provides friendlier names than the numbers used as IP addresses, both of which are widely implemented.

Public identifiers have four parts, combined into a single string and separated with double slashes (//). The first piece of a public identifier is a plus (+) or minus (-). If the identifier references a standard from the International Organization for Standardization (ISO), or a standards body recognized by ISO, this first field will be a plus. Otherwise, it will be a minus. Note that the W3C, the "standards body" of the Web and the creator of

XML, is not a standards body by this strict definition. All the public identifiers created by the W3C therefore start with a minus. The second part identifies the creator of the standard—W3C, for example, or SIMONSTL-COM (for the author's own work). Unlike the Internet's naming system, there is no central registry handing out these names, and no way to determine what a creator references. The third field is the name of what is being referenced, and the fourth field is the language used to describe it, using the ISO 639 language identifiers described in Chapter 21.

For example, the public identifier for the W3C's HTML 4.0 is:

```
-//W3C//DTD HTML 4.0 Final//EN
```

The minus indicates that this is not the product of ISO, the W3C identifies the keeper of the resource, "DTD HTML 4.0 Final" describes the resource—the DTD for HTML 4.0, and "EN" identifies the language used within the resource as English.

Because there is no generic way to "resolve" a public identifier to a resource, the XML specification requires that public identifiers be followed by a URI. The document type declaration looks like either:

```
<!DOCTYPE rootElement PUBLIC "publicIdentifier" "uri"
          [...declarations...]>
```

or, if there are no internal declarations:

```
<!DOCTYPE rootElement PUBLIC "publicIdentifier" "uri">
```

For example, to reference the XPDL DTD noted above, a document type declaration using a public identifier might look like:

```
<!DOCTYPE xpd PUBLIC "-//SIMONSTLCOM//DTD XPDL//EN"
          "http://www.simonstl.com/projects/xpdl/v1/xpd.dtd">
```

System identifiers tend to receive much wider use than public identifiers in XML applications that aren't based on older SGML models, but you can still use public identifiers. Generally, use the public identifier recommended in a specification if there is one. If there isn't, just use the system identifier approach, which is generally simpler to resolve. (There are some cases, notably in secure environments, where particular URIs may not be available to all users, and applications may need to use public identifiers supported by an internal catalog.)

The document type declaration lets you build a complete DTD from the combination of the internal and external subsets. Although it might have been convenient for the rules of both subsets to be identical (they do, in fact, use the same declarations), there are a few extra rules for the internal subset that will be covered in detail in Chapter 14. In short, all parameter entities inside the internal subset must contain complete declarations, while parameter entities in the external subset may use parameter entities within declarations as well. `INCLUDE` and `IGNORE` marked sections, described in Chapter 16, can only be used in the external subset. These differences can make it difficult to move DTD components between the two areas, and sometimes encourage the use of an external DTD.

The main advantage the internal subset retains over the external subset is that its declarations are given priority—when they are allowed, declarations in the internal subset can override declarations in the external subset. (Elements may only be declared once, so element declarations cannot be overridden.) The internal subset also has the advantage that all XML processors, both validating and non-validating, must process the declarations it contains. Non-validating processors aren't required to load external resources, so putting declarations in the internal subset is one way of ensuring their use in all circumstances. Declarations in the internal subset that reference external resources may also be ignored, so this doesn't solve all problems, but it can be helpful in some situations.

There are some serious questions still remaining, however, about the wisdom of putting declarations describing a document's structure within the document. "Self-describing" documents are convenient for many applications, but allowing documents to designate their structures on an individual basis (and, using the internal subset, to override some of those structures) makes it difficult for applications to rely on XML's built-in validation process to determine whether a document is suited for a given application's handlers. The document type declaration may be one of the first things to disappear as the W3C moves toward newer schema approaches, as described in Chapter 29. XML 1.0 documents may use this approach safely, provided that document designers and authors follow a few basic rules:

- Don't use the internal subset to override declarations from the external subset. There are many occasions when this may be useful (which will be noted), but in general, it's a potentially dangerous practice.
- Use the internal subset for document-specific extensions to the external subset, particularly entities. It may be convenient to declare entities that are appropriate to only a single document, but as soon as you find that they can be shared among multiple documents, move them to the external subset.
- Extending DTDs is generally better done in the external subset, where extensions can be shared among multiple documents and a wider set of tools is available.
- Occasionally documents may use the internal subset to declare parameter entities whose values control `INCLUDE`- and `IGNORE`-marked sections in the external subset. If you like `IGNORE` and `INCLUDE`, this may be nec-

essary, but there are often more readily controlled alternatives to these marked sections. (This issue will be described in more detail in Chapter 16.)

CHAPTER 3

Foundations: Elements, Attributes, and Namespaces

Elements, attributes, and namespaces do most of the work of markup. Elements define named structures in documents that contain information. Attributes provide annotation of elements and also contain named information. Namespaces allow you to avoid the dangers of overlapping names by creating unique identifiers that are applied to element and attribute names through prefixes. Elements and attributes provide the core structures of XML documents, breaking documents into pieces and identifying those pieces, while namespaces allow you to make those identifications more precise. The data modeling needed to build XML documents requires determining which structures to use when, and how to identify them. Although the many details of XML provide many more features, this core data modeling will largely determine whether your XML-based formats are successful.

"Sculpting" and "Designing" XML

There are several approaches you can take to create XML document structures, and determine the ways in which you'll use elements and attributes. No single approach is best in all circumstances, and those who claim otherwise are probably trying to sell something. Although XML may be ferocious about syntax, it is generous in providing room to experiment with structure. There are two levels of conformance to the XML 1.0 Recommendation: "well-formed" and "valid." Well-formed documents must meet all the syntactical rules, but aren't required to provide a description of their document structure. Valid documents must meet all the rules for well-formed documents, plus an additional set of rules that requires them to provide and live up to a description of their document structure. (For more on the differences between valid and well-formed documents and the parsers that process them, see Chapter 27.)

Because XML allows you to process XML documents without requiring a description of their structure, it's possible, indeed easy, to get started modeling data in XML by creating XML files containing those data. Typically, you start with a sample document—or many sample documents—and mark it up by hand, fragmenting the document as you go by adding elements and attributes that identify important structures. You can start with a memo, a database table, a spreadsheet—it doesn't have to be a conventional "document." After you've done this to a number of documents, you can then explore your results and create descriptions of the overall structure. If your goal is to create valid documents, you can then move on to the descriptive phase. Your original data is the block into which you'll "carve" description; this will emerge as a sculpted piece when the XML structure is complete.

Other people prefer to start with a description, formal or otherwise, that lays out the structure of what *should* go into the XML document. This approach is best used when you're creating a new format from scratch, with no prior documents to consider, but can be combined with an empirical examination of documents to add more grounding in existing formats. Working with abstracted descriptions is often easier for large groups of people working together than working with a set of particular documents. If you're integrating different types of information, or creating mechanisms for exchanging information among different types of users, this approach, where you design the documents rather than finding design inside the existing materials, is often more appropriate.

These two approaches don't have to be exclusive, and in fact they often feed into each other. An initial round of sculpting may lead to a basic design which is then abstracted and refined, only to be tested again in documents and refined again. The sculpting route is often an easier way to get started, especially for newcomers to XML, but one of XML's largest advantages is its support for both these approaches.

Elements

Elements provide most of the structure within an XML document. Elements create named hierarchies that may contain information. The beginnings and ends of elements are marked up directly in the flow of text, separated from the text by the ubiquitous delimiters < and >, and containing a name for the element and possible attributes. The name of an element must begin with a letter, underscore, or colon and may contain letters, digits, hyphens, underscores, and periods. (Also see the discussion of colons in the namespaces section below.) Element names may not begin with "xml," "XML," or any variation in case—these names are reserved for the W3C. Every element must have either a combination of a start tag and an end tag, or an empty tag that indicates the element has no content. Start tags begin with < and end with >, end tags begin with </ and end with >, and empty tags begin with < and end with />. For example, in:

```
<element>information...</element> <emptyElement />
```

`<element>` is the start tag, and `</element>` is the end tag. Together, they define an element named "element" that contains the content information.... `<emptyElement />` is an empty tag that defines an element named "emptyElement" that has no content.

Elements may contain textual content and other complete elements, and the body of an XML document must be contained in a single element. Elements are not allowed to overlap, ever. Every non-emplty element must conclude (have an end tag) before the end of the element that contains it. Every XML document is a set of containers (even if there is only one container). Creating XML document structures is primarily a matter of choosing among strategies for containing information and identifying the containers. Although XML's containment approach is fundamentally hierarchical, all kinds of structures can be built within that hierarchical framework, from highly structured tables and object representations to much more chaotic "traditional" documents. Containers are often structured using a small set of patterns that repeat throughout a document, making it easier to compartmentalize information for processing.

This hierarchical set of container structures comes with its own vocabulary, which derives from two different metaphors: *families* and *trees*. The two metaphors are commonly mixed, but are typically used to describe slightly different aspects of an XML document. The tree metaphors are limited to the extreme ends of the containment hierarchy, while the family references are used throughout. The "root element" of a document is the first element that appears, which contains all of the other elements. "Leaf elements" are elements that contain only text, with no other content. "Leaf nodes" are any kind of XML nodes that do not contain any further nodes. The textual content of an element, for instance, is a "leaf node." See the sample document below.

```
<label>
   <name>John Doe</name>
   <address>
      <street>123 Main Street</street>
      <city>Anytown</city>
```

```
    <state>NY</state>
    <zipcode>12345</zipcode>
  </address>
</label>
```

The element label is the root element, containing all the other elements. The name, street, city, state, and zipcode elements are leaf elements, which contain no other elements. The address element is neither a root element nor a leaf element. (Occasionally, the terms "branch" and "twig" are used to describe structures between the root and leaves.)

The family metaphors are used more broadly, describing larger portions of the document hierarchy. Elements may have parents, children, ancestors, descendants, and siblings. The term parent is used to describe an element that directly contains the current element. For example, the address element in the example above is the parent of the street, city, state, and zipcode elements, while the label element is the parent of the name and address elements. Similarly, child elements are directly contained by parent elements. The street, city, state, and zipcode elements are children of the address element, while the address element and the name element are children of the label element. Ancestors and descendants are much like parents and children, except that they can be further removed up or down the containment hierarchy. The street, city, state, and zipcode elements are descendants of both the address element and the label element, while the address element and label element are described as their ancestors. Siblings are elements that share a parent element. For example, the street, city, state, and zipcode elements are all children of the address element, and are therefore called *siblings*. Similarly, the name and address elements are siblings, sharing the common parent label. Because the label element is the root element, it has no siblings.

Although there are occasional references to aunt, uncle, cousin, grandparent, and grandchild elements, the basic "family" metaphors described above provide a core set of meaning and functionality that isn't likely to expand any time soon.

Attributes

Attributes provide additional information about an element within its start tag. (If the element is empty, this information goes in the empty tag.) Attributes are name/value pairs, and there may be any number of attributes associated with an element. The name of an attribute must begin with a letter, and may contain letters, digits, hyphens, underscores, and periods. (Again, see the discussion of colons in the namespaces section below.) Like element names, attribute names may not begin with "xml", "XML", or any variation in case—except for a few attributes defined by the XML Recommendation itself and other W3C Recommendations. An equals sign (=) must appear after the name of the attribute, immediately followed by a value for the attribute in quotes—either single quotes (') or double quotes (") are acceptable, but they have to match, and the use of quotes is mandatory. The value may contain any acceptable text characters, including the character and general entity references discussed in Chapter 12, but not <, >, & (unless used for a general entity reference), or the type of quote used to indicate the value. You may use single quotes within a value demarcated by double quotes, and vice versa. You may use any kind or amount of whitespace (spaces, tabs, line breaks, etc.) to separate attribute values within a start tag, and may also use whitespace between the name of the attribute, the equals sign, and the attribute value

For example, suppose the `label` element used in the example above came with some extra information about the source and type of the information it contained. Its start tag might then contain attributes describing the `label`, as shown below:

```
<label record="N2004" type="customer" source="list37">
```

Applications processing the `label` element could now find out that this label is record `N2004` from the source `list37` and that the information contained inside the label is for a customer. Attributes are containers for (typically) smaller chunks of information that is stored directly within an element's start tag, rather than as a child element. Attributes may contain only textual information—they cannot, for example, store small XML documents with their own element hierarchies. Typically, attributes are used to annotate elements or to store information in a more compact form than sub-elements provide. In particular, attributes are often used to supply additional meaning to empty tags. For example, all of the information in the XHTML `img` tag is supplied by the attributes:

```
<img href="mygraphic.gif" height="200" width="400" />
```

An HTML application would know that an image appears in the document when it encounters the `img` element, but which image and what size are key questions answered by the named attribute values.

Naming Your Elements and Attributes

While XML has very tight rules about structure, the rules it provides for naming things are very loose— it's up to developers to choose their own vocabularies. Naming is often just as important to a successful project as structure development. A good structure with obscure or inconsistent naming conventions can be very difficult to use. XML's insistence on case-sensitivity also requires that you hammer down conventions more tightly than is necessary in other environments. That insistence on case sensitivity doesn't require that you create all your names using the same case conventions, but it does mean that everyone will be stuck using the conventions that applications (and DTDs, in a validating environment) expect to see.

There are several competing traditions for markup naming conventions. Abbreviations (like P for paragraph or B for bold) are common, sometimes even necessary, but can become cryptic very quickly. Many of the reasons people consider HTML to be difficult "code" have to do with its inconsistent abbreviations. More verbose names can also be used, enhancing clarity at some cost in file size. Developers frequently mix and match, keeping short words, abbreviating long words, and hoping it all makes sense in the end. If you use abbreviations, make certain to document the full meaning. Remember that all the markup names you create—for elements, attributes, and everything else—is description that computers and most likely programmers and users are going to need to understand at some point. 100% consistency isn't necessarily an appropriate goal, especially if you're mixing terms from different sources, but a consistent approach can make documents and document structures easier for humans to understand, ultimately simplifying the task of getting those documents into application structures.

In matters of case, there are several competing viewpoints, each with its own roughly justifiable arguments. Some developers like to put names in UPPER CASE. Lots of HTML and SGML is already in upper case, and developers who handcode documents often find that it makes it easier to separate the markup from the content. Other developers prefer lower case, and most W3C activity seems headed this direction. Some developers use upper case letters to indicate the start of a word in a name composed of multiple words, like `salePrice` or `SalePrice`. Different systems and organizations have different rules for handling this issue, and you'll need to find approaches that can satisfy the users of your particular vocabularies.

Elements and/vs. Attributes (and Other Alternatives)

Both elements and attributes are named containers for information, and sometimes they can seem interchangeable. Attributes can be used as the equivalents of leaf elements, in cases where the parent element doesn't mix text with elements. For example, the `address` element presented above as:

```
<address>
   <street>123 Main Street</street>
   <city>Anytown</city>
   <state>NY</state>
   <zipcode>12345</zipcode>
</address>
```

can be redescribed as:

```
<address
   street="123 Main Street"
   city="Anytown"
   state="NY"
   zipcode="12345"
/>
```

The version using attributes is smaller—70 characters as opposed to 110—and stores the same information. For some uses—exchanging database tables in a compact format, for instance—this approach is probably just as good as using sub-elements. The information is equivalent, and it's not difficult to move from one version to the other if necessary.

The reverse is also possible. The attributes applied to the `label` element may be presented more verbosely as child elements:

```
<label>
   <record>N2004</N2004>
   <type>customer</type>
   <source>list37</source>
...
```

Although the examples above suggest that attributes and leaf elements are interchangeable, there are many cases where they aren't interchangeable, and an appreciation of those cases is important to the development of a consistent approach to using elements and attributes. Maintaining a consistent approach will simplify the creation of processors and style sheets for your XML documents considerably. Although elements and attributes are both named containers of data, most processors treat them very differently, and the tools for describing element and attribute types within a document type declaration are very different, as described in Chapters 7 and 8. The key differences include:

- Elements may contain other elements or text, while attributes may contain only text.
- The order of elements is always preserved; the order of attributes is not considered importnat. (Some parsers preserve order, others don't.)
- While elements may contain unnamed text nodes (when, for example, text is interspersed with elements), they may not contain unnamed attributes.
- Attribute type declarations allow you to declare default and fixed values for attributes, although there are no default or fixed values for elements.
- Attribute type declarations allow you to restrict the value of the attribute to a set of predefined choices. No such feature is available for elements.

- There are many more types of attributes (described in Chapter 8), each with its own set of possibilities and restrictions. Although elements may have declared content types, they have less meaning to the parser itself than attribute content types.
- Processors that use the SAX interface return attributes as a set with the start of an element, while child elements are returned one by one.
- An element may have only one attribute with a given name, although you can have any number of child elements of the same name, if not prohibited by your DTD.
- Over the years of SGML and HTML usage, the convention that element content is "presentable" content and attributes are "invisible" annotation has generally prevailed. The W3C's own XML-based presentation languages tend to reflect this convention, as does Cascading Style Sheets (CSS).

You will still have to choose between the two approaches on a case-by-case basis. In general, the path of least resistance is to treat element content as "real" content and reserve attributes for annotation of that content, or to reference content outside the element, like images or other documents. Default values and restraints on attribute content certainly give attributes a boost, but Chapter 8 will demonstrate some of the limitations of those restraints in XML 1.0. (The W3C's schema developments may expand the restraint options for both attributes and elements, reducing the differences between the two.) If you're building your own custom systems for handling your XML, you may of course make these choices however you'd like, but in the long run you may find it easier to adopt a single convention and stick with it. A key problem to remember is that switching from an element to an attribute or vice versa can be very difficult if you're working in a validating environment, so it's well worth taking the time to analyze current and future needs.

Another issue that frequently arises in XML design is the use of compound structures within a single XML element or attribute value. Notations like MM-DD-YYYY for dates and the convention in Cascading Style Sheets (CSS) for storing multiple properties in a single attribute both require additional processing of the results returned by the XML parser. This kind of processing may be appropriate in some cases—dates are often expressed by a convention, and expressing month, date, and year as separate elements or even attributes is unwieldy. For CSS, the centralization of inline style information into a single attribute helps separate presentation information from document content and simplifies DTDs considerably. The use of these types of conventions is frequently derided, however, by purists who would prefer that all parsing be done by the XML parser itself, to simplify the work of the application developer. This particular battle is far from over.

Namespaces

Namespaces are a controversial addition to XML, though it appears that they are here to stay. Namespaces allow the developers of XML vocabularies to uniquely identify their vocabularies with a Uniform Resource Identifier (URI). URIs include the familiar Uniform Resource Locator (URL) and Uniform Resource Numbers (URN). Because there is no consistent directory of URIs or URNs, many namespaces continue to be identified with ordinary URLs. Namespaces don't require that anything be stored at the URI they use; the URI is purely an identifier that connects to element and attribute names to make them unique.

Marking elements with unique URIs makes new classes of processors possible. An application could include sets of objects that apply to particular namespaces, and use those objects any time the namespace was encountered in a document. *Metadata* (information describing the document that isn't really part of its content) could be processed separately from the main body of the document, building a catalog of sites that have been visited, for example. XML-based graphics formats (like SVG) could be presented as graphics in a browser window. Applications could build on an XML application architecture that parses documents and passes off the results to the appropriate processor based on the namespace URI, juggling the applications as necessary.

Because element and attribute names can only use a restricted set of characters, and because URIs are typically long and unwieldy strings, the "Namespaces in XML Recommendation" (**http://www.w3.org/TR/REC-xml-names**) uses prefixes to connect namespace identifiers to element and attribute names, which are called "the local part." The prefix appears at the start of the element or attribute name, followed by a colon, and then by the element or attribute name. Prefixes must obey the same rules as element and attribute names: start with a letter or underscore (no colons!), and contain only letters, digits, hyphens, periods, and underscores. The prefixes are stand-ins for the URIs, and can change to accommodate conflicts between prefix names when information of multiple types is combined. At all times, the URI referenced by the prefix is the only thing that matters, and that URI is purely an identifier—it doesn't have to reference any kind of document, though it may.

Namespace prefixes are connected to URIs by attributes within a document. The attributes define that prefix for the element in which they appear and all of its contents. To define a namespace prefix for an entire document, for example, define the prefix in the root element. To define a namespace prefix for a portion of a document, define it within the element holding that portion of the document. You can define the same prefix multiple times within a document, and the processor should override the previous value for the prefix with the new value for all elements contained within the element overriding the old value. A default namespace is also available—the URI for this namespace will be applied to all elements that don't have prefixes (but not to attributes).

To declare a namespace, you create an attribute that begins with `xmlns:` and ends with the prefix name, and assign it a URI for its value:

```
<this:myElement xmlns:this="http://www.example.com/this/">
```

This declaration allows `this:myElement` to be processed into `http://www.example.com/this/` and `myElement`, identifying `myElement` as being in the namespace `http://www.example.com/this/`. (Some processors return this information as `http://www.example.com/this/^ myElement` or a similarly delimited form.)

You can declare multiple namespaces within a single element:

```
<this:myElement
   xmlns:this="http://www.example.com/this/"
   xmlns:that="http://www.example.com/yourthat/"
   xmlns:these="http://www.example.com/theirthese/">
```

To declare the default namespace, you create an attribute named `xmlns` that has a URI value:

```
<myElement xmlns="http://www.example.com/this/">
```

Note that like the previous declarations shown above, `myElement` will be recognized as using the namespace `http://www.example.com/this/`. All of `myElement`'s descendant elements will be recognized as using that namespace if they have no prefix and the default namespace is not redeclared.

Namespaces apply to both elements and attributes, but with a key difference: the default namespace doesn't apply to attributes. Attributes without prefixes are treated as attributes without namespaces. To specify that an attribute has a namespace, a prefix must be used. If you plan to use namespaces for your attributes, be aware that you will always need to use prefixes, or rely on processing (which isn't defined by the namespaces recommendation) that uses the element's namespace for unspecified attributes. The Namespaces recommendation also sets out rules for identifying attributes. If two attributes are in the same namespace and have the same local part, the usage is illegal (though the Recommendation doesn't say what error handling the processor should do at that point).

Namespaces and their interaction with validation processing will receive considerably more attention in Chapter 24.

CHAPTER 4

Documents, "Reality," and Modeling Models

Now that we've explored the foundation structures, it's time to consider how to apply them to modeling different kinds of documents and data. Information modeling is often presented as a "black art," a mysteriously complicated process that can bring your projects into paradise, doom them to the lowest levels of hell, or leave them stranded in purgatory for years. Although information modeling is critical to your successful use of XML, it isn't an impossible task best left to wizards. Smaller projects are usually much more manageable, especially early on, and no one should set out to use every tool that XML provides. Keeping it simple, at least at the start, will help you build coherent models that you can modify later if you need to. The information modeling process has many twists and turns, along with as many variations as there are practitioners. XML 1.0 has raised as many questions about information modeling as it has solved, but has made the process more accessible to a large number of people.

Structures, Reality, and Back Again

Most of the information modeling done using XML 1.0 isn't a direct mapping of "reality" to an XML document. Typically, XML document structures are based on the models we've already built for working with reality, from database tables to paper forms and books. The modeling process for an XML document is often a combination of conversion and enhancement, rather than starting fresh with a completely blank slate on which to recreate "reality." Because XML is a popular tool for integration, it needs to accommodate a wide variety of models, and is used in large part as a tool for moving information from one model to another.

There are some structures which XML's containment approach models "naturally." Component assemblies, where parts contain parts and connectors hold them together, may be modeled using XML's hierarchical structures to represent containment and naming conventions to represent connections across containers. Documents often contain hierarchies, and hierarchical organizations form the foundations of many writing and composition courses. Modeling these kinds of structures is typically a matter of identifying which components are important and how they fit together—not an easy task, but one that may be able to take some hints from the "natural" structures of the information being modeled. (Chapter 6 explores in more detail what some of these structures look like.)

In many cases, XML documents are used to recreate a model that someone else has already built for use in a different processing context. Those models may be paper forms, or they may be the results of complex database queries. Although you can start over (and in some cases it's worthwhile), it is often easier to integrate your XML processing with existing work if your XML documents themselves model existing models. This kind of model recreation is easiest, of course, with well-documented models (or at least models where the creators are available for comment and explanation). In such cases, recreating the model in XML is more of a translation than a modeling project, although some reconsideration of structure may be necessary.

Top-down or Bottom-up?

Since the beginnings of XML development, critics have been concerned about its potential for "anarchy." XML's amorphous nature lets users model all kinds of information using all kinds of vocabularies, with no guarantee that either the models or the vocabularies will be consistent. XML's allowing documents to be merely well-formed, with no requirement that they fit a particular schema's constraints precisely, pours gasoline on the flames of this concern about anarchy. In response, the XML community has typically pointed to the model used by SGML, in which SGML itself is used as a standard for building other standards. Rather than allowing developers to create their own models on an as-needed basis, SGML practice has encouraged the creation of models addressing general needs for a given class of problems. Government and industry committees have convened to create standards that used SGML, and then distributed those standards. An enormous amount of activity in the XML world has followed this approach, leading to the creation of committees (including committees within the W3C), the development of repositories for sharing standards, and general rhetoric encouraging industries to come together and agree on vocabularies rather than having individual companies go their own way.

XML does allow for a reversed approach, however. Instead of gathering experts together to build large-scale standards, the convergence of designs used for many small-scale implementations may lead to a better understanding of the processes and information being modeled, and provide flexibility unavailable to meetings trying to hammer out a single answer to a large problem. Seen this way, the "anarchy" of XML's open vocabulary is a benefit, not a hazard, allowing developers to find their own solutions to particular problems, and sort out the differences between their models when it matters. XML's easy transformability (described in the next chapter) reduces the costs of such differences in models, and makes it possible for organizations to use internal models that meet their needs better while still being able to communicate with the outside world. In cases where different participants in transactions have extremely different needs, this kind of approach may be the only way to create models that all participants find useful. (Always remember—if using a standard is more trouble than the benefits are worth, the standard is unlikely to stick.)

For more of my own opinions on this debate, see "Moving from the 'Community of Experts' to the Community," available at **http://www.simonstl.com/articles/doubting.htm**. Chapter 35 also explores another anarchic possibility.

The Document and Data Debate

In an important sense, *all* XML is documents containing data. Every XML document, whatever its content, is treated, to some extent, as a document, and contains some form of data. There are some important splits in the XML community between those who use XML for "documents" and those who use XML for "data", but the same tools can accommodate both camps. While this flexibility is fairly miraculous in its own right, it leads to some important and frequently argued questions about what exactly XML document authors and XML schema and DTD developers are doing. Some XML documents model documents, a fairly straightforward process. Other XML documents model information that already has a structure—like database tables. Yet other XML documents model processes, objects, and abstractions, making it difficult at times to figure out exactly how or why to choose one document structure over another. As abstract as this problem may seem, it has a significant impact on a large number of practical choices, and can become critically important when you are building document structures for interchange with large groups of people or organizations.

Document structures and data structures address slightly different needs, and tend to operate using different assumptions. Document structures often use element content to represent the actual content of the document, and attributes for annotation. In data structures, this separation is typically less important, and attributes or elements may be pressed into service to take advantage of particular structural features. In most document projects, data typing is an afterthought, a convenience that might make it easier to index documents but not a primary focus. In data projects, data typing is a crucial part of the "contract" backing up the XML document, telling all parties what to expect and how to handle the information being exchanged. Although the divide is somewhat artificial, and both kinds of developers can use the same set of tools—indeed, they may share the same set of documents—these different needs can become important stumbling blocks. Documenting your structures and explaining them as clearly as possible may at least reveal these potential conflicts, but often both sides of the debate will need to compromise.

How to Proceed?

The many options available for XML model development can be extraordinarily confusing. Top-down modeling that starts from the beginning may provide an effective solution for some problems, while translating existing data models into XML on an as-needed basis without much review may solve other problems. All of these approaches are going to be used for XML in the next few years, and it is entirely probable that no one school of thought will prevail. XML has no rigid guidelines for data normalization, and only the beginnings of a "best practices" approach.

If you want to explore different options before leaping into a project, several books do cover different aspect of and approaches to XML (and SGML) development. An excellent explanation of how to build large DTDs using a relatively tightly controlled process is available in Eve Maler and Jeanne El Andaloussi's *Developing SGML DTDs: From Text to Model to Markup* (Prentice-Hall, 1996). David Megginson's *Structuring XML Documents* (Prentice-Hall, 1998) explores five mature DTDs, analyzing the structures used in large-scale document standards. Rick Jelliffe's *The XML & SGML Cookbook: Recipes for Structured Information* (Prentice-Hall, 1998), includes a section on Software Engineering that addresses many of the tradeoffs discussed above. For examples of small scale "translations" from one model to another, my own *XML: A Primer, 2nd Edition* (IDG Books, 1999) may be useful.

CHAPTER 5

Processing Models and Document Structures

XML documents are designed to be highly processable. The strict syntactical requirements limit the number of structures that a parser can extract from a document, and ensure that different parsers will present similar pictures of the same document to their applications. Parser A should return the same document structure as Parser B, with some room for variation. (Non-validating and validating parsers may return different document information, and parsers sometimes break up text nodes into different-sized chunks.) Because of this heavy emphasis on structure, it's relatively simple to build software that takes one set of structures and converts them into another structure. XML's use of flexible hierarchies with identifiable names makes it possible to define transformations that use those named hierarchies to create other structures, from XML documents to database tables to graphics and presentation. By considering the many processing pathways your documents may follow, you may be able to make your document structures more adaptable to a wide variety of uses, including uses that haven't yet been specified.

Transformations and Their Importance

Although users deal with transformations every day, these have often been treated as an unfortunate nuisance rather than a powerful tool. Converting between the proprietary formats used for typical office software is error-prone at best, often losing critical information along the way. As a result, companies have often tried to minimize the cost of conversion by standardizing on single formats—while these were still proprietary, they worked very well as long as everyone had the same tools for working on them. Conversions were treated as a cost rather than an opportunity, and the developers of conversion tools had varying levels of motivation for accurate conversion.

XML promises to make transformation a powerful and ordinary tool rather than an occasional nightmare. The openness of XML documents is hard to break; only the most determined attempts at obfuscation (like encrypting data) can hide the information contained within them if the user has a clear picture of what the information should look like. Mapping from a well-understood input format to a well-understood output format is not especially difficult, and all kinds of processing can take place in between. XML provides several technologies for handling such conversions, including a scriptable and programmable Document Object Model (DOM) and the transformation language portion of Extensible Stylesheet Language (XSLT). Armed with an understanding of their starting and ending points, developers can create portable tools that convert information between XML formats (and even to and from other formats, although it requires more work) seamlessly.

Keeping Information Meaningful

Many of the rules that govern modeling for relational databases apply to XML, though in many cases the rules can be applied more flexibly. If transformation or other processing is going to be important to you, you'll want to make sure you data are as processable as possible, in small, well-labeled chunks. On the other hand, if your application is just producing output for human consumption, with no expectation of further processing, it may not matter how precisely you mark up your information.

A good general rule is that document structures should reflect every piece of information that might need to be referenced on its own. One "atom" of information per container (regardless of whether that container is an element or attribute) is a useful rule, although deciding which pieces of information stand on their own is sometimes difficult. If this were taken to an extreme, you could assign every letter of an XML document its own element, though this kind of verbosity is almost always unnecessary. In some cases, like modeling database tables, this work has (usually) been done for you by the database designer. In other cases, like determining how deeply to annotate text, it may be appropriate to provide different levels of markup to different users. Some users may only need paragraphs indicated, while others want all names, dates, places, and trademarks highlighted. The density of markup can have a dramatic impact on how difficult it is to "complete" the creation of an XML document, so dense markup may not always be practical.

The examples below demonstrates two levels of markup on the same sentence.

```
<sentence><person>U.S. President Richard Nixon</person> resigned from
office on August 9, 1974.</sentence>

<sentence><person><role><country>U.S.</country> President</role>
<firstname>Richard</firstname> <lastname>Nixon</lastname></person>
<action>resigned from office</action> on <date><month>August</month>
<day>9</day>, <year>1974</year></date>.</sentence>
```

The second version is considerably more verbose and much more thoroughly marked up, making it easy to look up by name, role, date, action, or country. It may or may not be appropriate to apply that level of markup to large quantities of information, however. If an automated process can provide that level of markup, it could simplify the work done by users getting the information later, though successful implementation of such a strategy would require an enormous amount of work, perhaps learning from humans as they marked up documents.

One practice that is typically frowned upon is the use of element or attribute content that requires the application to perform additional parsing above and beyond that performed by the XML parser. The style attribute, commonly used in HTML to apply in-line formatting information, is a popular target of this criticism. A common use might look like:

```
<H1 style="font-size:18pt; font-weight:bold; color:42426F;
font-family:sans-serif">Headline</H1>
```

The application is expected to interpret the property names and values in the style attribute. A more XML-centric approach might look like:

```
<H1 font-size="18pt" font-weight="bold" color="42426F"
font-family="sans-serif">Headline</H1>
```

Although XML purists find the first version disturbing, the use of a single parsed attribute using a separator may make sense—if only because it allows the style information to be separated from the structure, and significantly reduces the impact on the size of the DTD if the document needs to be validated. Nonetheless, using this kind of markup may make it difficult for your document to be interpreted correctly by simple applications—you don't always have control over the applications that will be processing your documents. "Smuggling" multiple pieces of information into a content area that "should" be a single atom of information will work, as long as you don't need to exchange your documents or if the standard you use is well understood (like CSS). However, the benefits of such an approach should outweigh the cost of the ease of processing XML promises for this to be worthwhile. It is rarely a good idea to use such an approach merely to skimp on a few bytes.

Middleware Possibilities

XML promises to open new frontiers in middleware, software that interacts with information between its origin and destination. Because it's possible to transform XML again and again and preserve (or add or subtract) both its structure and the information it contains, there may be times when it is appropriate to build infrastructures that rely on mediators to adjust the conversation between client and server. Middleware for XML is typically a transformation, whether filtering, adding information, changing the document structure and naming, or any combination of these. The simplest case is when middleware is used to convert XML output produced by a server into HTML that any Web browser can read, but there are many more cases where middleware can be used to connect large volumes of information being transported in different formats.

Middleware doesn't have to live on a separate computer between the client and the server. Transformational middleware can live on the client, the server, a firewall, or any system between the origin and the destination of the document. It can be highly generic, transforming documents according to style sheets specified within those documents, or tightly focused, designed to convert one format to another. Middleware could be invoked by the user in response to the arrival of a particular piece of information, or automatically by applications. One key aspect of XML's promise is that this transformation can be built in ways that are as portable as XML itself, allowing systems to perform work on clients or servers depending on the capabilities of those systems. A cheap PC may be wasting a lot of processor cycles while the user is browsing information, while an expensive server is groaning under the weight of transformation processing. By moving the processor for a particular user to the user's system, a developer or network administrator can make the most efficient possible use of resources.

"Terminal" Vocabularies

Not all XML vocabularies are equally processable. Some XML vocabularies, typically those designed to transmit presentation information, lack semantic information about their contents. The XSL Formatting Objects (**http://www.w3.org/TR/WD-xsl**) vocabulary is an extreme case, a destination vocabulary that is purely about presentation. HTML, especially in its current barely structured form, is another case. Scalable Vector Graphics (SVG), an XML graphics standard under development, is yet another, though not as extreme a case. All these are products of the W3C, the same organization that claims to be promoting the "semantic Web". Why create vocabularies that are difficult to process?

The answer in all three of these cases is that they aren't really about processability. Software that receives information in these formats is expected simply to present them, not to analyze them for semantic content. Users who want to search these documents can use the small amounts of semantic information available, attempt to interpret presentation information meant for human consumption, or resort to the approach used by most Web search engines today: ignore all the markup, and index only the text. SVG and XSL Formatting Objects (often called FOs) will be able to take advantage of many of the tools being developed for XML storage and management, as will XML-ized HTML documents built according to the W3C's XHTML development.

These "terminal formats" are the end of the line, or close to it. (Printouts and screen displays are really the end of the line.) Terminal formats are not designed for future transformation or processing; instead, they are intended to present a single view of a set of information. The view is what the markup describes, not the nature of the content itself. Depending on the nature of the application, this approach may be appropriate. In the case of SVG, XML provides a framework on which descriptions of graphics may be easily built. XSL FOs are intended to be the result of XSLT transformations as part of a formatting application, and may never actually be instantiated as XML documents within an XSL application (although it is, of course, possible). HTML has a more complicated heritage, but its structures were built to describe documents, not the contents of documents. That provided enough flexibility for users of many kinds to apply those structures to their own information and helped build the World Wide Web, but makes it difficult now to use HTML for applications other than display to human readers.

In general, the use of terminal formats should be avoided, although, as always, there may be cases where their use is unavoidable. Transmitting terminal formats severely limits the possibilities of the receiver, though this can be improved to some extent by annotating a format with additional semantic information that might allow its reconstruction. There are nondestructive tools for applying formatting, notably Cascading Style Sheets (CSS), but there really isn't an annotative alternative for creating graphics. If you focus on providing your users with as much meaningful information as possible and letting them transform it (perhaps with your tools), you'll likely have much happier users than if you send them information that they can use only for a limited range of purposes. Chapters 17 and 18 will examine different strategies for delivering information in as rich a form as possible.

CHAPTER 6

Common Document Patterns

Although XML provides considerable structural flexibility for your documents, many documents (or portions of documents) fall into common patterns. Understanding what these patterns look like—and being ready to apply them when appropriate—can simplify the process of converting information to XML. The descriptions given below are not hard-and-fast rules (one of them, in fact is a pattern with no consistent rules), but rather are things you can look for to build structures that might have much in common with other documents. The first few patterns are foundation patterns that appear throughout most XML documents, while later patterns tend to combine multiple structures.

Hierarchies

The "natural" structure of XML is definitely hierarchical, but only a few structures in the "real" world are nearly that hierarchical. (Most of those hierarchies are, like XML itself, the product of people explicitly organizing information.) Generally, hierarchies are recognizable by their emphasis on *containment*: the most important relationships in a document revolve around issues of which elements contain or are contained by other elements. If you're going to be asking questions like "is *x* a member of *y*?" on a regular basis, you have hierarchies to contend with. The existence of such questions doesn't always imply a strictly hierarchical document structure, but it does require some decision-making about how those relationships will be expressed.

Containment is an easy way to express hierarchical relationships, although it can break down if there are too many pieces of information being represented at once. Containment structures are often a useful way to present information that is a subset of a larger hierarchical tree, allowing for abstraction of information at upper layers in favor of details at lower levels. Trying to store a large set of related information in a single enormous document is often difficult, however. The example below demonstrates a biological taxonomy, using containment to represent "is-a-member-of" relationships down to the `species` element, where more detailed information about common names identifies names that both "belong" to the species.

```
<TAXONOMY>
<KINGDOM NAME="animalia">
<PHYLUM NAME="chordata">
<CLASS NAME="aves">
<ORDER NAME="gaviiformes">
<FAMILY NAME="gaviidae">
<SPECIES NAME="gavia stellata">
<COMMONNAME LOCATION="NA">Red-throated Loon</COMMONNAME>
<COMMONNAME LOCATION="EU">Red-throated Diver</COMMONNAME>
</SPECIES>
<SPECIES NAME="gavia arctica">
<COMMONNAME LOCATION="NA">Arctic Loon</COMMONNAME>
<COMMONNAME LOCATION="EU">Black-Throated Diver</COMMONNAME>
</SPECIES>
<SPECIES NAME="gavia pacifica">
<COMMONNAME LOCATION="NA">Pacific Loon</COMMONNAME>
<COMMONNAME LOCATION="EU">Black-Throated Diver</COMMONNAME>
</SPECIES>
<SPECIES NAME="gavia immer">
<COMMONNAME LOCATION="NA">Common Loon</COMMONNAME>
<COMMONNAME LOCATION="EU">Great Northern Diver</COMMONNAME>
</SPECIES>
<SPECIES NAME="gavia adamsii">
<COMMONNAME LOCATION="NA">Yellow-billed Loon</COMMONNAME>
<COMMONNAME LOCATION="EU">White-billed Diver</COMMONNAME>
</SPECIES>
<!--Information on loons came from a large number of (sometimes con-
flicting) sources including the American Ornithological Union checklist,
Peterson Field Guide to Eastern Birds, National Audubon Society Field
Guide to North American Birds, a list of birds at
http://www.hants.gov.uk/museums/ofr/birds_1.html, and "Obsolete Names of
North American Birds and Their Modern Equivalents", at
http://www.pwrc.usgs.gov/research/pubs/banks/obsall.htm -->
</FAMILY></ORDER></CLASS></PHYLUM></KINGDOM></TAXONOMY>
```

Similar patterns can be used for corporate organization charts, object-oriented program structures, and other fields where it is clear how one component is part of another. Although an approach like this one can be very useful when there are only five species listed at the end of a taxonomy, it can be difficult to digest larger quantities of information sent in such a format, and sometimes difficult to send fragments of information that supplement the hierarchy. In such cases, you can provide the information an application needs to use to build a hierarchy without necessarily relying on XML's built-in structures. If you'll be sending and combining fragments of information, this pattern may help:

```
<TAXONOMY>
<KINGDOM NAME="animalia" />
<KINGDOM NAME="plantae" />
<PHYLUM NAME="chordata" KINGDOM="animalia" />
<CLASS NAME="aves" phylum="chordata" />
<ORDER NAME="apodiformes" class="aves" />
<ORDER NAME="gaviiformes" class="aves" />
<ORDER NAME="strigiformes" class="aves" />
<FAMILY NAME="gaviidae" order="gaviiformes" />
<SPECIES NAME="gavia stellata" family="gaviidae">
<COMMONNAME LOCATION="NA">Red-throated Loon</COMMONNAME>
<COMMONNAME LOCATION="EU">Red-throated Diver</COMMONNAME>
</SPECIES>
<SPECIES NAME="gavia arctica" family="gaviidae">
<COMMONNAME LOCATION="NA">Arctic Loon</COMMONNAME>
<COMMONNAME LOCATION="EU">Black-Throated Diver</COMMONNAME>
</SPECIES>
</TAXONOMY>
```

Attribute annotation like this lets you make explicit statements about the relationships between components, rather than requiring all the information to fit into perfect containers. (Note the "unconnected" plant kingdom and a couple of extra orders of birds.) It also makes it easier to represent information that has different roles in different hierarchies, allowing programs to transform the information from one representation to another. In cases where you have multiple hierarchies or need to be able to support fragment processing, describing the hierarchy rather than building it directly may be more appropriate. (Matrix management systems, for example, often demand such markup because they deliberately refuse to fit a single "clean" containment model.)

Applications that make heavy use of hierarchies include directory structures, like the Internet's critical Domain Name Service (DNS) and the Lightweight Directory Access Protocol (LDAP), as well as classification and taxonomy systems covering all kinds of information, from business organization to the sciences.

Lists

Lists are among the most common structures in both the document and data worlds. Lists accumulate on refrigerators, in Palm Pilots, on post-it notes attached to monitors, deep inside relational databases, and generally any place that can store more than a single piece of information. XML provides excellent support for lists, allowing you to create lists of named information that can contain more structured information. Lists provide a basic framework for many different structures, even when they don't necessarily appear to be lists. A list is basically a sequence of information at the same level—and sequence may or may not matter, depending on the particular case. A list of instructions for assembling a product may require a particular order, while a grocery list may not.

Most lists in XML are represented as series of elements. For example, a grocery list might look like:

```
<grocerylist>
<item>macaroni</item>
<item>wheat bread</item>
<item>ketchup</item>
</grocerylist>
```

There is a little bit of hierarchy here—all the `items` are contained within the grocery list—but the main content is the list itself, which is bounded by the `grocerylist` element. Lists don't have to be a series of the same elements; we could be more specific and create a list that looked like:

```
<grocerylist>
<pasta>macaroni</pasta>
<bread>wheat bread</bread>
<condiment>ketchup</condiment>
</grocerylist>
```

A somewhat smart application could take this list and reorganize it to follow the layout of the particular store a shopper was visiting, for instance. Just as lists may contain multiple element types, those types may also vary in their content. For example:

```
<grocerylist>
<pasta brand="Barilla">macaroni</pasta>
<bread>wheat bread</bread>
<condiment size="64oz">ketchup</condiment>
<meat quantity="2 lbs." fat-content="93%">hamburger</meat>
</grocerylist>
```

The distinguishing characteristic of a list is a sequence of nodes at the same level. Those nodes (elements or attributes) may then contain further information, of course. An element containing attributes is a sort of list, though a limited one—attributes can't have the same names, nor are XML processors required to preserve the order of the attributes:

```
<grocerylist pasta="macaroni" bread="wheat bread" condiment="ketchup"
meat="hamburger"/>
```

This kind of list, although limited, is often used to represent database information in a compact form. This compact form is itself a sort of document pattern, useful in a limited number of cases for shrinking the size of files. However, you should explore the differences between elements and attributes described in Chapter 3 before making extensive use of this form, especially if you plan to create documents that need to go through validation.

Tables

Tables are lists of lists. Tables are usually described as rows and columns, reflecting the printed layout of most tabular information. In most cases, tables are built on the assumption that the lists contained within the table are *regular*—each of the lists has the same information in the same location. When you are describing relational database tables, the column structure usually defines the contents of the list, while the rows are lists that follow that structure. (In print, and in some other models, this relationship is sometimes reversed.)

The table below is a fairly typical set of tabular information (all people and information are imaginary).

First_Name	Last_Name	Title	Salary	Shares
Toni	James	President	$100,000	70,000
Jim	Robinet	Vice-President	$70,000	50,000
Jennifer	Spaulding	CIO	$70,000	50,000
John	Carothers	Java Developer	$90,000	10,000
Jenny	Douglas	XML Architect	$120,000	10,000

There are a number of ways we can model the information in this table. First, we can model the table itself, using elements with names like `table`, `row`, and `column`.

```
<table name="Personnel">
<row>
<column name='First_Name'>Toni</column>
<column name='Last_Name'>James</column>
<column name='Title'>President</column>
<column name='Salary'>$100,000</column>
<column name='Shares'>70,000</column>
</row>
<row>
<Column name='First_Name'>Jim</Column>
```

```
<Column name='Last_Name'>Robinet</Column>
<Column name='Title'>Vice-President</Column>
<Column name='Salary'>$70,000</Column>
<Column name='Shares'>50,000</Column>
</row>
etc...
</table>
```

If you'll be exchanging lots of tables and need a generic "table" format to simplify table interchange, this approach may be useful. This format can be compressed further by making the column information into attributes:

```
<table name="personnel">
<row First_Name='Toni' Last_Name='James' Title='President'
Salary='$100,000' Shares='70,000' />
<row First_Name='Jim' Last_Name='Robinet' Title='Vice-President'
Salary='$70,000' Shares='50,000' />
etc...
</table>
```

This compact form isn't much harder to use than the larger form above, although it's a bit more restrictive. Should you find yourself with identically named columns (unlikely or prohibited in many systems), you'll have a problem—you can't apply the same attribute name twice within an element. Also, you won't be able to create the extended tables described in the next section.

A different approach models the information rather than the table structure itself. Instead of a `table` element, we start with `personnel`. Instead of `row` elements, we have `person` elements, containing information about that person.

```
<Personnel>
<Person>
<First_Name>Toni</First_Name>
<Last_Name>James</Last_Name>
<Title>President</Title>
<Salary>$100,000</Salary>
<Shares>70,000</Shares>
</Person>
<Person>
<First_Name>Jim</First_Name>
<Last_Name>Robinet</Last_Name>
<Title>Vice-President</Title>
<Salary>$70,000</Salary>
<Shares>50,000</Shares>
</person>
etc...
</personnel>
```

And again, the list could be represented using attributes rather than child elements:

```
<Personnel>
<Person First_Name='Toni' Last_Name='James' Title='President'
Salary='$100,000' Shares='70,000' />
<Person First_Name='Jim' Last_Name='Robinet' Title='Vice-President'
Salary='$70,000' Shares='50,000' />
etc...
</Personnel>
```

There isn't always a single solution—you'll need to choose which structure best fits your project's needs. This doesn't have to be a permanently binding decision, foreclosing other possibilities, however—as noted in the previous chapter, XML's structures are relatively easy to transform from format to format, using tools like Extensible Style Language (XSL) or Document Object Model (DOM) processing. (Chapter 18 will provide more detail on these possibilities.)

Extended Tables

The basic table form described above can be mixed with a number of extra parts to describe more information than will fit into a strict table structure. There may be times when you want to insert additional information into a document that won't necessarily fit into a neat table, with the understanding that table processors can ignore the information (if indeed you expect it to go to table processors), but other tools can access the information. If, for example, the president of the company had some additional benefits, and some processor down the line needed a full listing, his/her `person` element might look like:

```
<Person>
<First_Name>Toni</First_Name>
<Last_Name>James</Last_Name>
<Title>President</Title>
<Salary>$100,000</Salary>
<Shares>70,000</Shares>
<Auto>Mercedes-Benz E8Y 4Z9</Auto>
<Healthclub>Gold</Healthclub>
</Person>
```

Meanwhile, the XML Developer has different information:

```
<Person>
<First_Name>Jenny</First_Name>
<Last_Name>Douglas</Last_Name>
<Title>XML Architect</Title>
<Salary>$120,000</Salary>
<Shares>10,000</Shares>
<DesktopSystem>Personal</Auto>
<Hours><Start>2000</Start><End>0600</End></Hours>
</Person>
```

There are many more sophisticated possibilities. XML's structures allow you to process information in ways that let you move beyond the old rules that defined delimited text and other interchange format. Adding extra material becomes a real possibility, opening up options for different levels of processing.

Messages

Messages intended for automatic processing have a lot to gain from XML, which provides an open standard for structuring information. Messages are generally small documents, although some messages are in fact quite large and contain many different parts. Typically, messages include headers describing the message, followed by the body of a message. XML can be used to build a similar structure, providing either flexibility (if message processors only expect well-formed XML and are designed to cope with variations) or thorough verification of message structure (if message processors validate each message). For one example of a protocol built on the sending and receiving of XML messages, see XML-RPC at **http://www.xml-rpc.com**.

Objects

Objects (the computer-programming variety) map very well to XML, typically using combinations of the hierarchical structures and list structures described above. There are a few important points to keep in mind when mapping objects to XML and back. XML 1.0 provides no type checking—everything is text. Although data typing is possible in schemas and DTDs, object processors built on XML 1.0 will need to add their own type checking processing. (See Chapter 11 for one way to do this with XML 1.0 and Chapter 29 for future developments that promise to make it easier.) A second set of issues involves different approaches taken by XML and object systems. Object systems use techniques like encapsulation to hide information, while XML shows everything in the document. Objects can connect to other objects, which connect to other objects, which can even be the original document, creating recursive structures that XML can't represent or structures with vague boundaries that make it difficult to decide what the "object" is actually composed of. The clear boundaries of XML documents are easily mapped to objects with relatively simple code, but the vaguer boundaries of objects are more difficult to map to XML documents.

Chaos: "Document Documents"

Most human-created documents are fairly chaotic. Books have varying numbers of chapters, which contain varying numbers of paragraphs, figures, footnotes, and other information. If you start marking up things like people's names, the variety in naming systems (and abbreviations for those naming systems) is remarkable. The more heavily marked up you make a human-readable document, the more complex its structure typically becomes. Lists, hierarchies, and loosely connected text combine to form chaotic and complex document structures that are often difficult to process automatically but closely reflect the information that humans create.

CHAPTER 7

Describing Foundations: Element Type Declarations

XML 1.0 provides a vocabulary for describing the structures you build with elements. Element type declarations provide a reasonably simple, readable, and compact form for describing a wide variety of possible structures. They are used by XML processors to define restraints, limiting the possible element names and structures within a document at validation time. They've also become a useful tool for building XML editors—armed with an understanding of what your documents *should* look like, XML editors can offer you a wide variety of appropriate structures during the process of document creation. Whether or not you intend to use validation on your documents to enforce your chosen structures, element type declarations provide a useful vocabulary for documenting those structures.

Describing Containers

XML element type declarations let you define element types that have a name and a content model. When you develop a set of XML element type declarations, you are creating a list of names associated with descriptions of the materials—emptiness, text, and other element types—that can go inside them. There is no mechanism for making claims like "the `xyz` element type may only appear in `tuv` elements." When you create element type declarations, you start by defining the parent and then you identify its children; there is no way to define a child element and specify in that declaration what element types its parents should be. (You can start by creating child elements and then describing parents that contain them, but the containment relationship is defined in the parent element type, not the child.)

Although this may sound like it limits XML development to strictly hierarchical document models, the content model options in element type declarations are flexible enough to accommodate all the patterns described in Chapter 6. Hierarchies use simple containment, while lists and tables use lists of possible content and restrictions on its appearance. Even the seeming chaos of document structures can be represented with XML 1.0 content models, although at times these may seem especially complex.

Basic Syntax

Element type declarations describe a class of elements that share a common name. An element type is a generic description of elements using a particular name, while an element is a specific instance appearing within a document. Element type declarations must appear inside the document type (DOCTYPE) declaration or a file referenced by that declaration, not in document content. All element type declarations use the same basic syntax:

```
<!ELEMENT elementName contentModel>
```

The element name must begin with a letter or underscore, and may contain letters, digits, hyphens, underscores, and periods. (You should avoid using colons unless you're using them for namespaces, but see Chapter 24 for a discussion of the many issues involved in integrating namespaces and DTDs.) Element names may not begin with "xml," "XML," or any variation of different cases—names beginning with these three magic letters are reserved for the W3C. If you use your element type declarations in validation, the element names declared here must match the element names used in the document in every detail, including case. The elements `tHis` and `thIs` are considered different—if you use both forms, you must declare both forms, and they are regarded as different at all times for purposes of attribute declarations and content model matching. In general, you'll find it much simpler to support only a single form of an element name. Using the same name with different capitalization can generate enormous confusion.

No element name may be used in more than one element type declaration within a DTD.

The EMPTY Content Model

The simplest content model you can declare for an element is the EMPTY content model. Elements with the EMPTY content model aren't allowed to contain any content whatsoever—no text, no whitespace, no child elements. (They may, however, have attributes.) For example, if you declared the element type emptiness with an EMPTY content model, the element type declaration would look like:

```
<!ELEMENT emptiness EMPTY>
```

Elements with the name emptiness could appear in the two legitimate forms for empty elements:

```
<emptiness />
<emptiness></emptiness>
```

The following forms would be prohibited, however:

```
<emptiness> </emptiness>

<emptiness>
</emptiness>

<emptiness>Oops! Here's some content!</emptiness>
<emptiness><myElement /></emptiness>
```

Element types declared with an EMPTY content must be genuinely empty.

The ANY Content Model

The ANY content model is as simple as the EMPTY content model, but far less restrictive. Element types declared with ANY content models may contain text and child elements in any order whatsoever. If you validate the document, all the child elements must have element type declarations of their own; ANY isn't a license to do anything you want, though it may seem that way. For example, to declare the anything element type, you might say:

```
<!ELEMENT anything ANY>
```

Instances of anything could use a variety of content models:

```
<anything />

<anything>Here's some text!</anything>

<anything>
```

```
</anything>

<anything>Let's mix text and <child>child</child> elements!</anything>

<anything>Let's do a lot of anything elements!
   <anything /><anything>
   </anything>
   <anything>Let's mix text and <child>child</child>
   elements!</anything>
</anything>
```

The possibilities are almost endless. ANY is frequently used when you're first starting out on a new model, although many DTD developers disapprove of its use in "final" DTDs. ANY is also used to add extensibility to a DTD, as discussed in Chapter 20.

Structured-Element Content Models

XML 1.0 provides a small set of notations that you can use to build very complex descriptions of element content. By combining these notations with the names of element types, you can specify possible element structures, balancing some flexibility (if appropriate) with a restricted set of allowed content. XML uses symbols to indicate group, sequence, and frequency of appearance, as shown in the tables below.

Table 7.1
Occurrence Indicators

Symbol	Example	Usage
+	(NAME+)	Specifies that the element type (in this case, NAME) must appear one or more times. This makes the element type mandatory and repeatable.
*	(NAME*)	Specifies that the element type (in this case, NAME) must appear zero or more times. This makes the element type optional and repeatable.
?	(NAME?)	Specifies that the element type (in this case, NAME) must appear zero or one times. This makes the element type optional but *not* repeatable.
none	(NAME)	Specifies that the element type (in this case, NAME) must appear exactly once. This makes the element type mandatory and *not* repeatable.

Table 7.2
Sequence Indicators

Symbol	Example	Usage
,	(NAME, TITLE)	Specifies that the element types listed must appear in sequence. In this case, a TITLE element must follow a NAME element. Multiple element types may appear in the list, separated by commas, but they may not be mixed with vertical bars
|	(NAME | TITLE)	Specifies that one, and only one, of the element types listed must appear. In this case, a TITLE element or a NAME element may appear, but not both. Multiple element types may appear in the list, separated by vertical bars, but they may not be mixed with commas.
( )	((A,B) | (C,D,E))	Parentheses allow you to group sequences to build more sophisticated combinations. In this case, the element sequence A,B may appear, or the sequence C,D,E may appear. Parentheses may also be given occurrence indicators; for instance (A,B)+ means that the sequence A,B must appear at least once, and may be repeated.

By combining element names and these symbols, you can describe the kinds of content permitted in particular element types. For example, to declare that a chapter element must contain a `title` element, followed by an `introduction`, then a series of `pgh` paragraph elements, and then a `conclusion`, the declaration below would be appropriate.

```
<!ELEMENT chapter (title, introduction, pgh+, conclusion)>
```

If the `introduction` and `conclusion` were optional, it might look like:

```
<!ELEMENT chapter (title, introduction?, pgh+, conclusion?)>
```

More complex models can be created by using the parentheses to create models within models. For example, if we wanted users to be able to mix pgh elements with figure elements and table elements, the structure might change to:

```
<!ELEMENT chapter (title, introduction?, (pgh | figure | table)+,
conclusion?)>
```

This would require that at least one pgh, figure, or table element appear (the chapter needs content after all), but they could be intermixed. The contents of the parentheses (which in this case allow for choice) must appear one or more times, as identified by the + following them. Alternatively, if you wanted to require a pgh element to appear, followed by any number of pgh, figure, and table elements, you might specify:

```
<!ELEMENT chapter (title, introduction?, pgh, (pgh | figure | table)+,
conclusion?)>
```

At some point this grows too complicated, and it makes sense to create a subelement containing the complications:

```
<!ELEMENT chapter (title, introduction?, body, conclusion?)>
<!ELEMENT body (pgh, (pgh | figure | table)+)>
```

XML 1.0 content models don't provide very much control over how many times a given component must appear. The restraints available support options of zero, one, or as many as the author of a document wants. Two or three may be sensible values at times, but specifying that in a content model is difficult and requires some extra writing. For example, we'll take the series `(A,B)`. If this sequence should appear zero or one times, it can be written `(A,B)?`. If it should appear only once, it can be `(A,B)`. To allow it to appear more than once, we can use `(A,B)+` or `(A,B)*`, depending on whether it has to appear at all. To restrain the sequence so it must appear twice, we can't use the indicators. Instead, we have to write `(A,B,A,B)`. To allow it to appear once or twice, we write `(A,B, (A,B)?)`. Similarly, for three appearances, it has to be `(A,B,A,B,A,B)`.

As you start writing more complex content models, you may run into the problem of ambiguity, which the XML 1.0 recommendation addresses in Section 3.2.1 and Appendix E. For compatibility with SGML, XML declares that "it is an error if an element in the document can match more than one occurrence of an element type in the content model." Thus, the examples in the paragraph above are acceptable, but: `((A,B) | (A,B,A,B))` is not. When a parser encounters that first `A,B`, it has no way of knowing which path (which side of the | bar) to follow for further processing. Simpler cases, like `((A | B) | (A,B))` cause similar problems. As your models grow more sophisticated, this can be important. If you encounter it, there is almost always a good way to solve it, but it may take some thinking. You'll need to determine which parts of your model describe the path the parser must take, and you may have to accept a less restrictive content model than the one you were aiming for. Using container elements (in place of parentheses) can often get you out of this problem.

Mixed-Content Models

Mixed-content models use some of the syntax of the structured models described above, but only a limited subset. Mixed-content models allow you to specify textual content for elements, possibly mixed with a selection of elements. XML doesn't allow you to specify content models that include text very precisely; the expressiveness of mixed-content models is explicitly limited by the XML 1.0 Recommendation. Content models that may contain text include `#PCDATA` (which stands for "parsed character data"). When `#PCDATA` appears, it must be the first (or only) item in a list.

The simplest mixed content model declaration available looks like:

```
<!ELEMENT textNode (#PCDATA)>
```

The element `textNode` could then include only text—no elements are permitted.

Text may be mixed with element content. When included in a mixed declaration, element names must be separated by vertical bars, and an asterisk applied to the end of the list:

```
<!ELEMENT mixedNode (#PCDATA | elementNode1 | elementNode2)*>
```

This indicates that instances of the element `mixedNode` may contain any combination of text, `elementNode1` elements, and `elementNode2` elements. The `elementNode1` elements and `elementNode2` elements must be declared someplace else in the DTD and may have their own content models. There is no way to limit how these components are mixed. For example, you are not allowed to declare:

```
<!ELEMENT mixedNode (#PCDATA, elementNode1, elementNode2+) >
```

or:

```
<!ELEMENT mixedNode (elementNode1, #PCDATA, elementNode2)+>
```

If you need to specify where text or elements should appear more precisely, creating *wrapper elements*—which only contain text or text and a few elements you don't need to control tightly—is usually the simplest answer. Those wrapper elements can then be included in structured content declarations, limiting their impact on your overall document structure.

For example, a memo structure could be declared as:

```
<!ELEMENT memo (#PCDATA | To | From | Cc | paragraph | name)*
```

This would allow the memo to have any mixture of To, From, Cc, paragraph, and name elements interspersed with text, which could lead to some unusual memo structures. More typically, the text is locked within the To, From, Cc, and paragraph elements, mixed with name elements:

```
<!ELEMENT memo (To, From, Cc, paragraph+))>
<!ELEMENT To (#PCDATA | name)*>
<!ELEMENT From (#PCDATA | name)*>
<!ELEMENT Cc (#PCDATA | name)*>
<!ELEMENT paragraph (#PCDATA | name)*>
```

By keeping the text out of the top level of the memo element, you can define a much stricter set of rules for document content.

Data Models

XML 1.0 doesn't include facilities for describing data models like numbers, dates, and other commonly used types. At present, that responsibility belongs to the application. If you want to create data descriptions for use with XML, see Chapter 11 (for tools you can use with XML 1.0) and Chapter 29 (for tools under development at the W3C).

CHAPTER 8

Describing Foundations: Attribute List Declarations

Attribute list declarations describe the attributes that may appear on particular element types. Validating parsers will report errors when attributes appear that weren't declared in the DTD. Although element type declarations contain a potentially complex content model, attribute list declarations contain a list of attribute names, types, and possibly default values. Attribute list declarations are more flexible in many ways than element type declarations—they can, for example, be declared repeatedly (though only the first one will be used) or contain no attribute names and types at all. This flexibility gives attribute list declarations a different sort of complexity than element type declarations, requiring a different approach to DTD design.

Describing Annotation

Attribute list declarations operate fairly differently from their element type counterparts. Because the order of attributes on an element doesn't matter for validation, and because elements can only have one layer of attributes, attribute lists are declared as additional parts for a particular parent element, not as independent components of their own. Every attribute list declaration includes the name of the element to which the attributes may apply, and any number of attributes may be declared for that element in a single declaration. This means that attribute declarations are local to particular elements—there is no reason built into XML 1.0 to assume that two attributes with the same name on different elements have anything in common. (Two child elements with the same name and different parents would have to have the same element type, and identical content models.) As we'll see later in Chapter 14, developers often use parameter entities to avoid the need to declare the same attributes repeatedly.

Although attributes may seem to have second-rate status because of this approach, they also have unique advantages. There are many more types of attributes, and each type has different constraints on the information it may contain. Also, unlike elements, attributes may be assigned default or even fixed values, and users may be required to provide content. These extra features often drive developers to use attributes in place of elements, taking advantage of the features built into attributes when they were considered a tool for annotating elements.

Basic Syntax

Attribute list declarations describe a list of attributes that apply to a particular element type. All of the attributes named in a declaration "belong" to the element type named at the start of the declaration. The basic syntax looks like:

```
<!ATTLIST elementTypeName
list_of_attributes>
```

The simplest possible attribute list declaration contains no attributes at all:

```
<!ATTLIST ElemWithNoAtts>
```

Although attribute list declarations like the one above are, to some extent, pointless, they often serve as placeholders in the early stages of XML 1.0 DTD development. By creating an attribute list declaration for each element, even if it's empty, developers make it easier to read through a DTD and figure out what's missing.

There may be multiple attribute list declarations for a given element type, and the same attribute may be declared repeatedly. When the same attribute name is declared for the same element type repeatedly, XML 1.0 uses a "which came first" approach that gives the internal subset priority over the external subset. This makes it easy, for example, for a document to change the default value of an attribute from the value specified in the DTD. (See Chapter 25 for a discussion of the implications of this feature.)

Naming Attributes

Attribute names within attribute list declarations follow the same rules as attribute names in documents. The attribute name must begin with a letter or underscore, and may contain letters, digits, hyphens, underscores, and periods. The name is case sensitive, as always. You should avoid using colons unless you're using namespaces, but remember that plain XML 1.0 parsers will not validate attribute or element names using the naming rules of namespaces. Although you can use namespaces as a layer on top of XML 1.0 validation, you can't take advantage of changing prefixes to avoid conflicts, for example. Also, the default namespace is not applied to attributes, which can create difficult interpretation challenges. Chapter 24 will provide a guide to the ins and outs of using namespaces in a validating context.

Attribute Types

XML 1.0 provides three broad categories of attribute types, with several subtypes, producing ten separate possibilities for attribute types. The XML 1.0 attribute types reflect XML's heritage as a document-oriented markup language—none of the types reflects "data types" in the sense that programmers and database developers typically understand them. (Chapter 11 will look at one way to add this functionality, however.) The XML 1.0 attribute types can be useful, however, to connect different parts of a document and to establish certain types of constraints on attribute content.

The most commonly used attribute type is the string type, `CDATA`, character data. `CDATA` applies the fewest constraints on content and suggests no assumptions about the meaning of the attribute. Using `CDATA` as your attribute type doesn't get you very much from the parser—the parser won't be able to tell if the contents of the attribute match what you actually wanted, and you'll often need to perform more sophisticated checking in your application. (Because everything in `CDATA` is treated as text, you'll need to make sure that attributes you expect to contain numeric values do in fact contain numbers, for instance.) Attributes declared as `CDATA` may contain any legal XML characters, as well as entities and character references. The characters `<`, `>`, and `'` or `"` (depending on which type of quotes you used to surround the attribute value) must be represented with the built-in entities described in Chapter 12. All white space will be normalized to single spaces, as described in Chapter 10. In a non-validating environment, all attributes are typically treated as `CDATA`, so in effect `CDATA` declarations don't add any extra work for the processor in a validating environment. (CDATA attributes are very different from the CDATA sections described in Chapter 9. The naming is unfortunate.)

The next category of attribute types, tokenized types, includes eight varieties of tokens and groups of tokens. These tokens may contain the same characters as element and attribute names—letters, digits, hyphens, underscores, and periods. The tokens used in these attribute types also contain colons. (The namespaces recommendation doesn't restrict the use of colons in tokens, but it would be consistent and perhaps wise to avoid using colons in tokens.) The simplest tokenized types are `NMTOKEN` and `NMTOKENS`. Attributes of type `NMTOKEN` may contain one token for their value, while attributes of type `NMTOKENS` may contain one or more tokens, separated by white space. While these types do have stricter restraints than `CDATA`, the tokens' meaning is left entirely up to the application. Validating parsers will indicate that these values are tokens, but they don't need to check them against the contents of any other part of the document.

The `ENTITY` and `ENTITIES` attribute types are used to reference unparsed entities, which are discussed in Chapter 15. These two attribute types must also contain a token (or tokens, for `ENTITIES`), but those tokens must be the names of unparsed entities declared elsewhere in the DTD, and validating parsers will report errors if they don't match.

The other three types of tokenized attribute types are used to mark and reference elements within a single document. The ID type is used to add unique identifiers to elements, while the `IDREF` and `IDREFS` attribute types are used to reference those identifiers. IDs may also be referenced by documents outside the document containing them, but the targets of `IDREF` and `IDREFS` must always be within the current document. Like the other tokenized types, all of these attribute types must meet the restrictions described above for tokens, and in addition, all of the tokens used in these types must begin with a letter or underscore. Unlike the other tokenized types, these types have restrictions of their own that require validating parsers to build a list of IDs during processing.

The ID attribute type is one of the most important pieces in XML, greatly simplifying the use of tools that need to manipulate document components. Element types may only have one attribute of type ID, typically (though not always) named `id`. ID-type attributes may not be assigned a default or fixed value—their values must be provided in the document itself, not the DTD. The values of ID-type attributes in a document must be unique—if there is duplication, a validating processor is required to report an error. These requirements make it easy to identify particular elements in a document, letting applications reference those elements directly rather than by describing the full path of parent elements that must be traversed to reach the element.

The `IDREF` and `IDREFS` attribute types are used to point from one element to another, using the ID value of the target. An element that provided notes about the content of another element might use an `IDREF` attribute to identify the element being described. Similarly, if the description applied to multiple elements, an `IDREFS` attribute might be more appropriate. `IDREFS` may be used in place of `IDREF` in all cases except those where you want to limit the number of ID references to one. `IDREFS` permits pointing at one or multiple targets, while IDREF permits pointing at only one. The tokens contained in attributes of type IDREF and IDREFS must match the values of ID-type attributes elsewhere in the document. Validating parsers will report errors if a token in an IDREF or IDREFS attribute doesn't match an ID. (It will usually have to wait until it reaches the end of the document to do so, however—until then, it hasn't finished building the list of all IDs.)

The last category of attribute types in XML 1.0 is enumerated types. These allow you to provide a list of acceptable values for an attribute. These values must be tokens—you can't provide values with spaces in them, for example. There are two kinds of enumerated attribute types—one which includes a simple list of tokens (that can mean anything), and notation type where the list must only include the names of notations declared elsewhere in the DTD. (For more on declaring notations, see Chapter 15.) In both cases, you'll need to provide a list of possible values, enclosed in parentheses and separated by vertical bars. You can also use white space between the tokens, parentheses, and bars, but it isn't required and doesn't affect the meaning. For example, if you wanted to limit the value of attribute to abbreviations for days of the week, you might present the list below as your attribute type:

```
(Sat | Sun | Mon | Tues | Wed | Thurs | Fri)
```

Alternately, you could use numbers:

```
(1 | 2 | 3 | 4 | 5 | 6 | 7)
```

If the values were notations, you could use:

```
NOTATION (gif | jpeg | png)
```

Enumerated types can't represent all constraints—the lists rapidly grow too long for easy processing—but they can be very useful in situations where a limited number of values are acceptable. Validating processors will report errors during the parse if the value in an attribute with an enumerated type fails to match the values in the list. (They will also report errors if the values in a list of notations don't match notations declared elsewhere in the DTD.)

Attribute Defaults

The final component in attribute declarations is known as the *default*. In fact, attribute defaults provide two services—the provision of a possible value and a statement about whether the attribute is optional, required, or has a fixed value. These services are provided using four varieties of keywords and syntax. The simplest default is just a value in quotes:

```
"defaultvalue"
```

If no value for the attribute is specified in the document, the parser will use the default value provided in the declaration; otherwise it uses the value spcified in the document. Alternatively, you can leave explicit declaration of the attribute within the document optional, but not provide a default value, using the #IMPLIED keyword. If you want to require that documents provide a value for an attribute, use the #REQUIRED keyword. Finally, you can fix the value of an attribute using the #FIXED keyword, as shown below:

```
#FIXED "fixedvalue"
```

Although it might seem odd to fix a value for an attribute, it does provide a means for alternate identification of element types. Two element types with the same fixed default values for the same attribute could be related, for example, despite their different names.

If you provide a default value, it must be appropriate to the rest of the declaration. You shouldn't, for example, use an enumerated list and then provide a default value that isn't in the list.

Putting It All Together

Now that we have the parts, let's see how they fit together in a variety of common situations. A common starting scenario developers use as a placeholder is to declare an attribute as CDATA and #IMPLIED; this minimizes the constraints on attribute content. For example, the initial declarations for an IMAGE element might look like:

```
<!ELEMENT IMAGE EMPTY>
<!ATTLIST IMAGE
   SOURCE         CDATA       #IMPLIED
   TITLE          CDATA       #IMPLIED
   BORDER         CDATA       #IMPLIED
   TYPE           CDATA       #IMPLIED
   DESCRIPTION    CDATA       #IMPLIED
   HEIGHT         CDATA       #IMPLIED
   WIDTH          CDATA       #IMPLIED
>
```

This initial state makes it easy to create documents and start exploring the possibilities of different structures. It doesn't commit users to taking advantage of features, and it doesn't restrict the ways in which they can attempt to access information. (Users are, of course, limited to the list of attributes actually declared.)

After some experimentation, it might be time to adjust the declarations. An IMAGE element without a SOURCE attribute isn't really an image—at best, it might be empty space, but other applications might not know how to handle it. So SOURCE will be marked #REQUIRED. For accessibility, it might be good to require authors to provide a TITLE, providing readers who can't see the image with textual information the computer could read. The BORDER attribute is difficult to work with unless a set of values with meaning is established. For right now, we'll offer 0, 1, and 2 as values, specifying the width in pixels. Because many images have no border, we'll set the default to 0. That brings us to:

```
<!ELEMENT IMAGE EMPTY>
<!ATTLIST IMAGE
   SOURCE         CDATA       #REQUIRED
   TITLE          CDATA       #REQUIRED
   BORDER         (0|1|2)     "0"
   TYPE           CDATA       #IMPLIED
   DESCRIPTION    CDATA       #IMPLIED
   HEIGHT         CDATA       #IMPLIED
   WIDTH CDATA    #IMPLIED
>
```

The TYPE attribute is difficult. If we want to identify what type of graphic we're referencing through the SOURCE attribute, we should probably use notations, taking advantage of the tools available in XML 1.0. (Notation declarations are described in Chapter 15. For now, just assume that we've declared notations named png and jpg.) There may be times, however, when we don't want to declare the type, and leave it up to the application to determine the type of graphic, using MIME content-types or another mechanism. It's a bit tricky (and not explicitly stated in the recommendation), but you can use a default of #IMPLIED to avoid having to declare the type. This way, if your element wants to declare the type, it can, but it isn't required. The same thing works with ordinary enumerated attribute types. You can't, however, provide an empty string as a choice in the list. This lets us declare the attribute list as:

```
<!ATTLIST IMAGE
   SOURCE         CDATA                    #REQUIRED
   TITLE          CDATA                    #REQUIRED
   BORDER         (0|1|2)                  "0"
   TYPE           NOTATION (png|jpg)       #IMPLIED
   DESCRIPTION    CDATA                    #IMPLIED
   HEIGHT         CDATA                    #IMPLIED
   WIDTH          CDATA                    #IMPLIED
>
```

It's difficult to do anything further with DESCRIPTION, HEIGHT, or WIDTH using XML's built-in capabilities. While DESCRIPTION might be text, it might also be a URL pointing to a more complete description of the image. HEIGHT and WIDTH should probably be numbers, but they might require additional labels to indicate what those numbers mean. We'll return to these issues in Chapter 11.

The IMAGE element might need to support an additional identifier—an attribute of type ID. This would let other elements within the document reference it safely, and would force the parser to ensure that the identifier was unique:

```
<!ATTLIST IMAGE
   id      ID      #IMPLIED>
```

ID attributes are typically, though not necessarily, identified with a name of lower-case id. In this case, it might be more consistent to use the upper-case ID. In either case, the declaration for the ID element could be made separately (as shown immediately above) or added to the larger list of attributes already declared for IMAGE.

We could also add a fixed attribute that identified the IMAGE element as an analog to the HTML IMG, possibly simplifying conversion among formats:

```
<!ATTLIST IMAGE
HTML-EQUIV      CDATA    #FIXED "IMG">
```

If we had an element named PICTURE that also had a fixed HTML-EQUIV attribute of "IMG", we might be able to determine that the two elements contained similar information.

Overriding Attribute List Declarations in the Internal Subset (and Elsewhere)

Attribute declarations, unlike element declarations, may appear repeatedly. This opens the door to authors' making significant changes using the internal subset, which will override declarations in the external subset. Although authors *can* make any changes they like—adding new elements, changing the type of an attribute, modifying the list of values in an enumerated type, or making required values implied—it's usually safest to stick to a limited number of different changes.

The most common change is the addition or modification of a default value for an attribute. If authors know that all the images in a document will be in PNG format, a declaration like the one below, appearing in the internal subset, would let them specify this without requiring constant explicit declarations in the document body:

```
<!ATTLIST IMAGE
   TYPE  NOTATION (png|jpg)   "png"
>
```

Similarly, there may be times when it is appropriate for a document to override an attribute value set in the DTD using a #FIXED default. By overriding the declaration, the document can substitute other fixed values, make the attribute optional, or provide a default that isn't mandatory.

DTD authors may find these tools will allow them to modify other DTDs without having to actually modify their content. The same use cases apply for DTD authors as apply for document authors, although DTD authors may be more likely to extend the original DTD with additional attributes. The implications of and mechanisms for this kind of extensibility will be explored more deeply in Chapters 14, 19, and 20.

All of these changes require some understanding of the application that will be parsing the document. If an application is relying on the parser to return documents that fit its needs precisely, getting the "wrong" value for an enumerated type may cause information to be lost or ignored, or worse, cause the application to crash. Although developers should at least build their applications flexibly enough to avoid a crash, lost information is a potential problem. If an application sorts out elements based on an attribute value, for example, it may simply discard elements with nonconformant values. Similarly, an application may not know to check for extra attributes, and discard their value during processing. The application thinks that validation against a DTD would check for this kind of conformance and notify it, but the internal subset provides document authors with as much power as the DTD's creator does when it comes to validation. Document authors should check to make certain their changes are acceptable, and not be surprised if seemingly minor changes cause odd behavior in their applications.

CHAPTER 9

Extras: Comments, Processing Instructions, and CDATA Sections

XML 1.0 provides some tools for putting information into documents "outside" the main document flow, as well as a tool for including information within an XML document that would normally cause well-formedness errors. Comments and processing instructions allow document authors to add information to documents that isn't elements or attributes, while CDATA sections allow authors to "escape" text that might otherwise require a large number of character references or entities to get through a parser. All these tools may be used in any well-formed XML document, including valid documents.

Comments

Comments let you add notes to documents that are intended for human consumption. Although parsers do process comments, they don't do anything with the content inside them. Ampersands and left angle brackets (<) don't cause problems within a comment, because comments aren't allowed to contain marked-up content. Entities will not be expanded inside comments. Everything within a comment is treated as text, until the comment is closed and the XML markup starts up again. Comments begin with the sequence `<!--`, and end with the sequence `-->`. (For compatibility with SGML, you shouldn't use the sequence `'--'` within an XML comment.) For example:

```
<!-- This is a comment. -->
```

Comments may appear in the prolog of a document, in the document type definition, in the document, or after the document. Comments may not appear within markup—they can't be placed in the middle of a tag, declaration, or processing instruction, for example. (If a comment appears within a CDATA section, it is treated as part of the text included in the CDATA section, and not interpreted as a comment.) Comments are commonly used to provide documentation for DTDs, and are often used within documents to report things like work that still needs to be finished. XML processors aren't required to report comments to the application, but many do anyway. Your applications would probably be smarter not to rely on comments for important processing information—processing instructions are a better tool for presenting such information.

Comments are a fairly limited tool for adding human-readable documentation to DTDs and documents. They provide no mechanism for identifying what they describe. A comment could describe the information that appears before it or after it or the element that contains it—only the author of the comment can be 100% certain. Using a convention—like always putting comments directly before the information they describe—can help alleviate this problem without always requiring authors to describe the target of the comment explicitly. In addition, if your application requires the use of different kinds of documentation, you should consider starting your comments with an identifier that describes the nature of the comment, typically something that wouldn't be entered by mistake. For instance, the XML Authority schema editor (see **http://www.extensibility.com**) represents its "notes" as comments that appear before their targets within DTDs. Notes describing how the element fits into the schema as a whole are comments prefixed with `#AUTHOR:`, while notes describing how the element is used in documents are comments prefixed with `#USAGE:`, and versioning notes are comments prefixed with `#CHANGES:` and the date of the change. For example:

```
<!--#AUTHOR: The paragraph element is the 'workhorse' element of this
schema, but is not to be used as a root element for documents.-->
<!--#USAGE: The paragraph element is used to represent paragraphs.
Use this element instead of or in addition to traditional whitespace
separation of paragraphs.-->
<!--#CHANGES:10-September-99 : Created -->
<!ELEMENT paragraph (#PCDATA | emphasis)*>
```

As XML does not allow comments within declarations (except the document type declaration, which contains many other declarations), conventions like these are the only way to document your DTDs reliably.

Although tools make it easy to stay within the conventions, authors writing DTDs by hand need to keep a close watch on comments to make sure they stay within the rules.

Processing Instructions

Although comments are meant for human interpretation, processing instructions, or PIs as they're often abbreviated, are intended for application interpretation. Applications may not be able to understand your processing instructions, but the parser is at least required to pass them to the application. If you have control over the application, you can add support for your own processing instructions, or you can stick to processing instructions that are in common use and hope that applications that could do something with your PIs understand how to use them. Like comments, processing instructions may appear in the prolog of a document, in the document type definition, in the document, or after the document—pretty much anywhere except inside markup. Processing instruction syntax is simple:

```
<?Target anything else ?>
```

There cannot be any space between the initial `<?` and the `Target`. The first piece of the processing instruction—the target—is fairly tightly restrained. It must follow the same rules that apply to element and attribute names: the target name must begin with a letter or underscore, and may contain letters, digits, hyphens, underscores, and periods. It may not start with "xml" or case variations on "xml." Colons should not be used in target names in documents that will be using namespaces. After the target, any content may appear inside of a processing instruction, even the characters `<` and `&`. Entities will not be expanded inside of processing instructions. The only content that may not appear within a processing instruction is the character sequence `?>`, which ends the processing instruction immediately—and could leave extraneous information floating in the document.

Processing instructions can be used for almost anything you'd like, although their use (even their existence) is somewhat controversial. Effectively, processing instructions are a huge escape clause for sending to the application information that is left completely unregulated. Processing instructions can appear anywhere in the content of a document, and have no effect on validation. Processing instructions can be used to "subvert" the strictly hierarchical rules of XML by telling applications to turn flags on and off outside the element structure. Even when the W3C has used processing instructions (to associate style sheets with documents—see **http://www.w3.org/TR/xml-stylesheet/**), the recommendation includes a serious warning label: *"The use of XML processing instructions in this speci-*

fication should not be taken as a precedent. The W3C does not anticipate recommending the use of processing instructions in any future specification."

Although it's probably best to avoid using processing instructions if possible, there may be circumstances when you want to include information targeted to a particular application that may not have a place in the document content itself. You might use processing instructions to describe a mapping between elements and program structures, that only works with a given set of tools. You might use the W3C's style sheet processing instruction, or you might in fact do something entirely new and different. If you plan to use processing instructions, it's probably best to use some sort of convention to make their contents easier for your applications to understand.

The W3C style sheet processing instruction provides useful tools for standardizing the contents of processing instructions. The target (`xml-stylesheet`) identifies that this is the processing instruction for associating style sheets with documents. (The W3C can, of course, start *their* PI target names with `xml`.) Following that target is a list of *pseudo-attributes* which, like regular attributes, may appear in any sequence. The pseudo-attributes are based on the attributes used by the HTML LINK element for associating style sheets with documents, and are written just like attributes. For example:

```
<?xml-stylesheet href="invoicestyle.css" type="text/css" title="Invoice
Style Sheet"?>
```

Browsers that support this recommendation will identify the processing instruction by its target (`xml-stylesheet`). They will then parse the rest of the PI's contents to extract the pseudo-attribute names and values. The parser itself will pass the application the contents of the PI verbatim—pseudo-attributes are a convention used within the style sheet recommendation, and not a part of XML 1.0, so the application will need to know how to interpret this PI and what its contents mean.

Processing instruction targets may also (but aren't required to) be associated with notations, described in Chapter 15.

CDATA Sections

CDATA sections are also an "escape clause," but fit into the structure of XML documents and don't generate the same kinds of controversy that processing instructions do. CDATA sections—not to be confused with `CDATA` attribute types, which are quite different—allow authors to include text content within an element that doesn't meet the rules for well-formedness. Typically, this means that it contains `<`, `>`, and `&`, though some CDATA sections protect generated content that *may* include these characters. CDATA sections may only appear within element content, and use the syntax:

```
<![CDATA[...content...]]>
```

The first occurrence of]]> will end the CDATA section, so be certain that your contents avoid this (relatively unusual) sequence. This means, among other things, that you can't represent a CDATA section inside a CDATA section. White space within a CDATA section is reported like any other white space in element content.

There are a number of cases where CDATA sections are useful. One of the most frequent uses is the inclusion of "sample" XML code within a document, thereby avoiding the use of lots of entities or character references:

```
<example>The XML below demonstrates two elements, one nested within the
other, as well as attributes and textual content:
<code><![CDATA[
<parent name="sample parent">
   <child name="sample child">CONTENT!</child>
</parent>
]]></code></example>
```

Another common use of CDATA is to keep the XML parser from misinterpreting < in scripts, where it is typically used to indicate "less-than." For example:

```
<SCRIPT><![CDATA[
a=20;
b=30;
if (a<b) {document.write("a<b");}
]]></script>
```

There are times in certain scripting languages where the sequence]]> may appear, as in JavaScript during an array comparison. Although CDATA can help with many of the simple cases, this is one that authors will need to watch for on their own and avoid.

Finally, CDATA sections may or may not be needed to protect text that represents binary information. Base64 encoding is sometimes used as a transformation to convert information from a binary format into text so that it can be transmitted as part of an XML document rather than referenced separately. Base64 is described in section 6.8 of RFC 2045, available at **http://www.ietf.org/rfc/rfc2045.txt**. Fortunately, Base64 only uses the letters (upper and lower case) of the English alphabet, plus digits and the +, /, and = characters. None of the characters used in Base64 requires escaping in a CDATA section, although it will probably be easier to manage your information if you put Base64-encoded material within its own element. However, if you choose to encode binary information using a different algorithm, you may need to use CDATA sections. If the algorithm may generate]]>, it should be avoided.

CHAPTER 10

White Space

White space may seem like the last thing that should generate controversy, but it has crept in to many XML discussions and generated a significant amount of confusion. The XML 1.0 recommendation answers and creates many questions about different types of white space, its role in XML and XML processing, when it should be significant and when it can be ignored, and, of course, ways to get around the rules put forward in XML 1.0.

An Introduction to White Space Handling

White space includes all the characters—regular spaces between words, line breaks, carriage returns, and tabs (although not non-breaking spaces, which are treated as regular characters)—typically used to format text in the absence of any other instructions, much as people used them on typewriters. Although some space in XML documents is clearly important—we don't want to lose the spaces between words, for example—it isn't clear that all of it is important, and there are many places where white space is treated more flexibly than other forms of text, as well as places where it is prohibited. In some cases, parsers are required to report all white space, while in others, the presence of white space is used to demarcate pieces which are themselves reported, but the specifics of the white space aren't.

The good news is that white space handling probably won't be an issue for most XML developers. Most of the rules for using white space within markup are quite clear, and although the rules for using white space in content are somewhat more confusing, application developers (and sometimes authors) can make their own decisions on how to handle it. Although XML processors (parsers) are required to report certain types of white space, there's no requirement that applications process that white space in any particular way. (Application developers should probably read the documentation that comes with the parser to see how exactly it behaves, however.)

A likely model for some XML application development is HTML. HTML browsers compress white space in element content, preserving it only in cases where they are explicitly ordered to (through the PRE element or with Cascading Style Sheets.) HTML editors often take advantage of this to format white space any way they like, with the understanding that the browser will ignore it. Although some XML applications may well adopt this approach, the XML recommendation itself makes sure that applications at least receive white space information in content, allowing developers to make their own decisions.

White Space in Declarations and Markup

White space is important within declarations and markup, but the particulars of that white space are not considered important. Where white space is required, it must appear, but any form or quantity of white space may appear: line breaks, spaces, tabs—whatever seems good to the author is acceptable to XML 1.0. For example, attribute type declarations are often written as:

```
<!ATTLIST myElement
   attribute1        CDATA       #IMPLIED
   attribute2        CDATA       #REQUIRED
   xattribute3       CDATA       #REQUIRED>
```

However, the same declaration could be written as:

```
<!ATTLIST myElement attribute1 CDATA #IMPLIED attribute2 CDATA
#REQUIRED attribute3 CDATA #REQUIRED>
```

It isn't as readable, but it is acceptable. On the other hand, the example below is forbidden.

```
<!ATTLISTmyElementattribute1CDATA#IMPLIEDattribute2CDATA#REQUIRE
Dattribute3CDATA#REQUIRED>
```

Although a parser might have a chance of figuring out what this was supposed to mean, the lack of white space makes that process uncertain, and some white space is therefore required. (White space is not required in element content models, which use other separators, but it is allowed.)

Within document markup, there are similar cases, as well as cases where white space is forbidden. For example, a typical start tag might read:

```
<elementName attribute1="example1" attribute2="example2">
```

elementName must appear right beside the opening <; no white space is allowed to appear there. There could be white space between the names of attributes, the equals sign (=), and the quoted value of the attribute, and there must be white space between the element name and attribute name/value pairs. White space may appear before the closing > or /> (for an empty tag), but white space may not appear between the / and > in an empty tag. The example below is another legal way to present the same start tag:

```
<elementName
   attribute1="example1"
   attribute2 = "example2"
>
```

End tags follow similar rules. There can be no white space between the opening </ and the name of the element, but there can be white space between the element name and the closing >. Again, it won't be reported to the application.

Processing instructions, as described in Chapter 9, allow no white space between their opening <? and the identifier of the processing instruction, or in the closing ?>, but white space may be used within processing instructions in a variety of ways. Similarly, white space within comments is preserved, although white space may not appear in the opening <!-- or closing -->.

White Space in Element Content

All white space in element content must be reported by the processor to the application, but, as noted above, the application is not obliged to do anything with it. There are two cases where white space usage is a bit complicated, both of which have to do with situations where there is no surrounding textual content.

In content models where only elements are allowed, document authors may use white space to separate element names. For example, let us say the element type CONTAINER has a declaration of:

```
<!ELEMENT CONTAINER (A,B,C)>
```

If white space were regarded as textual content, then the instance below would be illegal:

```
<CONTAINER>
   <A/>
   <B/>
   <C/>
</CONTAINER>
```

However, XML 1.0 explicitly allows such use of white space in element content, letting authors work with their elements in the manner of their choice.

When it comes to empty elements, however, XML 1.0 is not so forgiving. Stronger rules are enforced on the declaration:

```
<!ELEMENT EMPTINESS EMPTY>
```

`EMPTY` elements must be truly empty. The only two allowable forms of `EMPTINESS` are `<EMPTINESS />` and `<EMPTINESS></EMPTINESS>`. `<EMPTINESS> </EMPTINESS>` is forbidden.

White Space in Mixed Content

In textual content, XML processors are required to report all white space characters to the application as they appear, with one modification for end-of-line handling. Applications can preserve or ignore that white space as they find convenient, and possibly based on the `xml:space` attribute described in the section below. Although XML requires processors to pass white space to the application, this doesn't bind the application to do anything with it.

In an attempt to improve the consistency of that white space, the XML 1.0 recommendation specifies particular processing for handling line-feed and carriage-return characters, which together are used to identify the ends of lines and paragraphs. Different operating systems use different conventions to mark the ends of lines. UNIX systems identify end-of-line with a line feed (`#xA` in hexadecimal), Macintosh systems identify end-of-line with a carriage return (`#xD` in hexadecimal), while Windows systems use both—a carriage return followed by a line feed (`#xD#xA`). XML 1.0 processors should convert all occurrences of `#xD` and `#xD#xA` to `#xA`, "normalizing" everything to UNIX practice.

A Way to Sneak in #xD

If you really need to put a carriage return in an XML document's element content—perhaps a later part of the application expects to see one—you can use a character reference. Simply insert `
` wherever you need a carriage return.

xml:space

XML 1.0 provides a way for XML documents to signal to the application that white space within a particular element (and all its children, unless they declare otherwise) is significant and should be preserved. This doesn't obligate an application to preserve that white space, as some applications may ignore this flag. The `xml:space` attribute at least gives your document a chance to declare white space importance, however. The `xml:space` attribute accepts two values: `default` and `preserve`. The `default` value tells the application that it can do whatever it likes with the white space. The `preserve` value indicates that white space should be preserved.

The `xml:space` attribute must be declared like any other attribute in an XML document if you plan to use it in a validating processor. For example, to declare the `xml:space` attribute for an element type named `sourcecode`, and assign it the default value of `preserve`, you would declare:

```
<!ATTLIST sourcecode
    xml:space        (default|preserve) 'preserve'>
```

Because `xml:space` is defined in the XML 1.0 recommendation, you are allowed to declare it even though it starts with "xml."

White Space in Attribute Content

XML processors handle white space in attribute values differently from the way they handle white space in element content. XML processors compress all white space within attributes into single spaces between text. If three line breaks, a tab, and a carriage return appear inside an attribute value, the combination of all five characters will be reported as single space. If white space is important to you, store it in elements, not attributes.

In validating processors, white space is a required separator in attribute values that contain `NMTOKENS`, `ENTITIES`, or `IDREFS` content when more than one value is listed. Again, the amount of white space doesn't matter (and doesn't have to be reported to the application), as long as white space is present. The application should receive a list of items, with no concern for the white space that once separated them.

White Space on the Fringes: The Prolog and Epilogue

White space can appear outside of a document root element, either in the prolog, before it starts, or in the epilogue, after the root element closes. Although there is some debate about whether or not XML 1.0 requires that this white space be reported, this kind of white space is typically ignored. It is explicitly not part of the XML 1.0 Infoset Working Drafts at the W3C, although that could change before its emergence as a Recommendation.

Implications for Applications and Stylesheets

For some application builders, white space may matter enormously, while others may find it to be of little or no importance. Preserving white space is critical for some applications, like source code for certain computer languages, while it doesn't matter at all for others, like transfers of numeric data between databases. This flexibility is given to application designers, and they need to address (and document their handling of) such issues. Other XML users need to pay attention to how the tools they use handle (or don't handle) white space, to make sure they don't lose critical information along the way when multiple levels of processing take place.

CHAPTER 11

Data Typing in XML 1.0

At least one critical tool for developers who want to use XML for data interchange is missing from the XML 1.0 toolbox: a way to describe formal data types for elements and attributes. Element and attribute names can provide some hints, and it's possible to describe the data types in documentation. This doesn't go far enough, however, for a large number of developers whose primary focus is on data exchange and for whom those data types are as important as or perhaps more important than the tools for describing structures. Although XML 1.0's processing doesn't go far into data typing, you can take the tools XML 1.0 provides and build a data typing solution that both works with present XML processors and will be readily convertible to XML Schemas if you find later that you need to move that direction.

Extra Information

Storing information about data types within XML 1.0 DTDs requires two things: a standard way to describe that information, and a place to put it. XML 1.0 provides a standard way to create type identifiers—notations—but supports only a limited set of use cases for notation processing, as described in Chapter 15. The W3C's XML Schemas proposals include a separate document on data types (**http://www.w3.org/TR/xmlschema-2**)

that provides a core list of options that could readily be used as default data types for XML 1.0. XML 1.0 provides no standard place to put such information, however.

Supporting data types with XML 1.0 requires creating a set of conventions that can reliably hold information and providing fallback behavior for processing documents that don't support those conventions. XML Authority, a schema and DTD-editing product from Extensibility (**http://www.extensibility.com**), uses a set of conventions for storing this information as fixed attribute default values. Processors can then interpret these values after XML parsing is complete and supply their own data validation processing. Data validation becomes a step following document validation, but this extra step can be automated much the way that XML processing itself is automated, with a set of tools that takes information from one source, checks it against constraints, and passes the information along with a list of errors to the application. It requires an intermediate layer between the parser and the application (or perhaps some extra work within the application), but such processing can rest safely on conventions.

We'll start by looking at a simple DTD that uses data typing, first seeing it presented in the XML Authority interface, and then exploring the underlying convention and how it works. You don't need to have XML Authority to use these conventions—you can recreate their content in hand-coded DTDs or DTDs created with other tools. XML Authority is a convenient tool for creating DTDs that use data typing conventions, but by no means the only one.

The DTD we'll explore is a simple bill for bulk deliveries of goods. It contains an addressee, a date, information about shipments, and, of course, a total bill. In XML Authority 1.1, the element types are presented as shown in Figure 11.1.

Both elements and attributes can have data types assigned to them. Figure 11.2 shows the process of assigning the boolean data type to the paid attribute.

Most of the context for these declarations should be fairly clear—there are elements with XML content models, elements that just contain text (#PCDATA), and elements and attributes whose text also has a data type specified for it. The results of these choices are shown in the DTD below:

```
<!ELEMENT bill    (refNum , addressee , shipments , total )>
<!ATTLIST bill    dateSent CDATA        #REQUIRED
                  paid  CDATA           #IMPLIED
                  a-dtype NMTOKENS      'dateSent  date
                                        paid       boolean' >
<!ELEMENT refNum  (#PCDATA )>
<!ATTLIST refNum  e-dtype NMTOKEN  #FIXED 'int' >

<!ELEMENT addressee (CustomerName ,  CustomerAddress ,
 CustomerAddress2 ,  City ,  StateProvince ,  PostalCode ,  Country )>
```

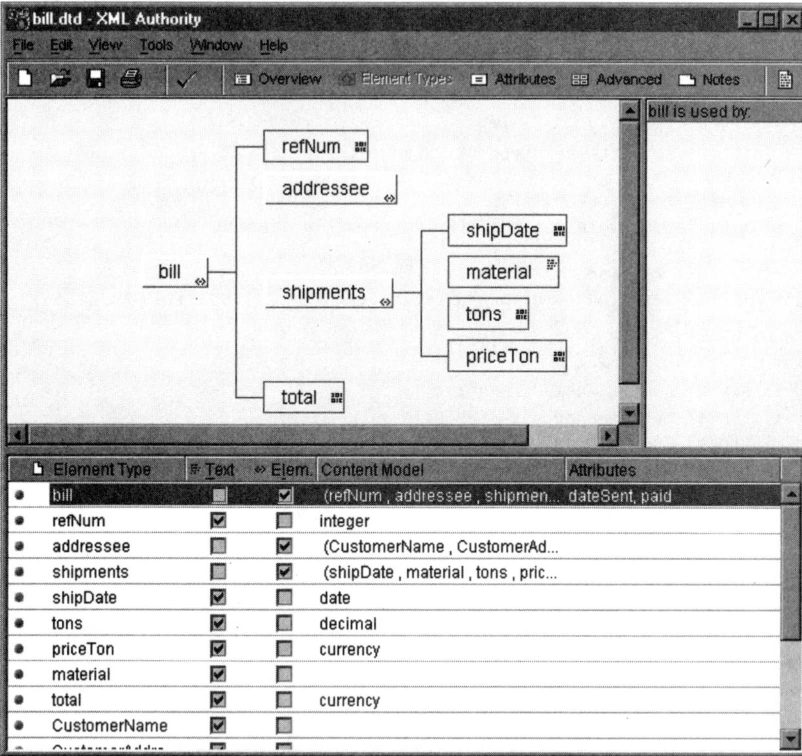

Figure 11.1 A simple DTD with element types in XML Authority 1.1

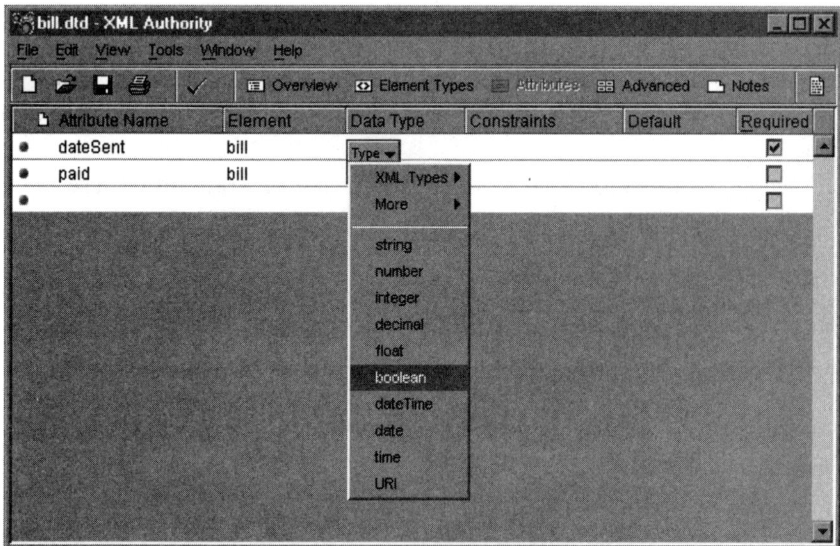

Figure 11.2 Assigning attribute data types in XML Authority 1.1

```
<!ELEMENT shipments  (shipDate ,  material  ,  tons ,  priceTon )>

<!ELEMENT total  (#PCDATA )>
<!ATTLIST total  e-dtype NMTOKEN  #FIXED 'fixed.14.4' >

<!ELEMENT shipDate  (#PCDATA )>
<!ATTLIST shipDate  e-dtype NMTOKEN  #FIXED 'date' >

<!ELEMENT tons  (#PCDATA )>
<!ATTLIST tons  e-dtype NMTOKEN      #FIXED 'decimal' >

<!ELEMENT priceTon  (#PCDATA )>
<!ATTLIST priceTon  e-dtype NMTOKEN   #FIXED   'fixed.14.4' >

<!ELEMENT material  (#PCDATA )>

<!ELEMENT CustomerName  (#PCDATA )>
<!ELEMENT CustomerAddress  (#PCDATA )>
<!ELEMENT CustomerAddress2  (#PCDATA )>
<!ELEMENT City(#PCDATA )>
<!ELEMENT StateProvince  (#PCDATA )>
<!ELEMENT PostalCode  (#PCDATA )>
<!ELEMENT Country  (#PCDATA )>
```

We'll start by examining the attributes assigned to the bill element. In addition to the declarations for the actual attributes, an extra attribute appears:

```
<!ATTLIST bill        dateSent   CDATA      #REQUIRED
                      paid       CDATA      #IMPLIED
                      a-dtype    NMTOKENS  'dateSent date
                                            paid      boolean' >
```

The `a-dtype` attribute contains a list of name value pairs, where the name corresponds to the name of an attribute, and the value is the name of the data type that attribute must contain. In this case, the `dateSent` attribute is assigned a data type of `date`, and the `paid` attribute is assigned a data type of `boolean`.

The declarations for the `refNum` element demonstrate how these types are applied to elements.

```
<!ELEMENT refNum  (#PCDATA )>
<!ATTLIST refNum  e-dtype NMTOKEN  #FIXED 'int' >
```

Instead of an `a-dtype` attribute, which would provide information about the attribute data types, we have an `e-dtype` attribute, which only contains a value describing the data type for the element. Similar patterns repeat throughout the rest of the DTD. (`Fixed.14.4` represents currency.)

This approach is derived from ISO/IEC 10744 (HyTime) "lextype" architectural forms, but doesn't require any understanding of the rest of HyTime to operate. The basic structure is simple. A small set of attribute names is used to assign data type information to attributes and elements.

If the information is about an attribute or set of attributes, the name of the attribute providing this information is prefixed with `a-`. If the information is about an element, the name of the attribute providing this information is prefixed with `e-`. `dtype` indicates that the information being provided is a data type, and the names of these data types are supposed to correspond to notations or a set of defaults. XML Authority supports some additional information about elements and attributes using `dsize` (for the size of the data), `pkey` (to identify the primary key of a database table), and `fkey` (to identify a foreign key to which an element or attribute refers). Using this technique, you can supplement the information supported by XML 1.0 DTDs with almost any information you like, though you'll need to have an application layer that understands how to process it. There are limits, because this technique adds overhead to every occurrence of an element that uses it, but for small pieces of information it can be useful.

Data Type Descriptors

To complete this system, developers need a set of data types they can use reliably. XML Authority provides support for the XML-Data data types (described at **http://www.w3.org/TR/1998/NOTE-XML-data-0105/#Datatypes**), and the XML Schemas Working Draft includes a core set of built-in and generated data types that could be similarly used, provided an application understood which vocabulary was in use. Applications need a stable set of tools for understanding the referents of data type declarations, and it looks like URIs may be the solution once again, much as they were for namespaces. Although namespaces aren't available in DTDs, notations are, so defining the data types using notations is probably the best approach. XML Authority 1.1's XML-data-based types can be expressed using notations including URIs that reference the XML-data specification, while data types that reference the XML Schemas work can use different notation declarations and URIs. Applications can then check the URIs behind the data type names to find out what a data type name actually refers to, and process the information appropriately.

Notations will be covered in more detail in Chapter 15. The mappings they establish between short names, which are easily referenced in the attributes described above, and URI values, make it easy uniquely to identify different types. In this context, they behave much like namespaces, mapping an abbreviated name to a URI (or public identifier, though URIs are more widely known). These conventions don't use the mechanisms XML 1.0 provides for `NOTATION` attribute types because those mechanisms are too restrictive, requiring an enumerated list, that all notations be declared, and that only one `NOTATION`-type attribute can appear on a given element. The use of `NMTOKEN` and `NMTOKENS` leaves the application with more work, although it is work the application will probably have to do anyway.

One final issue may cause problems for developers who want to use this data typing system—there are no "reserved spaces" for attributes like `a-type` and `e-type`. If your application encounters documents that use these attributes for something else, it may be confused. Unfortunately, there isn't any easy solution, given the variable compatibility of DTDs and namespaces described in Chapter 24. As a result, make sure to document what you're doing, and make sure the processors you use to check your data types are capable of dealing with unexpected information without a serious crash.

PART TWO

Elementary Principles of Composition

CHAPTER 12

Using Character References and Predefined Entities

XML 1.0 supports an enormous range of characters through Unicode, but most keyboards only provide access to a subset of those characters. A few characters (<, >, &, ", and ') have special meaning in XML and their use is tightly restrained. XML 1.0 provides tools for representing the entire range of characters without requiring any extra effort or foresight on the part of the DTD builder. All Unicode characters are accessible through character references, and the markup characters are also available through predefined entities, which come with more memorable names rather than numbers.

Identifying Characters—Character References

XML provides direct access to the ISO/IEC 10646 character set, which includes the Unicode character set defined in *The Unicode Standard, Version 2.0* (Addison-Wesley, 1996). Character references let document authors access characters directly without needing special entry devices or software tools. Character references may also let document authors include characters in documents that are not legal when included directly as text, like control characters. The main difficulty with character references is that they require users or tools to keep a list of the available characters handy. While *The Unicode Standard* is fun to browse, finding particular characters (especially getting the right character) can be challenging.

Once you know what character you need, XML provides two forms in which you can insert it into your documents. The first uses hexadecimal notation, and the second uses decimal notation. Character references that identify their characters with decimal values use the syntax:

```
&#Decimalvalue;
```

Character references that identify their characters with hexadecimal values use the syntax:

```
&#xHexadecimalvalue;
```

For example, the Euro character for the new European Union currency is 20AC hexadecimal or 8364 in decimal. To represent it with the decimal value, you would use:

```
&#8364;
```

To represent a Euro character with the hexadecimal value, you would use:

```
&#20AC;
```

Character references are always interpreted using the Unicode character value, whatever the encoding of the document as a whole. This makes character references a safe tool for use in any encoding, though there is no guarantee that the recipient of the document will be able to render the character, even though the character reference identifies it clearly. The implications of such character set issues will be discussed more thoroughly in Chapter 21.

Character references will be processed within element, attribute, and entity content. They will not be processed within CDATA sections, comments, or processing instructions, however.

Avoiding Collisions with Markup—Predefined Entities

Although character references can be useful, entering codes for characters that need to be handled on a regular basis can become a hassle quickly. XML 1.0 includes a set of predefined entities that provide more memorable references. The predefined entities are described using the same mechanisms as the general entities discussed in the next chapter, but users don't have to declare them to use them. Predefined entities are built into the XML processor. You may declare them in your DTDs if you like, to ensure interoperability with older SGML processors, but the declaration is not required.

The predefined entities are listed in the table below.

Entity	Usage in Document	Equivalent	Character Reference	Declaration
lt	<	<	<	<!ENTITY lt "<">
gt	>	>	>	<!ENTITY gt ">">
amp	&	&	&	<!ENTITY amp "&">
apos	'	'	'	<!ENTITY apos "'">
quot	"	"	"	<!ENTITY quot """>

The two most critical predefined entities are < and &, which must be used (or their equivalent character reference used) every time that < and & appear in element or attribute content. > is provided for consistency, and should be used anywhere within an element that]]> appears, to preserve compatibility with older SGML processors. (]]> is actually barred from all element content because of this compatibility issue.) ' and " may be used within attribute values to avoid ending the attribute prematurely. Predefined attributes provide an alternative to CDATA sections, allowing developers to "escape" markup text without needing to open and close sections. For example, to represent a less-than sign in code stored within an XML document, a developer might write:

```
if (a&lt;b) {
```

which the parser would report as:

```
if (a<b) {
```

Similarly, if ampersands were needed:

```
if (a &amp;&amp; b) {
```

would be reported as:

```
if (a && b) {
```

The apostrophe and quote entities are useful in a number of situations, mostly in attributes. For example, you might have:

```
<quote opinion='Ain&apos;t it the truth!'>
```

The parser would report the attribute value to the application as:

```
Ain't it the truth!
```

Although it's frequently possible to decide which type of quotes to use in an attribute based on its content, the built-in entities make it much easier for applications (and users) to protect these characters as they go into documents, without requiring consideration of what kind of quotes are used to mark the attribute's value.

Multiple Interpretation of Character References

The declarations for the `<` and `&` predefined entities demonstrate an issue that applies to both entities and character references. Entities and character references are resolved until all of the entities and character references will be resolved in multiple passes during DTD and document processing. This can be confusing, at times, but ensures that entities containing references to other entities will always be resolved. It also allows for the declaration of `<` and `&`, which would otherwise be made impossible by the requirement (described in the next chapter) that entity values must themselves be well formed. When an entity is declared, only one level of entities is processed; the whole set of entities or character references that are themselves referenced by that entity won't get processed until the document itself is processed. As a result, the declaration for the `<` entity starts out with the content:

```
&#38;&#60;
```

When this is declared in the entity, the processor will resolve it to:

```
&#60;
```

When `<` is encountered in a document, the processor will take the `<` character reference and finish resolving it to <. `&` is resolved using a similar set of steps. (Actually, an XML processor may just look for `<` in documents and replace it directly with <, but if it did go through a full set of entity handling, perhaps in an SGML parser, it would use the processing sequence described above.)

This multiple processing can also be used to create entities within entities, although only if you use the `&` character reference that represents an ampersand. (If you use `&`, the entity processing doesn't resolve it to an ampersand and you won't create any "new" entities.) Except for the complex cases described above, you shouldn't ever need to do this.

CHAPTER 13

Using General Entities for Reusable Document Content

In addition to providing basic syntax for creating documents, XML provides a mechanism for defining and reusing "shortcuts" to content, allowing you to include information in an XML document by reference. Sometimes this means that you can avoid enormous amounts of search-and-replace when a product name changes at the very last minute, and other times it lets you build documents out of other documents. General entities, often referred to simply as "entities," work only with XML (and text) content in the context of an XML document, not in the DTD. Although their syntax and typical usage is simple, there are a few tricks and traps to look out for.

Types of Entities

XML 1.0 categorizes entities in several different ways. There are *general* and *parameter entities*. General entities are used in document content, while parameter entities are used in DTD content. Parsed entities are expanded by the parser, while unparsed entities are passed as references to the application. Internal entities describe their content within the declaration itself, while external entities reference content in another file. This seems like it should create eight possible types of entities, but fortunately unparsed entities are subject to some serious limitations, appearing only in document content (therefore technically a subclass of general entities, although very different) and always referencing external content.

Parameter entities, both internal and external, are discussed in Chapter 14. Unparsed entities are described along with notations in Chapter 15.

Basic Syntax

General entities come in several varieties. Entities of the simplest type, internal general entities, are declared in the DTD using syntax that looks like:

```
<!ENTITY entityName "entityValue">
```

General entity names must always begin with a letter or underscore, and may contain letters, digits, hyphens, underscores, and periods. The name is case sensitive. Although XML 1.0 allows you to use colons in entity names, the Namespaces in XML recommendation declares that documents that contain entity names with colons are non-conformant. Even if you aren't using namespaces, it's probably wise to avoid using names with colons to keep your options open for future development.

The entity value in an internal entity may be text or markup, but it must be well-formed, conforming to the rules for content inside elements. No root element is necessary, but all elements that begin inside an entity declaration must also end within that declaration. If no start-tags appear, no end-tags should appear either. If start-tags appear, end-tags must also appear, and all elements must be nested properly. For example, the first three examples below are legal entity declarations, and the last three are not legal.

```
<!ENTITY legalEntity1 "this is just text">
<!ENTITY legalEntity2 "<sentence>This is a sentence.</sentence>">
<!ENTITY legalEntity3 "This <verb>is</verb> a sentence.">

<!ENTITY illegalEntity1 "this is mostly <text>text.">
<!ENTITY illegalEntity2 "<sentence>This is not a sentence">
<!ENTITY illegalEntity3 "<a><b/><c><d></c></d></a>">
```

The restriction on well-formedness assures users that they can drop your entities into element content without fear that they need to close or open elements. (Using general entities that contain markup will cause well-formedness violations if used within attribute values, however.)

There may be times when you want to include much larger chunks of information in an entity declaration, or simply want to include material within your document that someone else controls. Rather than stuffing large chunks of information directly into your documents and making the owner of the other material update your documents every time his or her own is updated, you can use external entities, which reference other information for inclusion in your documents.

External entities may be declared in two ways, using just a system identifier (the familiar URI) or a system identifier and a public identifier (the details of which were described in Chapter 2). External general entities are declared using the syntax below:

```
<!ENTITY entityName SYSTEM "entityURI">
```

or:

```
<!ENTITY entityName PUBLIC "entityPublicIdentifier" "entityURI">
```

In both cases, the resource described by the URI or the public identifier must be well formed in the same sense that internal entity content must be. Although it is not required to be a well-formed XML document, with a single root element, all the elements, character data, processing instructions, comments, and CDATA sections within the external entity must be complete and obey XML syntax.

The contents of external general entities must also be prefaced with an encoding declaration if they aren't encoded as UTF-8 or UTF-16. The encoding declaration is much like the XML declaration used for documents, except that use of the version or standalone declarations is prohibited. A typical encoding declaration might look like:

```
<?xml encoding="US-ASCII"?>
```

If an external entity's encoding declaration includes a version declaration or a standalone declaration, the parser will report a well-formedness violation when it retrieves the external entity content. (The same thing will happen if your external entity contains a document type declaration.) This unfortunately makes it difficult to include documents within documents. Also, external entities that are encoded in UTF-16 *must* begin with a byte order mark, the ZERO WIDTH NO-BREAK SPACE character (#xFEFF), so that processors can distinguish between documents in UTF-8 and UTF-16, the two encodings that all XML processors are required to be able to handle.

External general entities may not always appear in your document as planned. Non-validating parsers are not required to retrieve external resources, so your document may appear with the entity references left unexpanded in the text. Unfortunately, this behavior is explicitly allowed by the XML 1.0 specification, so there isn't much you can do about it except to hope that your documents using external general entities are either processed by validating processors (which are required to retrieve external resources) or processed by non-validating processors whose designers felt that retrieving external resources was a good idea.

All internal and external general entities—as well as unparsed entities—occupy the same namespace (in a different sense than the Namespaces in

XML recommendation describes). If you declare an internal general entity and an external general entity that have the same name, the first entity declaration (either first in the list of declarations or because a declaration appeared in the internal DTD subset) will have precedence over all others. This means that document authors can override the entity declarations made in the external DTD subset.

For example, if the declarations below appeared in an external DTD, the first declaration would assign the entity `myEntity` a value of `'kersploogedah'`.

```
<!ENTITY myEntity 'kersploogedah'>
<!ENTITY myEntity 'this is more sensible.'>
```

If the internal subset contained the declaration below, however, the entity `myEntity` would have a value of `'prim and proper'`:

```
<!ENTITY myEntity 'prim and proper'>
```

When referenced, whether inside the DTD (in an attribute default value or another entity declaration) or outside (in element or attribute values), the entity reference would be replaced with `'prim and proper'`. Parameter entities (described in the next chapter) occupy a different namespaces, and you can have parameter and general entities with the same name.

Using General Entities

General entities are included in element and attribute content through entity references. Entity references look a bit like the character references and predefined entity references shown in the previous chapter:

```
&entityName;
```

The ampersand preceding the name of the entity indicates that this is a general entity reference, and the semicolon marks the end of the entity. When parsers encounter general entity references in document content (or in attribute default values within the DTD), they process them by replacing them with the text contained or referenced by the declaration for that entity, "including" the entities. If an entity wasn't declared, validating parsers and non-validating parsers that retrieve external resources will report a well-formedness violation. (Non-validating parsers that don't retrieve external resources just leave the entity reference alone. They must notify the application that they recognized it but didn't process it, unless the standalone declaration was set to "yes.")

For example, if the entity declaration below appeared in the DTD for a document:

```
<!ENTITY myCompany "My Company, Inc.">
```

and the document referenced the entity as shown below:

```
<sentence>&myCompany; is doing very well.</sentence>
```

the application would receive:

```
<sentence>My Company, Inc. is doing very well.</sentence>
```

If the declaration changed to:

```
<!ENTITY myCompany "IBM">
```

the application would instead receive:

```
<sentence>IBM is doing very well.</sentence>
```

Similarly, if the entity declaration below appears in the DTD for a document:

```
<!ENTITY grocerylist SYSTEM "grocerylist.lst">
```

and the file `grocerylist.lst` contained the text below:

```
<toBuy>ketchup</toBuy>
<toBuy >toothpaste</toBuy>
<toBuy>crackers</toBuy>
```

A document that looked like:

```
<shoppingList>
<headline>Shopping List for <date/></headline>
&grocerylist;
</shoppingList>
```

would be reported to the application as:

```
<shoppingList>
<headline>Shopping List for <date/></headline>
<toBuy>ketchup</toBuy>
<toBuy >toothpaste</toBuy>
<toBuy>crackers</toBuy>
</shoppingList>
```

XML requires that all entities be declared before they are used. Most of the time, this isn't a problem for general entities—after all, most general entities are used in the document's content, after DTD processing is complete. When general entities contain other general entities, none of that processing is done until a reference to the entity actually appears in document content. There is one time, however, that a general entity may need to be processed inside of the DTD. When an attribute list declaration includes a default value that uses a general entity, that entity will be processed as soon as the attribute list declaration is encountered. If the entity hasn't been declared at that point, you may get an odd-looking error generated by this obscure well-formedness problem. The declarations below are legal:

```
<!ENTITY myCompany "My Company, Inc.">
<!ATTLIST company
   officialName CDATA "&myCompany;">
```

If you switch the order as shown below, however, the attribute declaration has no way to interpret the reference to the entity `myCompany`, and the parser will report an error.

```
<!ATTLIST company
   officialName CDATA "&myCompany;">
<!ENTITY myCompany "My Company, Inc.">
```

There may actually be times when this behavior can be helpful—it's certainly a good way to force users to define particular entities in the internal subset whether or not they actually use them in the document. If you leave such openings for errors, however, be certain to document them or your users may never figure out what's causing such problems.

Another error to avoid is the use of general entities within DTDs. The only places where general entity references may be used in a DTD are within other entity declarations and within attribute default values in attribute list declarations. General entities may not be used anywhere else in a DTD—attempting to do so will generate a violation of well-formedness.

Including Inclusions

Entities may be processed repeatedly, with the application reparsing the replacement text until all entities within it have been expanded. For example, the three entity declarations below represent two components and a larger whole that includes both of them.

```
<!ENTITY companyName "My Company, Inc.">
<!ENTITY companyWebSite "mycompany.example.com">
<!ENTITY companyListing "<Company>&companyName;</Company> <Website>&com-
panyWebSite;</Website>"
```

If a document then looked like:

```
<listing>&companyListing;</listing>
```

when entities are processed, the parser would first replace `&companyListing;` to produce:

```
<listing><Company>&companyName;</Company>
<Website>&companyWebSite;</Website></listing>
```

Then the parser would process this to:

```
<listing><Company> My Company, Inc.</Company> <Website>
mycompany.example.com </Website></listing>
```

The application would only see the final version, with all of the entity expansion complete.

Entities are not allowed to include references to themselves, either directly or through another entity. For example, the declaration below is illegal, and processors would report a well-formedness violation:

```
<!ENTITY a "&a;">
```

Similarly, the two declarations below are illegal, although a parser probably wouldn't notice it until it went to process a reference:

```
<!ENTITY a "&b;">
<!ENTITY b "&a;">
```

The entity a references the entity `b` which references `a` again, which could cause an endless loop except that the XML recommendation requires parsers to stop when they encounter this situation.

Using General Entities

Although they use the same reference mechanism and obey similar rules, internal and external general entities are typically used for very different things. Internal general entities are normally used for shortcut references, especially if a document's authors know that some key vocabulary in their document may need to change rapidly. Sometimes internal general entities are used to save keystrokes, while at other times they allow authors to rely on content provided by the DTD without requiring any active management from the author. External entities are more commonly used in document construction, helping authors to assemble large documents out of smaller, but still sizable, documents. At other times, external entities are used to reference information that is beyond the control of both the DTD creators and the document authors.

General entities provide one of the clearest cases for the existence of the internal DTD subset. Although some entities are declared as part of a larger DTD, typically information that is controlled by the DTD's editors, many entities are appropriate to only a few documents, not enough to justify processing their entity declarations in all documents of the same kind. By declaring general entities in the internal subset, authors can create their own convenient idioms, so they can simplify their work without interfering with the work of others sharing a central DTD. Internal general entities declared in the internal subset have the extra benefit of working across all parsers, whether or not they retrieve external resources. External general entities won't benefit in this regard from declaration in the internal subset, but their appropriateness to particular documents still makes the internal subset an attractive place to declare them.

There are some types of entities that may be better declared in the external subset or through an external parameter entity. Legal documents that rely on the same set of boilerplate text may want to use a common set of entity declarations across the entire set of documents, giving all the lawyers in an office access to the same material for writing wills, for example. This approach works well in fields where standardized forms are common, or across large document sets that all describe the same project.

Issues of Inclusion

As exciting a tool as general entities are, they raise some important problems about the nature of the documents that use them. Has a document changed if one of the external entities it reference changes? Or if internal entities declared in a central DTD changes? In some cases, notably archives, these kinds of changes, often made unintentionally, can have catastrophic consequences. Contracts, for example, are not supposed to change unilaterally, without negotiation. If an archive of contracts becomes corrupted because someone changed a file without realizing its impact on the archive, the participants in those contracts may become very unhappy. Their printed contracts (if they have them, of course) are going to have to be the binding contracts, making the archives useless for most automated processing.

Dealing with change issues requires planning ahead with a versioning and archiving strategy. Archive copies could be "parsed" versions of the documents created at their time of execution, stripped of any dependencies on resources that might change. Alternatively, your archive might take a snapshot of the document and its dependencies as they appeared at the time of execution, keeping all the information but preserving it against future changes in the documents on which it is dependent.

Change isn't the only problem facing included content, however. Ownership can cause equally difficult problems. Although external entities are a great way to include content that the author doesn't control directly, owners who find their material included in documents may not be very happy if they didn't grant permission. Within an organization, the use of external entities is fairly clear, and can follow existing rules for sharing information.

Outside an organization, the use of external entities may require prior agreement on the terms for including information, and possibly the creation of wrapper entities that mark the text being brought in from another source with its origin, ownership, and related legal information.

Entities provide excellent shortcuts, but they aren't an excuse to take shortcuts with other people's information. Asking first can spare you a lot of problems later. XML 1.0 provides the technology for inclusion, but provides no indemnity against its misuse.

CHAPTER 14

Using Parameter Entities for Reusable Declarations

Although general entities provide reusable content for use in documents, parameter entities provide reusable content for use in DTDs. Parameter entities may include declarations, lists of declarations, or fragments of declarations, allowing DTD creators to create modules for DTDs as well as smaller pieces like element content models, attribute enumerations and attribute default values. Although you aren't required to use parameter entities to create DTDs, they can simplify a large number of DTD creation and control tasks, as well as provide ways for document authors to assume some control over the DTD. Although their usage permits more "tricks" than general entities, their basic syntax is quite similar and the rules for their use only slightly more complicated.

Basic Syntax

Like general entities, parameter entities may be internal or external. Internal entities describe their content right inside the entity declaration that creates them:

```
<!ENTITY % entityName "entityValue">
```

The percent sign (%) identifies to the processor that this entity is a parameter entity. Parameter entities occupy a separate namespace from general entities—if a parameter entity and a general (or unparsed) entity happen to have the same name, they are still separate entities. (This has nothing to do with namespaces as used in the Namespaces in XML 1.0 recommendation.) Parameter entity names must always begin with a letter or underscore, and may contain letters, digits, hyphens, underscores, and periods. The name is case sensitive. Although XML 1.0 allows you to use colons in entity names, the Namespaces in XML recommendation declares that documents that contain entity names with colons are non-conformant. Even if you aren't using namespaces in your current work, it's probably wise to avoid using names with colons to keep your options open for future development.

The contents of parameter entities are less constrained than the contents of general entities—what matters is that those contents work in the contexts where they are used. Several basic rules apply, however. Parameter entities must either contain multiple complete declarations, or a fragment that can be used within a single declaration. (Parameter entities can't start in the middle of one declaration or end in the middle of another.) If parameter entities are used in the internal subset of the DTD, they must represent complete declarations, something that is rare with internal parameter entities.

Including complete declarations in internal parameter entities is unusual and generally pointless (we'll explore one case later in the chapter where it can provide enormous flexibility to document authors). Most often, complete declarations and lists of declarations are stored in external files, where they can be included by reference as modules of a DTD. External parameter entities are declared with syntax that looks much like their general entity cousins:

```
<!ENTITY % entityName SYSTEM "entityURI">
```

or:

```
<!ENTITY % entityName PUBLIC "entityPublicIdentifier" "entityURI">
```

In both cases, the resource described by the URI or the public identifier must contain complete DTD declarations that meet the same rules as external DTD subsets, containing complete declarations, parameter entities, white space, comments, processing instructions, and conditional sections. (It can also be empty, which is convenient when you're starting out and just need a place holder.) The contents of external parameter entities must also be prefaced with an encoding declaration if they aren't encoded as UTF-8 or UTF-16. The encoding declaration is much like the XML declaration used for documents, except that use of the version or standalone declarations is prohibited. A typical encoding declaration might look like:

```
<?xml encoding="US-ASCII"?>
```

If an external entity's encoding declaration includes a version declaration or a standalone declaration, the parser will report a well-formedness violation when it retrieves the external entity content. (The same thing will happen if an external entity contains a document type declaration.) External entities encoded in UTF-16 *must* begin with a byte-order mark, the ZERO WIDTH NO-BREAK SPACE character (#xFEFF), so that processors can distinguish between documents in UTF-8 and UTF-16, the two encodings that all XML processors are required to be able to handle. Fortunately, DTDs are just lists of declarations, without the structure or needs of XML documents that make including complete XML documents so difficult for general entities.

Like external general entities, external parameter entities may not always be retrieved for your document as expected. Non-validating parsers are not required to retrieve external resources, so your DTD may end up with the entity references left unexpanded. Because this behavior is explicitly allowed by the XML 1.0 specification, there isn't much you can do about it except to hope that your documents using external parameter entities are processed either by validating processors (which are required to retrieve external resources) or by non-validating processors whose designers felt that retrieving external resources was a good idea. Although it may not have the visible impact on your documents that leaving general entities unexpanded has, this behavior can cause more subtle problems, like missing default attributes.

All internal and external parameter entities occupy the same namespace (again, in a different sense than the Namespaces in XML recommendation describes.) If you declare an internal parameter entity and an external parameter entity that have the same name, the first entity declaration (either first in the list of declarations or because a declaration appeared in the internal DTD subset) will have precedence over all others. This means that document authors can override the entity declarations made in the external DTD subset. This can have significant implications for developers building modular DTDs—overlapping parameter entity names can cause chaos and errors that are difficult to trace. It also allows document authors to influence the document type definition by redeclaring parameter entities in the internal subset and using values that may be very different from what the DTD's creators intended.

As your parameter entities become more numerous and more important, keeping track of what's in them becomes more and more critical. Parameter entities with similar names can cause problems. In addition to naming your parameter entities, it's almost always worthwhile to document their intended purpose using comments. Other users who attempt to reference your parameter entities will have a better idea of what they were meant for, with more perspective than the minimal amount provided by their often-abbreviated names.

Using Parameter Entities

Parameter entities are included in DTD content through parameter entity references. Parameter entity references use the syntax shown below:

```
%entityName;
```

The percent sign (%) indicates that this is the beginning of a parameter entity, while the semicolon marks the end of the parameter entity name. Parameter entity references may appear anywhere within a DTD where their content is appropriate. It is uncertain whether parameter entities may be used within comments or processing instructions in a DTD. Although it seems the productions defining processing instructions and comments prohibit their use in this context, this practice is used in several W3C documents, including the DTD for the XML 1.0 specification itself. However, it is clear that parameter entities may not be referenced in document content, where the percent sign has no meaning apart from being a character. Attempts to use parameter entities in document content will leave the entity reference visible without the content it was supposed to reference being included. (Parameter entities may, however, be used inside of general entity declarations; this is demonstrated within the recommendation.)

Parameter entities are very simple things, but they open up an enormous number of possible strategies for DTD design, including strategies for getting around limitations imposed by the XML recommendation itself. Document authors can use them to circumvent the demands of DTD designers, and DTD designers can use them to force document authors to do things as well. Although they bring enormous flexibility, they may also bring problems to applications that are counting on a validating parser to return only "valid" content to their data model. We'll explore these tricks and traps as we go through the possibilities. Two general themes will emerge: the use of parameter entities to create "classes" of information that can be mixed, matched, and reused, and the use of parameter entities to supply naming and documentation for information that might otherwise be too complex to explain easily. The interactions between the internal and external subsets provide a third theme, but this is typically used only in a small number of cases.

Parameter entities are only allowed to use declaration fragments in the external subset of the DTD and this functionality makes it possible for DTD designers to create reusable components for many different aspects of DTD design. There are a few restrictions, however. XML parsers will append a space (#x20) to parameter entities when expanding them. This is to prevent declarations like the one below:

```
<!ENTITY % date "MONTH, DAY, YE">
<!ELEMENT DATE (%date;AR)><!--forbidden-->
```

The parser will end up with a content model for DATE of (MONTH, DAY, YEAR), which is illegal. The point of this "interference" is to ensure that parameter entities contain complete tokens, simplifying the work parsers have to do.

One of the most common uses for parameter entities is the creation of content models, or content model fragments, that can then be inserted in multiple-element type declarations. For example, an application might use a date format that splits dates into separate MONTH, DAY, and YEAR elements to allow easy formatting in a wide variety of environments. (These elements are all declared as #PCDATA.) That date format is then used in a number of elements, and the DTD contains separate FROMDATE, TODATE, and SIGNEDDATE elements. To allow all three of these elements to use the same date format, you could declare:

```
<!ENTITY % date "MONTH, DAY, YEAR">
<!ELEMENT FROMDATE (%date;)>
<!ELEMENT TODATE (%date;)>
<!ELEMENT SIGNEDDATE (%date;)>
```

All three elements would be assigned the content model (MONTH, DAY, YEAR). Or developer who needed to create DATE and TIME elements might use:

```
<!ENTITY % date "MONTH, DAY, YEAR">
<!ELEMENT DATE (%date;)>
<!ELEMENT TIME (HOUR, MINUTE, SECOND, %date;)>
```

This way the TIME element could include date information without having to include a DATE element and thereby adding an extra level of processing to the MONTH, DAY, and YEAR. Deciding when to use a parameter entity, instead of a containing element, can be difficult. Should (MONTH, DAY, YEAR) be handled as a parameter entity, or should it become a child elements, as shown below?

```
<!ELEMENT DATE (MONTH, DAY, YEAR)>
<!ELEMENT FROMDATE (DATE)>
<!ELEMENT TODATE (DATE)>
<!ELEMENT SIGNEDDATE (DATE)>
```

In many cases, it's up to the DTD author's preference. If containing dates in their own element feels more consistent with the approach of the DTD, this approach may be preferable. In other cases, the parameter entity approach makes sense. This is especially common where the parameter entity forms only part of the overall content model, or contains parts that follow in sequence without being related.

Parameter entities using fragments of declarations are also commonly used in attribute declarations. Parameter entities cannot be used inside default values (although they may contain default value declarations as part of a larger context). If entities are used inside default values for attributes, general entities must be used, as described in the previous chapter. Enumerations, however, can be specified with parameter entities. For example, if a number of attributes were going to be referencing days of the week, the entity declaration below might be useful:

```
<!ENTITY % days "Sat | Sun | Mon | Tues | Wed | Thurs | Fri">
```

That way, attributes which needed to reference a weekday could be easily constrained:

```
<!ATTLIST WEEKLY_MEETING
   day   (%days;) #REQUIRED>
```

When the parser expanded this, the declaration would look like:

```
<!ATTLIST WEEKLY_MEETING
   day   (Sat | Sun | Mon | Tues | Wed | Thurs | Fri) #REQUIRED>
```

If the `WEEKLY_MEETING` element also needed an option of `every` (hopefully just every weekday, not the weekend), it could declare:

```
<!ATTLIST WEEKLY_MEETING
   day   (%days; | every) #REQUIRED>
```

Now the `WEEKLY_MEETING` element could use all the day abbreviations specified in the `days` entity, plus `every`. If the parentheses had been included in the `days` entity, you couldn't do this, but since they weren't, it works well.

It is possible to use the same parameter entity within attribute declarations for the same element, though XML suggests that for interoperability (not compatibility, which is mandatory) with SGML processors, authors should avoid using the same tokens multiple times on an element. However, if you're confident that your documents won't encounter an SGML processor, you could do things like:

```
<!ATTLIST CHORE
   startday (%days;)  #REQUIRED
   endday   (%days;)  #REQUIRED>
```

If you're more conservative, you'll want to make sure you use the same parameter entity only on attributes for different elements.

On a larger scale, more like the element content models above, designers can use parameter entities to encapsulate sets of attribute declarations for use on multiple elements. Although this doesn't quite provide the functionality of assigning attributes across a set of elements, it can greatly simplify attribute management. For example, it's not unusual for a number of elements to share the possibility of ID values, and those are usually declared consistently throughout a document. Similarly, it may be useful for an element to cross-reference other elements using IDREF attributes. A parameter entity declaration like the one below makes it easy for authors to use IDs and references to IDs throughout their documents:

```
<!ENTITY % IDinfo "
   id      ID        #IMPLIED
   xref    IDREFS    #IMPLIED">
```

By including the entity reference %IDinfo; in the attribute declarations for all of your elements, you make them able to identify themselves and cross-reference others. Your application will still have to figure out what the cross-references mean, but you may have a head start on your document management.

```
<!ATTLIST paragraph
   %IDinfo;
   type (note | body) "body">
<!ATTLIST section
   %IDinfo;
   author CDATA #IMPLIED>
<!ATTLIST document
   %IDinfo;>
```

The parameter entity can be mixed with your other attribute declarations, as shown above. You do need to be a bit careful, and make sure you don't declare an additional ID attribute, which would generate a validity violation.

As was the case with general entities, you can include parameter entities (and also general entities, where appropriate to the content) in a declaration. For example, the declarations below are acceptable:

```
<!ENTITY % days "Sat | Sun | Mon | Tues | Wed | Thurs | Fri">
<!ENTITY % scheduleDays "%days; | every">
<!ENTITY % scheduleDaysDecl "day (%scheduleDays;) #REQUIRED"
<!ATTLIST WEEKLY_MEETING
   %scheduleDaysDecl;>
```

The parser will expand the %scheduleDaysDecl; reference to:

```
day (%days; | every) #REQUIRED
```

and that to:

```
day (Sat | Sun | Mon | Tues | Wed | Thurs | Fri | every) #REQUIRED
```

which will produce the final result:

```
<!ATTLIST WEEKLY_MEETING
   day (Sat | Sun | Mon | Tues | Wed | Thurs | Fri | every) #REQUIRED >
```

Like general entities, parameter entities must be declared before they are referenced. If these declarations were in any other sequence, the parser would find itself with a parameter entity reference it didn't yet understand, report errors, and be unable to properly construct the attribute list declaration for WEEKLY_MEETING.

Parameter entities are also commonly used to connect complete declarations to a DTD. Most of the time, these parameter entities are declared as external entities, referencing files, although it is possible (and occasionally useful) to create internal parameter entities that include complete declarations. Sometimes these external declarations are referenced on a small scale, to bring in a few common declarations (often for general entity sets relevant to a given documents), and other times they make up the body of the DTD. These entities may appear in either the internal subset of the DTD (inside the document's DOCTYPE declaration) or the external subset of the DTD.

Parameter entities make it possible for the designers of complex DTDs to break their creations into smaller pieces. These smaller pieces may be useful as a tool for assigning responsibility (individuals or teams each get their own pieces), simplifying reuse (a module may be referenced by different DTDs), or improving documentation (comments can describe the use of the module and its workings). The degree to which a DTD may be broken down varies, but typically some kind of functional or organizational principle is used. Some designers prefer to segregate parameter entity declarations that work across multiple modules to their own module, loaded before the rest of the modules, while others want each model to operate on its own, complete with its own set of parameter entities and dependent on nothing in the other modules. If modules may be reused in different contexts, the latter approach often makes more sense.

Remember, apart from a small performance penalty for processing repeated declarations, the same entity can be declared repeatedly. This usually works well until two modules need different values for the same entity name. This issue can be avoided with some forethought and the use of naming conventions. Although namespaces proper don't work with entities, there isn't really a need to ensure that entity names are uniquely identified beyond the edges of the DTDs in which they are used. Prefixing entity names with the name of the module in which they are used (or an abbreviation) and a dash will take care of most conflicts. If modules that come from DTDs outside the control of the designer are combined, this may not work (the prefixes may clash and require changing), but it should work in most situations.

Modularized DTDs are typically assembled in one of two ways. There may be an external DTD subset that references all the modules, building a single large DTD, or the internal subset may perform similar duties.

Assembling modules in the internal subset lets document developers use only the modules they need, but it can make it difficult to ensure that validation is meaningful—authors could always reference modules that weren't the "canonical" modules. Modules may also reference other modules, building dependency chains that further breakup the DTD, permitting more customized reuse of each of its pieces while retaining an overall hierarchical structure.

The internal subset's overriding priority can be very useful for making sure that certain modules, usually those including general entity declarations, are loaded before the contents of the external DTD subset arrive. Even though the parameter entities used to do this are "external" entities, by appearing in the internal subset they get priority over all declarations (internal and external) in the external DTD subset. Declarations included in this way will override declarations in the external subset—a great tool, unless you happen to load a module that contains element type declarations conflicting with element type declarations in the external subset. Then your parser will report errors and won't process your documents. In general, you'll probably be happiest if you reserve the internal subset for declarations that can be made repeatedly, and for references to such declarations. Don't declare element types in the internal subset or in modules loaded from the internal subset unless you're positive that they won't conflict with any declarations in the external subset.

This mechanism can provide a way to allow the internal subset to override element declarations. Although most DTD designers cringe at the thought of letting document authors modify the core of their designs (many aren't happy that the internal subset can override attribute and entity declarations), there may be times when this functionality is necessary. If you need to make it possible to override an element declaration, declare it as a parameter entity containing *only* that declaration, and then reference the entity. For example:

```
<!ENTITY % nameDecl "<!ELEMENT name (#PCDATA)>">
&nameDecl;
```

The document author could then override the declaration for `nameDecl` with a different declaration for the name element, if necessary. The document type declaration might look like:

```
<!DOCTYPE memo SYSTEM "myMemo.dtd" [
<!ENTITY % nameDecl "
<!ELEMENT name (given, family)>
<!ELEMENT given (#PCDATA)>
<!ELEMENT family (#PCDATA)>"
]>
```

The declarations for `given` and `family` could appear inside the entity or outside it—both approaches should work. Name elements for this document would be broken into two elements. If an application were just paying attention to the text as it appeared, this approach might be acceptable—applications that understood the child elements would get their child elements, and application just watching for text within the name element would get the text. Making this work requires cooperation between the DTD designer and the document author—the document author can't do this if the DTD designer hasn't created the opening.

The downside (or plus, depending on who you are and what situation you are in) is that the internal subset of the DTD can be used to override any parameter entity in the DTD, giving document authors the opportunity to wreak havoc or perform miracles (again, depending on your perspective). There is no way to turn off the internal subset. The external subset and external parameter entities may be ignored by non-validating parsers, but the internal subset is always read, in both validating and non-validating parsers. Any DTD that uses parameter entities may find its structures subverted by developers who override them at will. Applications that rely on the structural validation of XML 1.0 may find themselves getting "bad" or "wrong" data that don't meet their expectations, although the document is definitely valid. In short, the existence of the internal subset is a very good reason for application developers to provide their own mechanisms for checking data structures and handling such situations, rather than figuring that a validating XML parser will take care of all of these issues. Validation in these cases is inadequate, even for the kinds of structural checking that DTDs describe so well.

Parameter entities have one additional powerful use, managing conditional sections within DTDs. This usage will be covered, along with `INCLUDE` and `IGNORE`, in Chapter 16.

CHAPTER 15

Using Notations and Unparsed Entities

Notations and unparsed entities occupy some of the most obscure corners of XML 1.0, but these tools have significant promise for addressing some of the most basic problems developers have with the XML toolkit. Notations allow DTD designers to define types—file types, data types, processing instruction types, and almost any other "type" you'd like. Unparsed entities allow document authors (and DTD designers, to some extent) to reference non-XML content from within XML documents without having to implement a larger system like XLink. The XML specification gives little notice of the power of these two features, which together allow developers to significantly extend XML 1.0's own capabilities.

Basic Syntax

Notations may be declared by themselves, while unparsed entities are dependent on a supporting notation declaration. (You don't need to declare unparsed entities to declare notations, but you do need to declare notations in order to declare unparsed entities.) Notations are declared using syntax much like that for external entities:

```
<!NOTATION notationName SYSTEM "notationURI">
```

or:

```
<!NOTATION notationName PUBLIC "notationPublicIdentifier" "notationURI">
```

Notation declarations, unlike any other XML declarations, also allow the use of public identifiers without URI references:

```
<!NOTATION notationName PUBLIC "notationPublicIdentifier">
```

The resources identified by URI and the public identifier in notation declarations aren't meant to be retrieved; like the URIs in XML namespaces, they are only used as identifiers. There doesn't have to be anything at all at the target location, and if there is something, it may only be human-readable, not machine-readable. For example, you can build notations that describe file types using the Internet Assigned Numbers Authority's MIME media-types directory. To describe a file type of `text/html`, you could use:

```
<!NOTATION text_html
   SYSTEM 'http://www.isi.edu/in-notes/iana/assignments/media-types/
text/html'>
```

If you actually go to the URI listed in the notation's system identifier, you'll get a small document that says "See RFC 1866." Applications won't get a lot out of visiting that URI, but its status as a unique identifier for `text/html` is unquestioned. This approach can be useful for a wide variety of files commonly identified using MIME types, like the ubiquitous GIF file:

```
<!NOTATION image_gif
   SYSTEM 'http://www.isi.edu/in-notes/iana/assignments/media-types/
image/gif'>
```

John Cowan has provided a complete set of these MIME type notations at **http://www.ccil.org/~cowan/XML/media-types.dtd**. If your notations are describing commonly used file formats, this approach can make things much easier. If you need to describe your own data formats, and don't have the time (or need) to register them with the IETF (**http://www.ietf.org**), you can create notations that reference URI spaces that you control. For example, I could create a notation based on `simonstl.com`, my domain:

```
<!NOTATION myRecipeFormat
   SYSTEM 'http://www.simonstl.com/recipes/format/'>
```

Notations don't have to describe file formats, however. You can define notations to describe any type you like (although it will be up to your application to interpret them.) For example, you could create a boolean notation using the Java language specification:

```
<!NOTATION javaBoolean
   SYSTEM 'http://java.sun.com/docs/books/jls/html/3.doc.html#49652'>
```

A Java string type would look very similar:

```
<!NOTATION javaString
   SYSTEM 'http://java.sun.com/docs/books/jls/html/3.doc.html#101083'>
```

In both these cases, the system identifier leads to a clear explanation—in English—of what this information would be. Applications need to be hard-coded, however, to understand that these two URIs represent boolean values and string values, respectively. There is nothing intuitive for an application that states that 49652 has something to do with yes/no values, while 101083 has to do with string values.

The XML 1.0 specification isn't clear about what happens if the same notation name is declared repeatedly. An errata document in progress for the XML 1.0 specification (**http://www.alis.com/~yergeau/xml/ErrataAdd.html**) suggests that an extra validity constraint should be added, prohibiting such repeated declarations and making certain that XML remains compatible with SGML. Some parsers may exhibit more lenient behavior, especially those written before the errata were published. For consistency, always make certain that no notation is declared more than once in a DTD.

Unparsed entities are declared much like external general entities, except that they have an extra component: the `NDATA` token followed by the name of a notation:

```
<!ENTITY entityName SYSTEM "entityURI" NDATA notation>
```

or:

```
<!ENTITY entityName PUBLIC "entityPublicIdentifier" "entityURI" NDATA
notation>
```

Unlike notation declarations, unparsed entity declarations require a URI if a public identifier is used. Unparsed entities describe resources that may actually be retrieved by the application (although not by the parser), combining a location (the URI or public identifier and URI) and a description of format of the information at that location, specified by the notation. For example, an unparsed entity might be used to reference a graphic and identify its format as JPEG:

```
<!ENTITY myPicture SYSTEM "mypicture.jpg" NDATA jpeg>
```

The information provided by the entity declaration will be passed to the application when a reference to the entity is encountered in an attribute in the document.

Using Notations

Notations are typically referenced in documents through attributes of the enumerated NOTATION type, but can also be referenced in any attribute, provided the application knows where to look for it. (The data typing strategy described in Chapter 11 uses this approach to support multiple notations describing the data types for both elements and attributes.) In the "standard" approach, using notations only where explicitly provided by DTD conventions, notations can only be used to identify element and unparsed entity types. In a broader approach, with an application that understands more complex conventions, notations can be used to identify attribute types as well, significantly increasing the power of notations.

As noted above, all unparsed entities must have a notation included in their declaration, following the NDATA keyword. XML 1.0 also supports notation attributes, using enumerated attribute types that are identified as notations. The XML 1.0 recommendation is a bit lax with notation attributes, ignoring a compatibility constraint from SGML that limits elements to one attribute of type NOTATION. The errata document for the XML 1.0 recommendation (**http://www.w3.org/XML/xml-19980210-errata.html**) states that an extra validity constraint should be added, prohibiting multiple NOTATION-type attributes on a single element type. Because this change was made in the errata, not all parsers may enforce it. Sticking to one NOTATION-type attribute per element will ensure that your DTD works with all validating parsers, however.

Notations may be declared at any point in the DTD, even after they have been used in declarations. As long as the notation is declared someplace in the DTD, the notation declaration is fine. The validity constraint governing NOTATION-type attributes states only that the notation name must have a matching declaration, not that the declaration must be made before the attribute list declaration. This gives you extra flexibility to include notations at any point in the DTD you choose and still have a validatable DTD.

You can use notations to describe information both within NOTATION-type attributes and outside those attributes, although the latter approach (required for the data typing described in Chapter 11, for instance) requires your application to do some work beyond that of the parser. NOTATION-type attributes can be used to describe the contents of elements (in which case something like the javaBoolean or javaString described above might be useful), or to describe something those elements refer to. The XML 1.0 specification states that "A NOTATION attribute identifies a notation, declared in the DTD with associated system and/or public identifiers, to be used in interpreting the element to which the attribute is attached." The application needs to figure what the notations refer to in the end, so either usage is possible. The example below uses the MIME type declarations to describe the kind of file referred to by an image element.

```
<!NOTATION image_gif
   SYSTEM 'http://www.isi.edu/in-notes/iana/assignments/media-types/
image/gif'>
<!NOTATION image_jpeg
   SYSTEM 'http://www.isi.edu/in-notes/iana/assignments/media-types/
image/jpeg'>
<!NOTATION image_png
   SYSTEM 'http://www.isi.edu/in-notes/iana/assignments/media-types/
image/png'>
<!ELEMENT image EMPTY>
<!ATTLIST image
   href  CDATA       #REQUIRED
   type NOTATION (image_gif | image_jpeg | image_png) #REQUIRED>
```

The image element will have to include both an href attribute and a type. For example, it might read:

```
<image href="mygif.gif" type="image_gif" />
```

or

```
<image href="mypng.png" type="image_png" />
```

This would tell an application (if it understood what the image element was for) that the image was stored at a relative URI of mypng.png, and it was of type image_png—in other words, that it was a Portable Network Graphics (PNG) file, as defined by the W3C.

There are other ways to identify file types that don't rely on notations, especially if you're working in an environment (like the Web) where applications can determine file types from MIME identifiers passed during transactions or from file type extensions. If for some reason you're working in an environment where that information is unavailable, requiring explicit labels inside the documents making the reference may be appropriate. (This is the approach taken by XML unparsed entities, described below.)

You can also use notations to indicate the type of the element itself. If an element could contain boolean values (true or false), you could indicate that with the declarations below.

```
<!NOTATION javaBoolean
   SYSTEM 'http://java.sun.com/docs/books/jls/html/3.doc.html#49652'>
<!ELEMENT myBoolean #PCDATA>
<!ATTLIST myBoolean
   type  NOTATION (javaBoolean) "javaBoolean">
```

Applications processing this might note that myBoolean elements had a NOTATION attribute identifying them as being Java boolean values. They would accept elements that looked like:

```
<myBoolean>true</myBoolean>
```

or

```
<myBoolean>false</myBoolean>
```

but would reject elements that looked like any of those below:

```
<myBoolean>0</myBoolean>
<myBoolean>1</myBoolean>
<myBoolean>yes</myBoolean>
<myBoolean>no</myBoolean>
<myBoolean>hello there!</myBoolean>
<myBoolean />
```

It is all up to the application. You could also have used the conventions for data typing described above to identify this element as a `javaBoolean`, using the declarations shown below:

```
<!NOTATION javaBoolean
   SYSTEM 'http://java.sun.com/docs/books/jls/html/3.doc.html#49652'>
<!ELEMENT myBoolean #PCDATA>
<!ATTLIST myBoolean
   e-type    NMTOKEN #FIXED "javaBoolean">
```

Applications that used the conventions described in Chapter 11 would still have to understand what the URI behind `javaBoolean` meant, but if they understood this notation, they'd be able to process it along with the rest of the data types. The only advantage `NOTATION`-type attributes provide over the `e-dtype` approach above is the ability to specify a data type within the document itself rather than in the DTD. If you need that functionality, you'll like enumerated `NOTATION`-type attributes. Otherwise, you may want to leave `NOTATION` processing up to the application or components that can work within a given set of conventions.

Notations can also be used to provide extra information about the format of processing instructions. The target of a processing instruction, the first piece of text that appears, is required to be an XML name, following the same rules that apply to names of notations. You can give your applications extra guidance in deciphering the rest of the processing instruction by creating notations that have the same name as the processing instruction target and provide information about the format of the processing instruction. You could, for instance, tell an application that the characters following the PI represent JavaScript (standardized as `ECMAScript`) instructions though that would be an approach that moved well beyond current rules for HTML and XML document handling. The notation declaration might look like:

```
<!NOTATION ECMAScript SYSTEM "http://www.ecma.ch/stand/ECMA-262.htm">
```

A processing instruction that then used this notation might look like:

```
<?ECMAScript {document.write("Hello, World!");}?>
```

XML 1.0 actually changed the processing instruction rules so that the terminating sequence was ?>, instead of just >, to accommodate scripts and similar processing. Although you should probably stick to the rules for specifications that already have spaces for scripts, like XHTML, the processing instruction solution is handy for cases where you may not be able to modify the DTD but still want to include scripts inside documents. (You can make the notation declaration inside the internal subset of the DTD if necessary.) If you wanted to identify some other format for processing instructions, you could define another notation. Remember, however, that the application needs to understand first that you are using notations to describe PI targets, and beyond that, it needs to map the URIs you provide to some kind of behavior. Processing instructions and this kind of usage will be explored in more depth in Chapter 26.

Using Unparsed Entities

Like notations, unparsed entities are processed by the application, but they have a lot less flexibility. Unparsed entities actually refer to resources, not just identifiers. Unlike parameter and general entities, unparsed entities are included in documents through attribute values (of type `ENTITY` and `ENTITIES`) rather than through direct references. Although unparsed entities are technically a kind of general entity, using the name of an unparsed entity in a general entity reference (`&name;`) is illegal, generating a fatal error. (Similarly, attempts to use the names of general entities in attributes meant for unparsed entities will generate a fatal error.)

Using unparsed entities in a document is somewhat like the image example presented above, except that the element itself only needs a reference to the unparsed entity, which contains both the URI and the notation identifying the type of the resource to be retrieved. Unparsed entities are a tool for encapsulating resources effectively, making them available for documents without requiring that extra information be provided within the document body itself. Using an unparsed entity requires several components to be available. First, notations supporting the unparsed entity are needed. These notation declarations may appear in an external DTD file, which gives developers a chance to build applications that recognize the DTD's particular set of notations. Second, the unparsed entity itself must be declared. This is typically done in a portion of the DTD for documents that share common resources (a logo, for example) or in the internal subset of the DTD for resources that are only used by a single or a few documents. Finally, an element must be available that contains an attribute of type `ENTITY` or `ENTITIES`. That element and its attributes is typically declared in the external subset of the DTD.

To put all this together into an `unparsed_image` element, we'll need to start with some declarations in the external subset of the DTD:

```
<!NOTATION image_gif
   SYSTEM 'http://www.isi.edu/in-notes/iana/assignments/media-types/
image/gif'>
<!NOTATION image_jpeg
   SYSTEM 'http://www.isi.edu/in-notes/iana/assignments/media-types/
image/jpeg'>
<!NOTATION image_png
   SYSTEM 'http://www.isi.edu/in-notes/iana/assignments/media-types/
image/png'>

<!--Please display the image described by the unparsed entity in the
content attribute of unparsed_image -->
<!ELEMENT unparsed_image EMPTY>
<!ATTLIST unparsed_image
   content ENTITY #REQUIRED>
```

These notations provide a framework applications can expect, giving developers a roadmap of what each application needs to support. The `unparsed_image` element fills in the picture for those developers, telling them where they'll need to be ready to handle an unparsed entity. The comment above `unparsed_image` also provides a hint about what kind of processing behavior is expected. (You could alternately let document creators specify behavior through an enumerated attribute or something similar.)

All that remains is to declare the unparsed entity—probably in the internal DTD subset of the document that uses it—and reference it in an element. The very simple document below does just that.

```
<?xml version="1.0" encoding="utf-8"?>
<!DOCTYPE unparsed_image SYSTEM "unparsed_image.dtd" [
<!ENTITY myGif "mygif.gif" NDATA image_gif>
]>
<unparsed_image content="myGif" />
```

This document reaches out to the DTD shown above for the notation declarations and the declaration for `unparsed_image`, then defines an unparsed entity called `"myGif"`, and then references that entity in an otherwise empty `unparsed_image` element. If an application had been built around the DTD and the directions it contained, the picture contained in the file `myGif.gif` would probably appear on the user's screen when this document was opened.

Unparsed entities may seem counterintuitive to Web developers, who are used to the infrastructure provided by the HTTP protocol and MIME media types, but they can be useful in certain situations. Unparsed entities provide a useful tool for creating a library of resources, from images to text to multimedia. This library can then be referenced from any document that includes it as part of the DTD, and used in documents. If the resources described by the unparsed entity move to a different location, the library maintainer can make changes to the DTD in one location, rather than having to figure out a search-and-replace strategy for every document (which documents?) that referenced the resources. By defining the notations used by these resources within the library, application builders can get a clear picture of what they'll be expected to support for users working with this library. (Users can still cause mischief within the internal subset, but a foundation level of functionality can be developed by reading the DTD.) In systems where information about file types is hard to come by (no file extensions, no MIME Content-type headers), the notation information can be invaluable.

Unparsed entities haven't received a lot of emphasis, however. In a Web context, much of their functionality is being absorbed by XLink, a proposal under development at the W3C (and described in Chapter 23). Applications have to do extra work to make unparsed entities do anything for the user, and undoubtedly some developers have been confused when loading an XML document to find that their unparsed entities didn't appear anywhere in it. Like notations, unparsed entities are a set of tools for extending XML's core functionality, and like notations, those extensions need application-level support in addition to the parser-level foundation XML 1.0 provides.

CHAPTER 16

Using Conditional Sections: INCLUDE and IGNORE

Parameter entities and the internal subset allow document authors to exert significant control over the contents of DTDs, but sometimes a more complete and flexible set of tools is needed to let DTD designers give document authors a cleaner set of options. Conditional sections, which only operate in the external subsets of DTDs, allow developers to create sets of optional declarations. These optional declarations, created by the DTD designer and, we hope, supported by applications, can then be used by document authors with much less risk than other approaches that use the internal DTD subset to directly override the external DTD subset.

Basic Syntax

Conditional sections must contain complete declarations, and may only appear in the external subset of the DTD. They may not start or end in the middle of a declaration. Conditional sections use the syntax:

```
<![INCLUDE[...complete declarations...]]>
```

or

```
<![IGNORE[...complete declarations...]]>
```

For example, to INCLUDE an element type declaration, you could use:

```
<![INCLUDE[<!ELEMENT myElement (#PCDATA)>]]>
```

This element type declaration would be included in the DTD, making the INCLUDE section the equivalent of the declaration below.

```
<!ELEMENT myElement (#PCDATA)>
```

To IGNORE an element type declaration and an attribute list declaration, you might write:

```
<![IGNORE[
   <!ELEMENT myElement (#PCDATA)>
   <!ATTLIST myElement
      myAttribute CDATA #IMPLIED>
]]>
```

Both these declarations would be ignored, as if they had never appeared. White space within a conditional section doesn't matter any more than white space within a DTD normally does, so you're free to use line breaks and indent in any way that makes your declarations more readable.

Unlike CDATA sections, conditional sections may be nested. XML parsers are responsible for figuring out where the "proper" end of the conditional section is, and don't simply stop at the first occurrence of]]>. For example, the conditional sections below are valid:

```
<![INCLUDE[
   <!ELEMENT myElement(#PCDATA)>
   <![IGNORE[
      <!ELEMENT yourElement(#PCDATA)>
   ]]>
]]>
<![IGNORE[
   <!ELEMENT ourElement(#PCDATA)>
   <![INCLUDE[
      <!ELEMENT theirElement(#PCDATA)>
   ]]>
]]>
```

Even if you nest an INCLUDE section inside of an IGNORE section, its content will still be ignored. Unlike namespace processing or other XML processing that allows child elements to override parents, INCLUDE and IGNORE sections are constrained by any IGNORE statement that contains them in the DTD. In the example above, this means that only the element type declaration for myElement is processed. yourElement is inside an IGNORE statement, as is ourElement. Although theirElement is inside an INCLUDE statement, that INCLUDE statement is itself contained by an

IGNORE statement, and its content is therefore ignored and the declaration for theirElement is never processed.

This nesting capability means that all the syntax inside a conditional section, even an ignored section, must meet XML's expectations. For example, even though the content of the conditional section below is "ignored", parsers will report a validity constraint violation:

```
<![IGNORE[No one can see me!]]>
```

Using Conditional Sections

In their basic form shown above, conditional sections seem to be a nuisance, at best. INCLUDE is essentially meaningless, and IGNORE is useful mostly to turn off sections of a DTD you are replacing. However, most uses of conditional sections combine them with parameter entities, which makes them much more powerful. Basically, a parameter entity's value is set to 'INCLUDE' or 'IGNORE', in the DTD, and document authors can change those values in the internal subset as appropriate. (DTD designers may also leave the declaration of the parameter entity entirely up to the document authors, but usually providing a default is a good idea.) For example, a DTD designer faced with the problem described in Chapter 14, where a set of documents needed a different declaration for the element, might start with a pure parameter entity approach. The DTD reads:

```
<!ENTITY % nameDecl "<!ELEMENT name (#PCDATA)>">
&nameDecl;
```

and the document type declaration for the affected documents reads:

```
<!DOCTYPE memo SYSTEM "myMemo.dtd" [
<!ENTITY % nameDecl "
<!ELEMENT name (given, family)>
<!ELEMENT given (#PCDATA)>
<!ELEMENT family (#PCDATA)>"
]>
```

If the DTD designer wanted to accommodate both declarations for name, but didn't want to leave the content model for name entirely up to the whims of the document author, he or she could use parameter entities to control conditional sections instead of replacing declarations. It would require two parameter entities instead of one, but it would be much simpler than the current parameter entity used in the internal subset. Because the default declaration is the simpler form (where name is just PCDATA), the DTD designer could specify values for the parameter entities controlling the conditional sections. The portion of the external DTD dealing with this element would look like:

```
<!ENTITY % nameDeclSimple "INCLUDE">
<!ENTITY % nameDeclComplex "IGNORE">
<![%nameDeclSimple;[ <!ELEMENT name (#PCDATA)>]]>
<![%nameDeclComplex;[
   <!ELEMENT name (given, family)>
   <!ELEMENT given (#PCDATA)>
   <!ELEMENT family (#PCDATA)>
]]>
```

This is a more complex DTD, but it would spare document authors' having to make the same declarations, perhaps repeatedly, within the internal subset. If the internal subset doesn't override either of the parameter entities, the declarations above will be resolved to:

```
<![INCLUDE [ <!ELEMENT name (#PCDATA)>]]>
<![IGNORE [
   <!ELEMENT name (given, family)>
   <!ELEMENT given (#PCDATA)>
   <!ELEMENT family (#PCDATA)>
]]>
```

which is the equivalent of:

```
<!ELEMENT name (#PCDATA)>
```

The `name` element will get the simplest possible declaration. If, however, the document author needs the more complex model, he/she can include a document type declaration that looks like:

```
<!DOCTYPE memo SYSTEM "myMemo.dtd" [
<!ENTITY % nameDeclSimple "IGNORE">
<!ENTITY % nameDeclComplex "INCLUDE">
]>
```

Then the conditional sections will resolve to:

```
<![IGNORE [ <!ELEMENT name (#PCDATA)>]]>
<![INCLUDE [
   <!ELEMENT name (given, family)>
   <!ELEMENT given (#PCDATA)>
   <!ELEMENT family (#PCDATA)>
]]>
```

which is the equivalent of:

```
   <!ELEMENT name (given, family)>
   <!ELEMENT given (#PCDATA)>
   <!ELEMENT family (#PCDATA)>
```

Although this approach is a bit more work for the DTD designer, it also makes it much simpler for the document author. The DTD designer gains some control over the document structure, and the document author trades that control for simplicity. Instead of relying on document authors to populate the internal subset with complete information, DTD designers can provide a set of (presumably well-documented) switches for document authors. For example, if a DTD included a set of entities in multiple languages, document authors could signal (via a parameter entity declaration in the internal subset) which set of entities should be used. The external DTD might read:

```
<!ENTITY % french "IGNORE">
<!ENTITY % spanish "IGNORE">
<!ENTITY % english "IGNORE">
<!ENTITY % german "INCLUDE">
<![%french;[ <!ENTITY % boilerplate SYSTEM "descfr.dtd">]]>
<![%spanish;[ <!ENTITY % boilerplate SYSTEM "descsp.dtd">]]>
<![%english;[ <!ENTITY % boilerplate SYSTEM "descen.dtd">]]>
<![%german;[ <!ENTITY % boilerplate SYSTEM "descde.dtd">]]>
%boilerplate;
```

The document authors who wanted to use the German version of the entities wouldn't have to make any declarations in the internal subset. Document authors who wanted to use the French, Spanish, or English version of the entities would define the appropriate entity to read `'INCLUDE'`, as shown below for a document author who wants the entities to appear in English:

```
<!DOCTYPE contract SYSTEM "myContract.dtd" [
<!ENTITY % english "INCLUDE">
]>
```

Although the document author might also define the `german` entity to read `'IGNORE'`, this isn't necessary, because the declaration using the English form of the entities appears before the version for the German form, and the first declaration of `boilerplate`—in this case, the English one—will win out. The declarations will end up looking like:

```
<![INCLUDE [ <!ENTITY % boilerplate SYSTEM "descen.dtd">]]>
<![INCLUDE [ <!ENTITY % boilerplate SYSTEM "descde.dtd">]]>
%boilerplate;
```

which will resolve to:

```
<!ENTITY % boilerplate SYSTEM "descen.dtd">
<!ENTITY % boilerplate SYSTEM "descde.dtd">
%boilerplate;
```

The entities listed in the file `descen.dtd` will be loaded. This approach works well with entity and attribute declarations, but you should be careful not to use it in cases where element declarations are enclosed by the conditional sections. In those cases, you should always make sure that only one set of declarations is used to prevent an error when the same element is declared repeatedly.

Conditional sections are one of the trickier parts of XML, a tool that allows document authors and DTD designers to negotiate degrees of flexibility. Their inclusion in XML 1.0 was questioned by many, because they can significantly complicate DTD processing and make it difficult to debug. However, if you're a DTD designer who needs to provide flexibility, conditional sections can simplify your work considerably, making it easier to communicate the available options to authors and providing a consistent mechanism for implementing these options. `INCLUDE` and `IGNORE` sections also make it difficult to describe schemas completely, because they allow for significant changes at runtime rather than designtime. If you use `INCLUDE` and `IGNORE` sections be certain to document their use, explaining to both application designers and document authors the options available.

PART THREE

A Few Matters of Form

CHAPTER 17

Types of Markup: Semantic to Application Specific

Although every markup language created with XML has its own semantics and vocabulary, each of these markup languages can usually be described as embodying a certain type of markup, depending on what the target application is like and how much emphasis is given to presentation. There's a wide spectrum of possibilities from markup languages that describe only the data to markup languages that describe only a particular application of information, often (although not always) presentation. Despite the loud rhetoric that came with XML about separating content from presentation, XML is quite capable of supporting a range of possibilities.

Semantics, Semantics, and More Semantics

The word "semantics" is commonly thrown around in XML discussions, but its meaning changes frequently. Because semantics is basically an advanced word for "meaning," this situation is somewhat ironic. In some cases the word semantics is used to describe the fact that XML markup provides a description—a meaning of some sort—for the document. In other cases, the word semantics is reserved to describe XML markup that provides a description of the content represented by the XML. A `PRICE` might be semantic markup, while a `BOLD` might not be, according to this usage. The finer grained the information provided by the markup becomes, the higher the level of semantic content.

Developers who attempt to pin down the meaning of every piece of information often become frustrated, finding themselves caught in a maze of meanings every bit as complex as those in natural languages. While some of those cases are easily resolved, others are not. Even `PRICE`, a seemingly understandable concept, has surprising depth when looked at closely. For starters, there are currency issues. One U.S. dollar and one U.K. pound have very different actual values, and even "dollars" are not all alike, with different values for dollars from Canada, Australia, and Hong Kong, for instance. For many purposes this level of detail is sufficient, but there are still other possibilities. Is this price a sale price? Does it have an expiration date? What are the terms that define how this price may be used? Do I have to pay cash? Does it cost extra to leave the item there for a week? Does the price include shipping? All these may seem like details about the transaction, but in some cases they may be part of a more extended understanding of what a price actually is.

Even if developers leave out the deliberately perverse questions, it is easy to question the implications of a particular name in XML. To some extent, this can be resolved through documentation and pre-existing understanding, much as they are in the "real world." Prices in American supermarkets are typically fixed and not negotiable, while prices at an American used car dealer are rarely truly fixed. Stock market prices are fleeting, often fluctuating wildly to meet changes in supply and demand. XML documents can provide structures for expressing these differences, but the differences remain and must be dealt with. To some extent, this work can be passed to lawyers rather than XML document designers, but it can rarely be completely escaped.

Although finding real meanings is always difficult, XML at least provides a good set of tools for expressing such meanings. Its nearly boundless vocabulary gives developers the opportunity to create vocabularies with meanings for particular cases, and its namespace facilities provide ways to keep different vocabularies from clashing. If my `PRICE` is negotiable and your `PRICE` is not, we'd probably do well to have a way of telling them apart. XML provides both ways to identify the information as a price and ways to identify the context of that identification. Armed with those tools, we can at least begin to describe information in terms that we (and, we hope, a broader base of users as well) understand.

There is definitely a spectrum of possible descriptions, ranging from descriptions that focus on things as they exist in the real world to descriptions that focus on structures we commonly use to represent those things, to descriptions of how information should be presented in a very particular context. Although it is difficult to say that any one part of the spectrum is better in general than any other part of the spectrum, different projects may be better suited to different parts of the spectrum. As a general rule, the information in an XML document becomes less easily reused as you move from a focus on meaning to a focus on presentation. It's easier to say "print all sale prices in bold red" and have it work than to say "everything in this document that is marked in bold red is a sale price." Someone may have slipped a note into the document using the same presentation format as prices, leaving the computer stuck with a mystifying item that might be a price but probably isn't. Although reusability isn't always the primary goal, it's often a goal worth considering.

Focus on Meaning

Many developers come to XML looking for a way to create documents that describe their content in more meaningful ways than is possible in other formats. XML allows developers to create flexible named structures, and the ability to create "more appropriate" names for things has been one of its strongest selling points. Information that carries its own description fuels Tim Berners-Lee's vision of the "semantic Web," while simultaneously exciting the developers of computer desktop management tools, database administrators who need to exchange information between dissimilar systems, and programmers who need to transfer requests from one computer to another. All of these visions focus on XML's ability to represent content as a set of labeled structures. The process of creating labels and structures is given special priority in XML, as it sets XML apart from other tools like HTML, word processors, and page layout programs. Developers who create vocabularies that aren't seen as describing the contents of their documents as closely as possibly are frequently told that they're doing a bad job of modeling. Meaning is definitely privileged in XML, in part as a reaction to its best-known predecessor (HTML), in part as a way to differentiate XML from potentially competing projects.

To explore what a seriously meaning-oriented document structure might look like, we'll investigate the PRICE element's many possibilities once again, and attempt to pin down at least one set of possible meanings for a price. To keep things somewhat sane, we'll limit the discussion to retail prices, cutting out wholesale and auction possibilities while still preserving perhaps too many options. A basic PRICE element might be connected to its target (the commodity it describes) through containment—a price describes its commodity. We'll create a simple COMMODITY element with a few features so we have something to work with and a PRICE element that is the main focus of our work.

```
<!ELEMENT COMMODITY (NAME, DESCRIPTION, PRICE)>
<!ELEMENT NAME (#PCDATA)>
<!ELEMENT DESCRIPTION (#PCDATA)>
<!ELEMENT PRICE (#PCDATA)>
```

The actual price of the commodity will be stored in the content of the price element. Our simplest PRICE element, before we've added any clarifying attributes, might look like:

```
<PRICE>1.00</PRICE>
```

A price of 1 isn't very clear, though. We'll need to add at least a currency type, for starters.

```
<!ATTLIST PRICE
   CURRENCY  (USD | UKP | CAN | AUS)   #REQUIRED>
```

Our sample PRICE element grows a bit, but at least we know the denomination we're worried about:

```
<PRICE CURRENCY="USD">1.00</PRICE>
```

Even in retail, many prices are good for only a limited time. We'll add a start date and end date for which the price is good:

```
<!ATTLIST PRICE
   STARTDATE   CDATA    #IMPLIED
   ENDDATE     CDATA    #IMPLIED>
```

Because not every product has a start date and an end date, we leave these attributes optional. The sample PRICE element has grown a little more:

```
<PRICE CURRENCY="USD" STARTDATE='12 Dec 1999' ENDDATE='19 Dec
1999'>1.00</PRICE>
```

If this is a sale price, it may need special highlighting when presented, and it may be more convenient to store personnel to see a list of what's on sale. At the same time, the store may have a policy forbidding extra discounts on some sale items, so we'll need attributes to support these two needs:

```
<!ATTLIST PRICE
   SALE  (YES | NO)   "NO"
   EXTRADISCOUNT     (ALLOWED | PROHIBITED)    "ALLOWED">
```

Note that because we've provided default values for both of these items, the PRICE element may not need to declare them explicitly. In addition, if some items in the store have negotiable prices, while most have fixed prices, we'll need to represent that, using the same strategy of providing a default value.

```
<!ATTLIST PRICE
   TYPE  (FIRM | NEGOTIABLE)  "FIRM" >
```

(Using `firm` instead of `fixed` makes it easier to read the DTD—it doesn't look like the attribute value is `#FIXED`. If you'd prefer to use `FIXED` or `fixed`, that's fine, too. All these issues should be covered in documentation.)

Now that we have all these parts, it's time to put them together:

```
<!ELEMENT COMMODITY (NAME, DESCRIPTION, PRICE)>
<!ELEMENT NAME (#PCDATA)>
<!ELEMENT DESCRIPTION (#PCDATA)>
<!ELEMENT PRICE (#PCDATA)>
<!ATTLIST PRICE
   CURRENCY  (USD | UKP | CAN | AUS)   #REQUIRED
   STARTDATE CDATA    #IMPLIED
   ENDDATE   CDATA    #IMPLIED
   SALE  (YES | NO)   "NO"
   EXTRADISCOUNT      (ALLOWED | PROHIBITED)    "ALLOWED"
   TYPE  (FIRM | NEGOTIABLE)  "FIRM" >
```

The `PRICE` element now contains an enormous amount of information, capable of representing pricing information for these two very different commodities:

```
<COMMODITY>
<NAME>Super Sucker</NAME>
<DESCRIPTION>A lollipop that lasts all day.</DESCRIPTION>
<PRICE CURRENCY="USD">1.00</PRICE>
</COMMODITY>
<COMMODITY>
<NAME>Super-Stacked Car</NAME>
<DESCRIPTION>A fine little automobile that was only driven by an elderly
parishioner going to church on Sundays at very reasonable
speeds.</DESCRIPTION>
<PRICE CURRENCY="USD" STARTDATE="1 Dec 1999" ENDDATE="31 Dec 1999"
SALE="YES" EXTRADISCOUNT="PROHIBITED"
TYPE="NEGOTIABLE">10,000.00</PRICE>
</COMMODITY>
```

The Super Sucker costs a non-negotiable US$1.00, is always that price, is not on sale, and extra discounts may be applied. The Super-Stacker Car, on the other hand, is on sale (aren't they always?), has a price good for the month of December 1999, and a negotiable $10,000 price that can't get knocked down after the negotiations by a smart customer with a discount card.

This kind of markup is what gets a lot of potential users of XML excited, but it's not the only kind of markup available.

Focus on Structure

HTML started out as a markup language for representing documents. Rather than modeling the content of what was inside every single document, HTML provided a general model that was useful for documents in general. This "good enough" solution took the world by storm, providing one of the foundations of the World Wide Web. HTML represents in many ways a compromise position between representing content directly and representing presentation. In its early days this compromise worked well, because HTML provided an easily implemented format for sharing information of all kinds. As the Web grew and more and more presentation-oriented Web sites were built, many complained that HTML's formatting tools were too weak for real use, and then XML appeared with its promise of content-specific vocabularies. Despite the complaints and the competition, HTML represents a strategy that can work for many types of information, allowing people to communicate without worrying too much about the details of either the content or the presentation.

One of the key reasons for HTML's overwhelming success was that it modeled a very simple form that most people could understand without great difficulty. Although it was never really strong enough to provide heavy support (equations, graphs, etc.) for the scientific papers it was supposed to support, the form of those papers (expressed in a vocabulary influenced by Annex E of the SGML specification) struck a balance between sophistication and simplicity. HTML had enough information about documents to get people started, without overwhelming them with options. By modeling a particular kind of document, it kept things simple, describing a very flexible container instead of its contents.

On the other hand, HTML's lack of content-oriented features does make it a bit difficult to express the PRICE information shown above. The two commodities demonstrated above don't have quite the same structure in HTML, and a lot of the information has to be spelled out as (fine print?) text.

```
<HTML>
<HEAD><TITLE>Commodities</TITLE></HEAD>
<BODY>
<H1>Super Sucker</H1>
<P>A lollipop that lasts all day. - <STRONG>US$1.00</STRONG></P>
<H1>Super-Stacked Car</H1>
<P>A fine little automobile that was only driven by an elderly parish-
ioner going to church on Sundays at very reasonable speeds. -
<EM><STRONG>US$10,000.00</STRONG></EM><BR>
<SMALL>Price Stands from 1 Dec 1999 to 31 Dec 1999. No extra discounts
permitted at close of negotiations.</SMALL> </P>
</BODY>
</HTML>
```

There are a few compromises here. Prices are marked as `STRONG`, and sale prices are marked as `EM` and `STRONG` for that enticing bold italic look. Pricing details are now fine print (`SMALL`), and written in English that may be hard for an automated tool to understand.

As long as your target audience is people, HTML like that shown above should work fairly well. It's easily generated from databases or even the

XML document in the previous section, and it is in a format flexible enough to work on screens and paper of all different sizes. An aural reader would get enough clues from the HTML markup to provide different levels of emphasis to people listening to the document rather than reading it visually. It's not a bad compromise, though it certainly is a compromise. Similarly, the interfaces HTML presents for collecting information—forms and hypertext links—represent a compromise between the sophisticated interfaces possible in today's GUI environments and the simplest approach users can learn quickly. Compromises often work wonders.

Focus on Applications

The bogeyman of XML is application-specific markup, where data structures are entwined so deeply with structures pertaining to a particular use of that information that it is often difficult or impossible to extract the data and put them back into a more generically useful form. Typically, this is done with a focus on presentation, but there are plenty of other opportunities to use XML in a way that is more about a particular application than about the information in the document.

Designers who felt that HTML didn't have enough formatting information should be very pleased with the Extensible Stylesheet Language's Formatting Object vocabulary. Formatting objects (or FOs, as they're often abbreviated) use an XML vocabulary that is entirely about presentation. No abstractions like headlines, emphasis, or paragraphs are provided—all the information included in an XSLFO document is about putting text and other content into a presentation, not about describing it in any other way. As XSL formatting objects are expected to be derived (through XSL transformations) from other XML documents that are less presentation oriented, this is considered a benefit, not a problem. (This approach to formatting will be discussed further in the next chapter.) Writing FO documents directly isn't impossible, and the approach is hardly new—page layout programs like QuarkXPress and other page description formats like Adobe's PDF store their information in much the same way.

Because XSL is a moving target as of this writing, we'll just explore a (very simple) version of the HTML document shown above as expressed using the formatting objects vocabulary from the 21 April 1999 XSL Working Draft (**http://www.w3.org/TR/1999/WD-xsl-19990421**). In the early drafts of XSL, formatting objects were abstract, a vocabulary without explicit XML expression. By this draft, they had become an actual XML vocabulary, usable outside of the context of XSL transformations.

```
<fo:root xmlns:fo="http://www.w3.org/XSL/Format/1.0">

<!--set up basic page layout -->
<fo:layout-master-set>
   <fo:simple-page-master page-master-name="simple">
```

```
      <fo:region-body />
    </fo:simple-page-master>
  </fo:layout-master-set>

  <!--connect that layout to this presentation-->
  <fo:page-sequence>
    <fo:sequence-specification>
      <fo:sequence-specifier-single page-master-name="simple"/>
    </fo:sequence-specification>

  <!--Start the text flow-->
  <fo:flow flow-name="xsl-body">

  <!--Lollipop Headline-->
  <fo:block font-size="24pt" font-family="sans-serif">
  Super Sucker
  </fo:block>

  <!--Lollipop Description-->
  <fo:block font-size="12pt" font-family="serif">
  A lollipop that lasts all day. - <fo:inline-sequence font-
  weight="bold">US$1.00</fo:inline-sequence>
  </fo:block>

  <!--Used Car Headline-->
  <fo:block font-size="24pt" font-family="sans-serif">
  Super-Stacked Car
  </fo:block>

  <!--Used Car Description-->
  <fo:block font-size="12pt" font-family="serif">
  A fine little automobile that was only driven by an elderly parishioner
  going to church on Sundays at very reasonable speeds. - <fo:inline-
  sequence font-weight="bold" font-style="italic">US$10,000.00</fo:inline-
  sequence>

  <fo:inline-sequence font-size="6pt">Price Stands from 1 Dec 1999 to 31
  Dec 1999. No extra discounts permitted at close of
  negotiations.</fo:inline-sequence>
  </fo:block>
  </fo:flow>
  </fo:page-sequence>
  </fo:root>
```

This is a very lightweight version of the document. It could have provided a variety of different media-handling supports, specified block placement, indentation, letter spacing, word spacing, line spacing, padding, or any of several hundred other possibilities. Instead, it just defines enough formatting to display headlines and descriptions, put prices in boldface and sale prices in italic boldface, and made sure the small print is tiny. This version is a lot more verbose than either the original semantic version or the HTML version, though to some extent that can be blamed on XSLFO's more explicit element and attribute names. Nonetheless, trying to process this document for any purpose other than its intended use in presentation is difficult. Documents that explicitly position text on a page (rather than just letting it flow) can be even harder to process, forcing analysis tools to figure out what the page looks like. That kind of analysis is a task better done by humans than by computers, because it is very difficult to process the information in XSLFO documents in any way that uses the structural information provided by the elements and attributes.

NOTE
XSLFOs are somewhat controversial. For one perspective on why, see Håkon Wium Lie's "Formatting Objects Considered Harmful" at http://www.operasoftware.com/people/howcome/1999/foch.html.

Presentation is a common target of critics objecting to "improper" uses of markup, but there are thousands of other possibilities with similar requirements and consequences, and many of them are in fact quite useful. Building user interfaces by writing code is one of the most painful tasks a programmer encounters, mostly because of the repetition involved in creating things like menus, windows, and dialog boxes. Although there are tools for creating interfaces, most of them store their information either directly as application code or in proprietary formats that can't be edited by hand.

XML resource files can simplify all this. XML documents can easily represent the nested object structures used to create these interfaces. The interfaces described in these documents can be edited easily, with either a dedicated graphical tool or a simple text editor, giving programmers of all kinds easy access to the interface design. Programs themselves can save their object information back to an XML file, allowing users to customize their applications' appearance as they use them.

There are several approaches to this problem, using different levels of application specificity. A generic interface markup language might describe menus, windows, and dialog boxes, while a markup language tightly bonded to a particular development tool would express that information in terms of the objects provided by that tool. The process of transferring information from the files to the tool can be simplified if, for instance, the names of elements and attributes in the XML correspond to the names of classes and properties in the tool. However, using the same information with a different tool may require significant structural modifications or even hand editing to make the conversion work.

XWingML, from Bluestone Software, uses element and attribute names tightly connected to Java's Swing API for creating user interfaces. A sample of XWingML code looks like:

```
<JMenuBar>
   <JMenu text="File" mnemonic="F">
      <JMenuItem icon="mennew.gif" text="New..."
```

```
 mnemonic="N" accelerator="VK_N,CTRL_MASK"
 actionListener="NewFile"/>
<JMenuItem icon="menopen.gif" text="Open..."
 mnemonic="O" accelerator="VK_O,CTRL_MASK"
 actionListener="OpenFile"/>
<JMenuItem icon="mensave.gif" text="Save" mnemonic="S"
 accelerator="VK_S,CTRL_MASK" actionCommand="save"
 actionListener="SaveFile"/>
<JMenuItem icon="mensaveas.gif" text="Save As..."
 mnemonic="A" actionCommand="saveAs"
 actionListener="SaveFile"/>
```

By reading it closely, you can figure out that this XML fragment is describing a File menu and its first four entries, `New`, `Open`, `Save`, and `Save As`. The information is encoded to be as tightly connected to the Java program as possible. This makes Java Swing developers feel at home—the names are just as they expect them, and the structures are clear parallels to things they already understand. Other developers may not be so lucky, however—creating a more generic menu description out of this will require figuring out the difference between `actionCommand` and `actionListener`, not to mention decoding the cryptic `"VK_S,CTRL_MASK"` accelerator attributes. Without a good understanding of how Swing is structured, it's hard to tell what these things mean.

XML is clearly capable of supporting many different styles of markup. While striving for more generic and meaningful semantics is often worthwhile, creating usable vocabularies often involves tradeoffs. If you feel that an application-specific vocabulary has more to offer in the long run, because of convenience, familiarity, or other reasons entirely, that may be an appropriate choice. Going that route makes it more difficult to automate reuse of your information, but there are many cases worth pursuing where specificity has greater benefits than costs.

CHAPTER 18

Planning for Transformation and Presentation

XML's flexibility makes it possible to design information models with little concern for how that information will be presented to an application or a user at the "end" of XML processing. This doesn't mean that you can design documents using any form you want and other applications will figure out what you mean; rather, it means that if you model your information in a way that's easy to process, other applications down the line will be able to transform it or annotate it to meet their needs. HTML forced developers to test code in every browser to make sure it would look the way the designer wanted. With XML, if you design well-atomized document structures you can build presentations and transformations separately. Then you can worry about testing the results, not the document structures. Making this work requires understanding the processing your documents may face and keeping their structures flexible and useful enough to support that processing.

When Transformation is Useful

Transformation is useful in a much wider range of circumstances than "mere" presentation. Because XML lets developers create documents in infinitely different formats, there can be multiple representations of the same information. Conversions among formats are a common staple of

XML development, with a number of different methodologies. Transformations may also be useful for reorganizing information—the order in which an XML document was originally written may not be appropriate for all comers. Transformation also permits changing the structure of documents, replacing sets of structures as needed. Filtering information can be another useful aspect of transformation, showing only the information that fits particular criteria.

Perhaps the most important thing to remember about transformation, whether or not you actually use it in your documents, is that it provides an escape clause that allows you to develop information in the format you consider appropriate, without having to conform precisely to everyone else's expectations. This doesn't mean that you can ignore everyone else's standards—you still need to provide all the information that a destination format needs, if you hope to be able to make the conversions. It does mean, however, that you can work with formats you're comfortable with, from simply translated element and attribute names to thoroughly revised structures that store information using very different kinds of models. It also means that if you receive XML documents in a form you've never seen before, you may be able to automate the processing of those documents into your own structures rather than forcing the sender to conform to your preferred format. You may still have to negotiate about the information they send you, to make certain they send you everything you need, but you don't need to force them to obey your own conventions, however industry-standard they may seem.

Different Kinds of Transformation Tools

There are two main varieties of transformation tools available to XML developers. The procedural tools conventionally used by most programmers remain available—writing custom programs for converting XML from one format to another isn't especially difficult. Another kind of transformation, based on declarations in either a DTD or a separate document, lets developers specify transformations without necessarily writing code. Both approaches have their loud supporters, and there are a huge number of different possibilities within each approach. The approaches can also be combined at different levels of processing, opening up even more possibilities.

The first set of tools uses conventional programming techniques, where XML documents are manipulated either as text or as parsed application structures by a program written in Perl, Java, C++, C, Omnimark, Python, Basic, Pascal, or whatever seems appropriate, and a new XML document is generated as program results. These kinds of transformations can be extremely powerful, giving developers as much power as they want to convert from one format to another. Transformation capabilities may be buried in a program through the "traditional" Save As... style dialog box, where internal structures can be saved to files using a number of different formats, or they may be the sole purpose of a piece of code that just transforms documents all day.

There are two general models for handling XML transformations within procedural frameworks. For some transformations, handling the XML as text and applying textual transformations is adequate. Tools like regular expressions provide sophisticated matching and replacement capabilities that can often handle simple tasks with very little work. Perl was an important tool in the SGML arsenal even before XML existed, and the icon of the "Desperate Perl Hacker," manipulating XML as text, was an important factor kept in mind by the XML Working Group throughout the development of XML.

The other model for transforming XML requires working with a parsed version of the document rather than the raw text. Parsers feed the information into an application, which manipulates the information internally and then exports that manipulated version as a new XML document. There are several different approaches to this kind of transformation. In some cases, the application loads the entire document into an in-memory representation (typically as a Document Object Model—DOM—tree, described in Chapter 28) and then manipulates that representation. With a complete picture of the document, the application can make decisions about the new direction for the document, and either make changes to the original representation in memory or create a new tree entirely. When the application is done manipulating the tree, it can convert the results into an XML document, completing the transformation. (It could also pass the transformed tree to another process in the same application space, instead of reserializing the tree into a document that would require another parse for processing.)

If an application doesn't want to build an entire tree in memory, it can process an event stream (typically using the Simple API for XML, also described in Chapter 28) and make changes to the document as it passes through. There are limitations to this approach, because an application can't base transformations on any information that appears later in a document than its current position. Event streams read the document from start to finish, limiting the application's knowledge of the document to what has already appeared, excluding what hasn't yet appeared. Event stream transformations, often implemented with filters, are very useful, however, for many simple tasks like changing element and attribute names, stripping out unwanted information, or converting one well-understood and static structure to another.

The other kind of transformation processing relies on declarative descriptions of the transformation to be performed rather than explicit code that performs the transformation. The processors that perform these transformations have procedural code at some level, but users don't need to see those details. The processor is a black box that accepts documents and descriptions of how they should be transformed, and returns transformed documents (and possibly error messages, on a bad day). Users can focus on the describing their needs, and not on how to rebuild an attribute node within a DOM tree into an element node. The tools for describing these needs can be quite complicated themselves, but for many users and developers they represent a plausible, necessary, or delightful alternative to traditional programming.

There are three main streams of declarative transformation processing. Extensible Style Language Transformations (XSLT), the standard developed at the W3C, is the latest representative of the approach that seems most popular lately, using a template-based system for describing transformations. A different stream of thought uses declarative documents to configure filter processing, using the declarations as a thin layer on top of the procedural processing described above. Yet another approach uses information stored inside DTDs to indicate equivalencies and facilitate conversion from one format to another.

Template-based transformations are definitely the model supported by the W3C. Extensible Style Language (XSL—**http://www.w3.org/Style/XSL**) began as a project to bring a simplified version of ISO's Document Style Semantics and Specification Language (DSSSL) to the Web, but it has rapidly moved beyond presentation. Although DSSSL was primarily used for its formatting of flow objects, the transformation side of it received little use. The transformation side of XSL, its descendant, has proceeded far more rapidly than its formatting side and received a large number of implementations from a variety of vendors, including Microsoft and Lotus, as well as open-source implementations which are widely used. (See **http://www.xslinfo.com/software/** for a complete list.) Although XSL transformations were originally built to convert XML information into formatted documents, they have found use in many different environments. XSLT isn't the best tool for every task, although it is finding use throughout the XML world. (For an authoritative overview of its limitations, see the posting by its editor, James Clark, at **http://www.mulberrytech.com/xsl/xsl-list/archive/msg06180.html**).

XSLT uses templates to define both structures in the origin document and how those structures should be represented (or rebuilt) in the target document. XSLT uses XPath, another W3C project, to create match patterns that are used to find information in the origin document. For each match pattern, XSLT developers must provide a template showing the output that XSLT should produce. That template may include references to further processing, letting information pass through several levels of templates to build a complete document. XSL style sheets are lists of these templates, providing a complete framework for converting information from the origin format to the target format. XSL processors read the origin document into memory (a complete tree representation, though not necessarily a DOM tree) and then apply style sheets. Documents may identify their own style sheets using the mechanism specified by the W3C (**http://www.w3.org/TR/xml-stylesheet**) or an application may assign a particular style sheet to a document. Style sheet identifiers within documents are commonly used for work on presentation within Web browsers, while applications focused on transformation tend to assign the style sheets they consider appropriate. (Origin documents may not even be aware of the target format.)

Using declarative documents to configure procedural processing is a very different process, although once again processors receive origin documents and a document describing how that document should be processed. The description is effectively a style sheet similar in purpose though not in form to XSLT. One system that uses this approach is MDSAX (**http://www.jxml.com/mdsax/**), which provides a set of filters for document processing. It can produce a document (or documents) or a Java object structure or both from a given origin document and instructions. The instructions for MDSAX are written in ContextML, a markup language that describes filter structures. Developers using ContextML don't need to know anything about how the filters work—they just need to know which parameters are available and what effect they have on the output. These filters are capable of the same transformations (in fact they are the same filters) as the event stream filters described above. This approach is extensible—adding new procedural filters opens new possibilities, and even ContextML itself can be supplemented. For some projects, especially those making a transition from procedural to declarative approaches, this kind of configuration approach can add flexibility without compromising power. This approach also has the advantage of being able to include the other approaches as filters inside its overall structure.

The last approach takes a very different tack from the other two. Architectural forms, originally used for SGML processing, use information stored within the DTD of the origin format to describe its relationship to the DTD of the target format. The DTD that actually describes the origin format is the "client", or "derived" DTD, considered to be just one implementation of the *meta-DTD* or base architecture—and there may be multiple meta-DTDs and corresponding base architectures. Information about the relationship between meta-DTDs and client DTDs is stored as fixed attributes within client DTDs.

Architectural forms processing treats declarations in the client DTD as announcing that "X type in the client DTD is really an implementation of the form described by Y in the meta-DTD." Transforming from X to Y is then a fairly simple matter of mapping. Architectural forms can't provide the level of transformation that XSL or filters can—among other things, architectural forms don't modify the content of documents (although they can convert attribute to element content and vice versa). For conversion among various formats for information, however, they can be very useful. A SAX filter implementation for using architectural forms in XML is available at **http://www.megginson.com/XAF/**. For an introduction to architectural forms, see *Structuring XML Documents*, by David Megginson (Prentice-Hall, 1998).

Annotative Presentation

Many XML documents don't provide any information about how their content should be displayed, and most applications won't understand the documents that do provide such information without some additional tools. Cascading Style Sheets (CSS—**http://www.w3.org/Style/CSS**), a standard for presenting information in XML and HTML documents, allows developers to provide descriptions telling applications how to display document content. Applications (at this point, mostly browsers) parse the document and display the information it contains according the rules laid out in the style sheet. A `HEADLINE` element might be specified as appearing in 24 point bold sans serif black text, while a `FOOTNOTE` might be specified as 8 point normal serif text. CSS provides support for positioning and formatting element content, and more recent developments are adding support for behavior, user input, and more sophisticated handling of text in different languages. Because CSS sticks to descriptions, it is very easy to combine different descriptions or override particular descriptions, allowing CSS processors to "cascade" multiple style sheets together to create a unified result.

CSS doesn't provide very much support for changing the structure of documents. The "annotative approach" is focused on adding style information to documents, not changing their organization. CSS does provide some support for text inserted before and after particular elements, and limited access to attribute values for inclusion as content, but won't reorganize a table or convert a document into a graph. For those kinds of activities, you'll need to use one (or more) of the transformation tools described in the section above. For many XML applications, this isn't a problem. Many documents don't require structural modifications, and are intended to have only one content flow—that used by the original document. For other applications, especially data-oriented ones, these limitations are a large problem, as filtering and document construction become tasks that must be done before the style sheet is actually applied to the document.

Transformative Presentation

Extensible Stylesheet Language (XSL) is also about presentation, but it takes a very different approach. Instead of annotating documents with information about how they should be formatted, XSL processes documents into entirely new document trees consisting purely of presentation information, using the Formatting Objects vocabulary discussed in Chapter 17. Applications which understand that vocabulary then display the results of this transformation. Although converting element structures into formatting structures is a key part of the transformation, structural transformations—reordering, filtering, rebuilding, numbering, and more—can take place simultaneously. All the document transformation capabilities of XSLT are available during transformations to formatting objects, making it possible to integrate structural transformations with formatting into a single style sheet.

XSL's transformative approach provides an important advantage to document designers. It frees them from having to consider presentation order when they structure their documents, allowing them to leave that job to style sheet creators. Although it is still important to make sure that information is stored in a way that XSL style sheets can easily manage, developers can worry less overall about making the way their documents are structured reflect the way they are presented. This also allows document designers to provide information within documents that will result in different structures emerging from the style sheet processors, providing a greater level of control.

Staying Flexible

No matter what kind of output you hope to produce from your XML documents, whether it be database entries, printed documents, hypertexts, or music, you'll want to structure your documents so that you can make the most of the tools described above. For the most part, it isn't very difficult, but a number of issues can cause problems. Some involve how you represent your information, while others require being prepared for a variety of circumstances. Although some of these issues may feel like inconveniences, none of them needs to detract from good design.

The first thing you can do to make styling and transforming your documents easier is to atomize your information as much as possible. This doesn't mean assigning every letter its own element; it means breaking down your documents into the smallest pieces that it would be reasonable to process as a unit. In some ways this process is similar to normalizing databases, but you may find that even the units you've used within databases are too large or too inflexible and that you need to break them into smaller components. In some cases this might be readily fixed by using XML within the text content of your databases, while in others it might mean extra processing when database information is converted to (or from) XML. Finding the proper balance between fragmenting your documents completely and leaving chunks too large to process can be difficult.

Several techniques may be helpful. Soliciting information from potential users about how they'd like to view or process information can give you some idea of the granularity users really need. In some cases, documents are chopped up beyond the needs of users by an overzealous document designer, while in other cases the document designer wasn't aware of the needs of certain groups of users. Although many development processes start by collecting input from users about the information they need, it's not unusual for developers to assume that they can figure out how that information should be chopped up. Getting more feedback about how users would like the information broken down can help make your projects a success.

Although you can't always tell what transformation and styling environments your documents will have to operate in, learning about as many style languages as possible may help you understand the kinds of processing your documents need to be prepared for. Although it might be nice to think that the document architect just creates the best design and then hands it off to graphic designers to make it beautiful and application developers to integrate it with other projects, an understanding of the work other people are going to do on your documents can make it easier to communicate with them, as well as substantially improve your ability to choose appropriate structures. If you're familiar with XSLT match patterns (XPath) and CSS selectors, you have a better chance of creating documents that work easily with both. Architectural forms are more in the realm of document designers, and a basic understanding of those may change the way you structure your DTDs.

Perhaps most important is the need to accept the fact that you may not always have control over where and how your documents are processed, and to design them to accommodate as many different approaches as possible. Even if you're a die-hard XSL fan who never expects to see a document processed with CSS, it's probably still a bad idea to create documents that always need extensive transformation merely to become intelligible. Similarly, developers whose only needs are periodic filtering of their documents shouldn't be surprised when someone else wants to transform their information into something else. By making flexibility a key goal in your document structure development, you can leave these critical doors open and make it easier for others to take advantage of your application of XML.

CHAPTER 19

Building Modular DTDs

As DTDs grow larger and more complex, it often makes sense to break them into smaller chunks. Developers typically fragment DTDs for a number of reasons: to allow reuse of smaller portions, to make the DTD easier to manage and work with, or to divide responsibilities among a number of users. XML parsers will combine all the modules when it is time to process the document, knitting together parts that may come from disparate sources all over the Internet. Creating these modules is not especially difficult, once you've mastered parameter entities (discussed in Chapter 14), but dividing up your DTD in a way that makes sense for the long term may be more complicated. Various XML processing rules can complicate the situation, as anyone trying to track down a duplicate element type declaration can testify. Building a modular DTD requires figuring out how best to use the tools provided by XML 1.0 in a given situation, and there may be several different worthwhile approaches. Choosing the approach that best fits your needs can be tricky.

Manageability vs. Reusability

Although it is often possible to create modules that both meet management needs and are easily reused within other DTDs, achieving both goals is difficult. Breaking down DTDs for simpler management is typically related to assigning responsibility and organizational convenience, while creating reusable DTD fragments is more often concerned with finding "natural" breaks in data structures and creating self-contained structures with as few dependencies on other modules as possible. Organizing a DTD for easier management might involve centralizing sets of parameter entities that are then used by other modules, while organizing a DTD for reusability might involve breaking down those sets into locally declared entities with scope inside a single module. Users of an application that only needs a single module might not appreciate having to wait for the parsing of hundreds of declarations for entities relating to tasks it will never perform. Although it may not be noticeable on a small scale, parsing hundreds, thousands, or millions of documents that refer to the same unnecessary declarations can become a performance irritation, if not necessarily a crisis.

To some extent, these conflicts can be alleviated by exploring the options early, and by choosing an overall approach to development that assigns projects in a way that reflects potential for reuse. If your DTD breakdowns reflect the hierarchies that actually appear in your documents, you may be able to assign management on a module-by-module basis, and make certain that your libraries of reusable content (typically, your parameter entities) reflect that approach. If you can, avoid having reusable content that crosses module boundaries. As tempting as it may be to create `%id;` once, and use it in every attribute list declaration, even seemingly benign dependencies like this can cause problems for developers who want to use modules in a different context. If you do create such dependencies, make certain that you document them thoroughly, so that other developers are spared a search of your files for the right declarations.

Limitations

Although the structure of your DTD is critically important, there are a few rules imposed by XML 1.0 that can force you to take certain approaches to module design. The most important of these are the limitations on names, and the rules describing what happens if declarations for the same name are made more than once. Additional rules governing the sequence in which certain declarations must appear impose further constraints. Keeping names and sequences organized is therefore a critical task in modular DTD creation.

Although most declaration types are fairly tolerant, allowing repeated declarations on a "first-come-first-served" basis, element type declarations and notation type declarations (according to the errata discussed in Chapter 15) can only be made once for a given element or notation name. Declaring the same element or notation type repeatedly will make your DTD fail, returning errors every time you try to parse a document that uses it. There are ways around this, notably the parameter entity encapsulation of such declarations discussed in Chapter 14. Even these tricks have their limitations, however. Modules can't change parameter entity values that have already been declared. Although the internal subset is a useful tool for overriding such values, requiring every document that uses a particular set of modules to carry additional declarations in the internal subset isn't likely to be very reliable. This may require that certain modules be included before others. This is often acceptable, but it is a technique that should be documented. Other developers, presented with a simple list of modules, may not be able to find the dependencies between them, especially if they are subtle.

Similar problems exist for other types of declarations, although without the same kind of loud error that duplicate element and notation type declarations cause. If a module needs to override declarations made in another module, that module must appear before the module being overridden. This may involve using the internal subset (the guaranteed way to insure priority) or it may just mean being careful when creating the external subset. If modules need to override each other's declaration, the problem is probably serious enough to deserve a thorough analysis of what the "dueling modules" are up to and probably a restructuring. Sorting out these problems is often difficult, because the failures may take place silently. Figuring out where a module stepped on your module's declarations isn't always easy, especially when multiple modules may be guilty of the same problem.

The other rule that can trip up schema developers is the requirement that parameter entities be declared before they are used. In a single-file DTD, this is fairly easy to track, but it can become difficult in larger sets of modules. Dependencies need to be documented thoroughly, and changes in those dependencies communicated. Again, moving a module up or down (by moving the parameter entity that references it) within a DTD can have significant, sometimes dire, effects. Managing this change process requires keeping track of all of the dependencies, and making certain that developers know when changes are made.

Naming Conventions and Namespaces

Although namespaces provide some level of protection for element and attribute types, no similar facilities exist for parameter entities or processing instructions, leaving DTDs to cope with potential conflicts. (The lack of integration between the Namespaces recommendation and the XML 1.0 recommendation also leaves some room for conflict, as discussed in Chapter 24.) Keeping modules within DTDs from stepping on each other's declarations may requiring establishing conventions at the start of development.

A good first step is the use of prefixes on a per-module basis. These prefixes may correspond to the namespace prefixes used by your element and attribute names, but they don't have to. Although prefixes don't provide any guarantee of universality like namespaces proper, they do insure that the `story-xref` and `picture-xref` parameter entities don't cause collisions between the story and picture modules of your DTD. Consistent names for every component in a module can save your developers time, reduce the amount of documentation needed to explain potential conflicts, and make your DTDs both more readable and more reusable. They can help with versioning, allowing you to reference newer and older versions of declarations by changing a prefix slightly, and simplify searching for the declarations you actually need.

Documentation

Once you start breaking down a DTD into smaller components, that breakdown requires documentation that goes beyond the documentation for the declarations themselves. Modular reuse is much easier if potential users can read about the module to learn about its contents and its requirements before moving forward with inclusion. The level of documentation required will vary with the complexity of the module and its potential interactions with other DTDs. If a module is itself composed of modules, not an unusual situation in a hierarchically organized DTD, those dependencies need to be explained. For most cases, textual explanation is adequate, but in some large and complex cases, you may need to provide maps to your DTD.

Mapping

Although DTDs are processed into sequential lists of declarations, they often have more complex internal structures before all the parameter entity references are expanded. If your DTDs use multiple levels of modules, or if there are dependencies between your modules, it may be worthwhile to create graphical maps of your DTDs, identifying hierarchies (containment) and dependencies (sequence). Especially complicated DTDs may tempt you to work in three dimensions, but simple hierarchical diagrams may be adequate for many projects. For example, a base DTD might be composed of three parameter entities and references to them:

```
<!ENTITY % paragraph "paragraph.dtd">
<!ENTITY % figure "figure.dtd">
<!ENTITY % table "table.dtd">
<!ENTITY % chapter "chapter.dtd">
<!ENTITY % book "book.dtd">
%paragraph;
%figure;
%table;
%chapter;
%book;
```

Inside `paragraph.dtd` we find a similar pattern:

```
<!ENTITY % textual "text.dtd">
<!ENTITY % reference "reference.dtd">
%textual;
%reference;
```

We could present a map of our DTD like Figure 19.1 below.

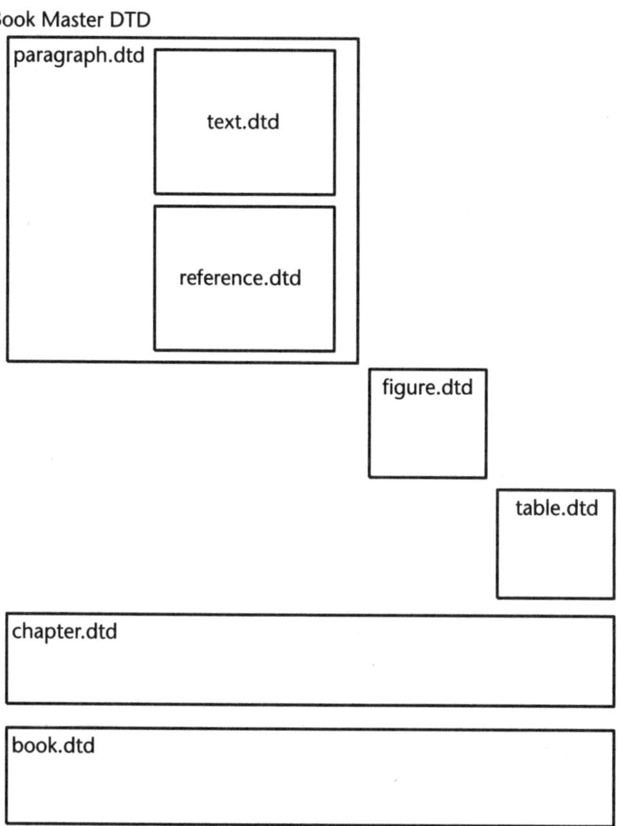

Figure 19.1 A DTD map indicating containment and sequence

More complex maps may need to grow more sophisticated. Dependencies in this DTD only flow down the chart, and there aren't any cases where a later module is dependent on (or independent of) different sets of modules than its parents'. As DTD structures grow more complex, you may find yourself adding lines or colors to these diagrams, and indicating specific dependencies where possible. Especially complex DTDs are much like hypertexts themselves, with the internal relationships forming links.

CHAPTER 20

Leaving Room for the Future: Extensible DTDs

Creating DTDs that others can extend is a somewhat different problem than creating self-contained modules that others can use. XML 1.0's validation constraints don't leave a lot of openings for modification of element declarations, so DTD developers need to plan ahead if they want later developers to be able to extend their work without having to modify the "core" DTD. Although XML stands for "Extensible Markup Language", creating markup languages that are genuinely extensible (or shrinkable) requires planning, careful implementation, and clear explanation.

Easy Extensions

There are a few ways to extend document type definitions that are quite easy. You can always declare additional and overriding general and unparsed entities, and you can declare additional attributes or override existing declarations for attributes, either in the internal subset or in an external file. As long as you don't want to change element content models or notation declarations, extending an XML DTD is fairly simple.

Valid XML's Closed World

At the heart of the extensibility problem is XML's requirement that every element, attribute, and entity in a valid document must conform to a declaration made in the DTD. Validation is an all-or-nothing deal (although applications may choose to ignore validity problems). Most validating parsers treat violations of validity constraints the same way they treat violations of well formedness, not even giving the applications the opportunity to decide if the violation is significant. Although it is possible in XML 1.0 to say that "any declared element or text may appear here," it not possible to say that "any element, declared or not, or text may appear here." This (along with the frequently present injunction to finish a job "right") encourages developers to build complete models of every bit of a document, effectively closing out potential variations.

If developers build complete models, latecomers can't modify them easily. Because a given element type may be declared only once, there is no easy way to override an element declaration. (The technique described in Chapter 14 makes it possible, but still requires the advance knowledge of the DTD designer.) XML 1.0 only leaves two easy possibilities for extending element models, both of which require the designer to use particular tools in the original DTD. If the designer of the original DTD declines to leave these doors open, the only way you can extend a DTD's structure is by rewriting the DTD or confining your additions to attributes. (You can always add extra attribute list declarations and override existing attribute declarations. Conveniently, most applications can safely ignore extra attributes.)

Opening the Doors: ANY and Omitted Declarations

The first door that designers can leave open is the `ANY` content model. Element types with a content model of `ANY` can include any *declared* element type or text. Developers who want to extend the DTD just need to include declarations for their extra element types and any supporting pieces. This can be done either in the internal subset or in an external file that references the original DTD. Using `ANY` has a number of advantages. It's the most obvious way to create an extensible content model—just search the DTD for occurrences of the word `ANY`. The original DTD designer can go ahead and create elements to be used in that space, without having to create extensions to a core DTD. It also makes the DTD look complete. Although `ANY` doesn't say very much about an element's content, it does a least fill a gap in the DTD that would otherwise be there, allowing DTD designers to say that they've defined content models for 100% of their element types.

The second approach involves deliberately leaving element types undeclared. This may seem a little less satisfying to those who want complete

DTDs, but it has several advantages. The main plus is that the developers creating extensions can specify more complete content models for those extensions, rather than being stuck with ANY. For example, if a DTD used an ANY content model for its extensions element, the declaration would look like:

```
<!ELEMENT extensions ANY>
```

Once that declaration has been made, later developers have no way to constrain the contents of extensions more tightly. A developer might want to modify extensions so that its element type declaration read:

```
<!ELEMENT extensions (structural, documenting, ignorable)>
```

If the extensions element type had been declared previously, this declaration would be illegal, its constraints unenforceable.

Another potential benefit of completely omitting the definition of extensions from the core DTD is that you can trap designers who neglect to define extensions. Requiring the designers of extensions to your DTD to consider the content model of what they are adding may help you focus them more closely on the expectations of application processing for your document type, for example. Because they'll need to take the extra step of reading your documentation to find out which element types they need to define in order to extend your DTD, you have an opportunity to warn them of potential consequences to extensions and to describe other tasks they'll have to complete in order to build applications that can process their extensions.

Notes on Notations

Although the rules that a given notation declaration can only be made once appear in the errata, and not the main XML recommendation, it's worth playing by the rules. (Among other things, it ensures that your XML can go through SGML parsers without unexpected problems.) If you just need a notation of a particular kind for an unparsed entity, you can define a notation that is used only by that unparsed entity without worrying about overriding anything.

Adding to the NOTATIONs declared in an attribute type or modifying them is more difficult. Attribute type declarations of NOTATION require that all of the enumerated possibilities correspond to notation declarations—none can be missing. If, for some reason, you need to leave open the possibility of changing a notation referenced through an attribute, there are two approaches. If you really want to change the value of the notation, you can enclose the notation declaration in a parameter entity and then reference the entity. For example:

```
<!ENTITY % myNotationEnt
'<!NOTATION myNotation SYSTEM "http://www.example.com">'>
%myNotationEnt;
```

If, for some reason, you need to change the meaning of myNotation, you can override myNotationEnt in the internal subset of the DTD or in an earlier declaration, and the notation will reflect your override.

The other option, which is frequently simpler, is to redeclare the attribute type, which you can do anywhere before the declaration that needs to be changed appears. This is probably the only approach you'll have available if you need to add a notation to the list of options someone else created. This simpler approach isn't always going to work, however, if your documents are occasionally processed by applications that use non-validating parsers and rely on the notation name information they get rather than the full system or public identifiers returned by validating parsers. In general, application compatibility will probably determine which choice is best.

(Also worth noting is that applications which use notations but don't use NOTATION attributes, like the data typing scheme described in Chapter 10, are much more flexible. It will be up to the application, not the parser, to see if you declared all the notations, and the parser may not care.)

Dependencies and Other Structural Issues

Extensible DTDs face many of the same problems as the modular DTDs described in the previous chapter. In both cases, developers are working with sets of components over which they may not have complete control. XML 1.0's rules for handling naming conflicts, even when they aren't as harsh as the rules prohibiting duplicate element and notation type declarations, can cause confusion when different developers deliberately or inadvertently override each other's declarations. The results can be chaos, especially for simple-minded applications that can't handle changes to the structures of the documents they process. Tracking down dependencies can be complicated, especially if multiple modules and their extensions need to be integrated.

Some of the same techniques that help keep modular DTDs manageable can be applied to DTD extensions. Prefixing the names of any entities you declare with a unique identifier (something better than ext-, for "extensions" probably) can help keep your declarations out of the way of the "core" declarations. Thorough documentation by the original DTD developers identifying requirements and dependencies can help extenders figure out how best to build on an existing DTD. Depending on both the scale of the original DTD and the scale of the extensions, direct correspondence between developers may be very useful.

Documenting Extensibility

As noted above, extensibility issues are an opportunity to communicate with the developers who are building on your DTD. Noting which parts of a DTD are extensible is important, but also provides a chance to describe the impact of extensions and how applications processing these documents are expected to react to extended documents. In many cases, you'll just be noting that applications may ignore extensions, but in other cases the DTD designers may already have specific extensions in mind and be planning on building application that handle such extensions more flexibly. Planning ahead for extensions and describing them thoroughly is an excellent way to preserve the integrity of your core DTD while allowing other designers to customize it to meet their needs more thoroughly. Extensibility can be a selling point for a well-crafted document structure, a promise to other developers that the structure is flexible enough to accommodate changing requirements.

Shrinkability

There may also be times when you want to cut a DTD down to a smaller size. Subsetting DTDs isn't especially difficult, but XML 1.0's built-in tools don't provide much help. You'll need to change content models on a large scale, pruning away features you don't want. You'll need to create a separate DTD for your subset. If you want to retain compatibility with the larger DTD, you'll need to test documents against multiple DTDs. Comparing DTDs visually is often good enough for small projects, but shrinking large DTDs that contain mazes of parameter entities and multiple modules can be a complicated task.

Perhaps the best places to start are in the documentation for the original DTD and in document sets representing the features you want to use. The documentation should be able to help you decipher the dependencies within the original DTD, sort out the tasks of various pieces, and figure out the "whys" behind the DTD design. You may find that features you'd planned on removing are in fact useful, that additional pieces can go. A set of documents gives you test cases for comparing against both your new DTD and the original DTD. When they are available, applications that were built for the original DTD can give you a good idea of how your documents will fare once they get beyond the parser. Your subsets may require special-purpose applications, or you may be able to use existing applications, depending on the nature of your cuts and the approach taken by the applications.

Another possibility you can leave open when you create subsets is creating extensible subsets, even subsets that can be supplemented to rebuild the original, larger DTD. This can be a first step in the re-creation of a large DTD, reforming its basic structures on a different and potentially simpler model that combines extensibility with the modular approach described in the previous chapter. These kinds of changes may be appropriate as a DTD reaches maturity and starts to show its age. A rebuilding of this kind may be able to preserve compatibility with older documents and applications, while paving the way for both documents that use smaller portions of the core DTD and documents that extend it beyond its original borders.

CHAPTER 21

Developing for an International Audience

Although the tools provided in XML 1.0 aren't going to solve all the world's internationalization (commonly abbreviated i18n) and localization (l10n) problems, they provide a solid foundation for building applications and formats that can be used in multiple language environments. Unicode 2.0 support provides a foundation on which documents in many languages can be created, and the extra power of the `xml:lang` attribute makes it easy to identify which language is used in a document or document fragment, simplifying translation tasks and allowing for language-based styling. Creating documents and document structures that can work in multiple environments requires extra work, however—very little of this functionality comes free. You may need to track down operating system support, fonts, and special software to work with some languages, and even marking default languages in XML documents takes a bit of effort.

Unicode 2.0 and ISO10646

XML's "native" format is the Universal Character System ISO10646, a standard for representing characters using two bytes (called UCS-2) or four bytes (called UCS-4) per character, providing access to 65,536 character positions (or over two billion in the four-byte version.) ISO10646 includes

Unicode 2.0, a standard created by the Unicode Consortium (**http://www.unicode.org**). Typically, discussions of XML character sets focus on Unicode, which is the better known of the two standards, and the ISO standard (so far) tends to track Unicode. All XML processors are required to accept UTF-8 and UTF-16, which are both UCS Transformation Formats. XML processors may accept documents stored in other character encodings, but this is entirely at their own discretion.

XML 1.0 uses Unicode is defined in *The Unicode Standard, Version 2.0* (Addison-Wesley, 1996), which describes the character set, the transformations of that set, and rules for conforming to the Unicode standard. Most of the book is devoted to tables of characters, displaying the many possibilities Unicode makes available. Unicode has not filled in all 65,536 available positions with characters, and controversy regularly flares about which characters are available and which are not. Some languages, like English, get along well with a relatively tiny set of characters. (Most needs for English are addressed in the first 128 character positions, which have the same values as the ASCII characters that are the standard for English.) Others, like Chinese, Korean, Japanese, and Vietnamese, need regular access to tens of thousands of characters. In some cases, custom characters may be critically important. XML avoids this controversy by following the Unicode standards. Although it doesn't give everyone all the characters they want, it at least keeps the character set controversies with the character set specialists.

XML doesn't use the entire set of legal Unicode characters. Most control characters (those with values below 32) are expressly prohibited, and cannot even be represented with character references. The use of compatibility characters, which typically represent compromises with existing character encodings but duplicate other characters, is "discouraged" in Section 2.2 of the XML Recommendation. Appendix B, "Character Classes," assigns the legal characters to particular categories used throughout the XML 1.0 recommendation, including Letters, Base Characters, Ideographic Characters, Combining Characters, Digits, and Extending Characters. Any characters which are defined as letters in this description can, for example, be used within an element name or even to start it, whatever their language. It may take some looking up to figure out if the character of your choice is acceptable, but the XML lists should be familiar to those used to working with Unicode.

XML doesn't limit you to working with Unicode, although the UTF-8 or UTF-16 encodings of Unicode will always be your best bet for interchange with unknown XML processors. A wide range of encodings, which may be specified in the encoding declaration of the XML declaration, is available to support the character sets of your choice. A few of the more commonly used encodings are listed in Table 21.1 below.

Table 21.1
Character Encodings Commonly Used in XML

Encoding	Bits Per Character	Usage
UCS-2	16	Universal Character System – 2 bytes
UCS-4	32	Universal Character System – 4 bytes
UTF-8	8	UCS Transformation Format – 8 bits
UTF-7	7	UCS Transformation Format – 7 bits (used for mail and news)
UTF-16	16	UCS Transformation Format – 16 bits (provides access to 32-bit characters)
ISO-8859-1	8	Latin alphabets No. 1 (Western Europe and Latin America)
ISO-8859-2	8	Latin alphabets No. 2 (Central and Eastern Europe)
ISO-8859-3	8	Latin alphabets No. 3 (Southeastern Europe and Miscellaneous)
ISO-8859-4	8	Latin alphabets No. 4 (Western Europe and Latin America)
ISO-8859-5	8	Latin and Cyrillic
ISO-8859-6	8	Latin and Arabic
ISO-8859-7	8	Latin and Greek
ISO-8859-8	8	Latin and Hebrew
ISO-8859-9	8	Latin and Turkish
ISO-8859-10	8	Latin, Lappish, Nordic, Eskimo
EUC-JP	8	Japanese (with multi-byte encoding)
Shift_JIS	16	Japanese (with multi-byte encoding)
ISO-2022-JP	7	Japanese (with multi-byte encoding; for mail and news)
US-ASCII	7	Early standard used for English

continued on next page

Table 21.1
continued

Encoding	Bits Per Character	Usage
EBCDIC	7	IBM standard used for English
Big5	16	Chinese, used in Taiwan
GB2312	16	Simplified Chinese, used in mainland China and Singapore
KOI6-R	8	Extended Russian

There are many more encodings available. The list of all the character sets registered with the Internet Assigned Numbers Authority (IANA), at **http://www.isi.edu/in-notes/iana/assignments/character-sets**, is enormous. Most Java-based parsers use Java's built-in support for encodings, and can process all the encodings supported by Java, listed at **http://java.sun.com/products/jdk/1.2/docs/guide/internat/encoding.doc.html**. However, support for any character encodings in XML beyond UTF-8 and UTF-16 will always depend on the parser you use. Check the documentation that comes with your XML parser and any applications you plan to use to edit or process your XML to make sure that they can handle the encodings properly. Internally, XML parsers should convert other encodings to Unicode to be able to check constraints like character and name legality, and applications should expect Unicode output from their parsers.

Application support for a particular encoding will let you process that encoding safely, but doesn't mean that you'll be able to display, edit, or print information stored in that encoding. "Real" support requires operating system support and fonts that can represent the characters. Although several fonts covering large sections of the Unicode character map are available, no single font presently covers the entire space. Making documents displayable requires deploying an infrastructure that goes well beyond XML.

The XML 1.0 Recommendation only referred to Unicode 2.0. Unicode 3.0, which arrived in September 1999, may require some revisions to XML 1.0, mostly in the character list, but it remains to be seen how the W3C will go about handling this process. Another possible snag in transmitting XML documents in various encodings is communicating enough information to the parser to get it started processing. This communication outside the document is described in RFC 2376 (**http://www.ietf.org/rfc/**

rfc2376.txt). Use of the `charset` parameter is strongly recommended for documents that are transported as either of the XML MIME types (`text/xml` and `application/xml`). For `text/xml`, use of the `charset` parameter will (typically) prevent wrongful interpretation as the default text encoding, which is US-ASCII. For `application/xml`, it will help the processor figure out what kind of encoding it has and simplify processing.

TIP

The Chinese XML Now! site, at http://www.ascc.net/xml/, provides information in both English and Chinese (using several encodings, at that) on XML processing with Chinese language encodings, as well as links to other resources about encodings. If you need a detailed guide to East Asian language processing in particular, try *CJKV Information Processing*, by Ken Lunde (O'Reilly and Associates, 1999). Rick Jelliffe's *The XML and SGML Cookbook* (Prentice-Hall, 1998) provides extensive resources on internationalization and character encoding issues in a markup environment.

Beyond Character Encodings: Identifying Languages

Character encodings and Unicode support are critical features for opening XML to a wider range of languages, but they don't furnish answers to every question in order to provide support for multilingual documents. A single character set, even a relatively small character set like ASCII, can be used to represent multiple languages. Latin, for example, can be represented with a subset of ASCII, which was originally designed for American English. Applications which need to identify the languages used in documents, whether for machine translation or just for styling, need a better guide to which language is being used than a character encoding can provide. Although automated tools are capable of identifying particular languages through character sequences, a mechanism that allows document authors (and perhaps even DTD authors, through default) to identify the language being used in a document or a part of a document can greatly simplify the process.

XML 1.0 defines the `xml:lang` attribute as a place to store information about the language of the content stored within an element. (It isn't clear whether the "content" described by the values in `xml:lang` attributes includes attributes or only element content, but it definitely applies to element content.) Using the `xml:lang` attribute in a validating environment requires that you provide an attribute type declaration for it. Although you normally aren't supposed to define attributes starting with "xml", `xml:lang`'s status as an attribute name specially identified in the XML 1.0 specification makes this permissible. The `xml:lang` attribute should be declared as an `NMTOKEN`, as shown in the recommendation, but there is no constraint requiring that. A sample `xml:lang` declaration is shown below.

```
<!ATTLIST stanza
   xml:lang NMTOKEN #IMPLIED>
```

Like the `xml:whitespace` attribute, the `xml:lang` attribute applies to all descendants of the element that used the `xml:lang` attribute unless those descendants make their own declarations, in which case those declarations apply to all their descendants, subject to the same limitation. If most of your documents only use a single language, it's easy to declare `xml:lang` in the root element (or even specify a default attribute value for it in the DTD) and forget about it.

XML 1.0 uses a standard for language identifiers originally laid out by RFC 1766 (**http://www.ietf.org/rfc/rfc1766.txt**). The contents of `xml:lang` are a combination of language codes and country codes, and potentially even other subcodes for extra precision. This structure lets you distinguish American, Australian, Canadian, and UK English from each other, or French, Belgian, and Canadian French. Even simple tasks like spell-checking can become much simpler when languages are identified at this level of precision. Those who need to identify languages even more tightly, perhaps linguists interested in regional dialects, can use additional subcodes further to describe the language, although the format for those is left unspecified by the XML 1.0 recommendation.

XML 1.0, following RFC 1766, uses two sources for language codes and one for country codes. The first source is ISO 639, which defines two-letter codes for identifying languages, shown at the end of the chapter in Table 21.2. An explorable list of these codes is at **http://www.dsv.su.se/~jpalme/ietf/language-codes.html**. The second source is the IANA, which has a much smaller set of registered languages, listed at **http://www.isi.edu/in-notes/iana/assignments/languages/tags**. There are far fewer IANA codes than ISO 639 codes. For country codes, XML relies on ISO 3166. A complete and updated list of ISO 3166 country codes (which are added to and updated frequently) is available at **http://www.din.de/gremien/nas/nabd/iso3166ma/codlstp1.html**; Table 21.3, also at the end of the chapter, shows a list of ISO 3166 country codes that is current as of this writing. It's usually worth checking a table to make sure get the country codes right—the United Kingdom, for instance, is GB (for Great Britain), not UK.

We'll explore two examples, one of which uses the inheritance features of `xml:lang`, the other of which uses country subcodes to identify the language more closely. In the first example, from Shakespeare's Julius Caesar, Caesar's dying words in Latin are supported with a translation for readers who might otherwise be confused.

```
<speech xml:lang="en">
<speaker>CAESAR</speaker>
<line><fragment>
   <original xml:lang="la">Et tu, Brute!</original>
```

```
    <translation>And you, Brutus!</translation>
  </fragment>
  Then fall, Caesar.</line>
  </speech>
```

The language identifier for the `fragment` element marks "Et tu, Brute!" as being in Latin, allowing style sheets to perform tasks like presenting it in italic, a traditional English-language approach to identifying quotes in foreign languages. "Et tu, Brute!" is the only content marked as Latin in this document, though if there were any child elements involved they would inherit the `xml:lang` value from the original element. The `translation` element, like the rest of the document fragment, is in English, inheriting its `xml:lang` value from the speech element. The translation element might be hidden by the style sheet, or used as a pop-up when a user ran a cursor over the Latin text.

In the next example, `xml:lang` is used to differentiate two different flavors (or flavours) of English, American and British. The entire fragment is marked as being in English, but only in the child `ASSERTION` elements are the details of which country's English indicated.

```
<CONTRADICTIONS xml:lang="en">
<ASSERTION xml:lang="en-GB"> The colour of money is varied.</ASSERTION>
<ASSERTION xml:lang="en-US">The color of money is green.</ASSERTION>
</CONTRADICTION>
```

Both the `ASSERTION` elements here would have inherited a value for `xml:lang` of "`en`"—English—had they not provided more specific details. An application with a language-sensitive spelling checker could, for example, acknowledge both colour and color as correct in their respective contexts.

Beyond XML: Style Sheets and More

The W3C is busily developing tools that will let you display information in different languages the way it's meant to be displayed. More than fonts is at stake here—the next generation of style sheets is supposed to move beyond the Western-centric model that CSS1, CSS2, and even XSL formatting objects have provided so far. Cascading Style Sheets has long provided support for relatively simple internationalization features like bidirectional text, but is only getting started in its support for text written vertically (instead of horizontally). The W3C is moving forward on support for a wide range of additional features to help move the WWW out of its initial bias toward Western languages. The International Layout (**http://www.w3.org/TR/WD-i18n-format**) draft is currently only focused on Cascading Style Sheets, but should have an impact on Extensible Style Language, and provides a grid-based layout system for languages that use vertical presentation. The Ruby (**http://www.w3.org/TR/ruby/**) project is creating support for typography used in Japanese and Chinese where one run of text is associated with another, "base" run of text. The W3C is also coordinating with the Unicode Consortium to describe the interactions between certain types of Unicode characters and markup. The joint Unicode in XML and Other Markup draft (**http://www.unicode.org/unicode/reports/tr20**) identifies character types used to control structure and formatting that should be supplanted by markup to avoid potential collisions.

Table 21.2
Two Letter Language Codes from ISO 639

Language	Code	Language	Code	Language	Code
Abkhazian	ab	Hindi	hi	Romanian	ro
Afan Oromo	om	Hungarian	hu	Russian	ru
Afar	aa	Icelandic	is	Samoan	sm
Afrikaans	af	Indonesian	id	Sangro	sg
Albanian	sq	Interlingua	ia	Sanskrit	sa
Amharic	am	Inuktitut (Eskimo)	iu	Scots Gaelic	gd
Arabic	ar	Irish	ga	Serbian	sr
Armenian	hy	Italian	it	Serbo-Croatian	sh
Assamese	as	Japanese	ja	Sesotho	st
Aymara	ay	Javanese	jw	Setswana	tn
Azerbaijani	az	Kannada	kn	Shona	sn
Bashkir	ba	Kashmiri	ks	Sindhi	sd
Basque	eu	Kazakh	kk	Sinhalese	si
Bengali; Bangla	bn	Kenya, Rwanda	rw	Siswati	ss
Bhutani	dz	Kirghiz	ky	Slovak	sk
Bihari	bh	Kirundi	rn	Slovenian	sl
Bislama	bi	Knupiak	ik	Somali	so
Breton	br	Korean	ko	Spanish	es

continued on next page

Table 21.2
continued

Language	Code	Language	Code	Language	Code
Bulgarian	bg	Kurdish	ku	Sudanese	su
Burmese	my	Laotian	lo	Swahili	sw
Byelorussian	be	Latin	la	Swedish	sv
Cambodian	km	Latvian, Lettish	lv	Tagalog	tl
Catalan	ca	Lingala	ln	Tajik	tg
Chinese	zh	Lithuanian	lt	Tamil	ta
Corsican	co	Interlingue	ie	Tatar	tt
Croatian	hr	Macedonian	mk	Tegulu	te
Czech	cs	Malagasy	mg	Thai	th
Danish	da	Malay	ms	Tibetan	bo
Dutch	nl	Malayalam	ml	Tigrinya	ti
English	en	Maltese	mt	Tonga	to
Esperanto	eo	Maori	mi	Tsonga	ts
Estonian	et	Marathi	mr	Turkish	tr
Faeroese	fo	Moldavian	mo	Turkmen	tk
Fiji	fj	Mongolian	mn	Twi	tw
Finnish	fi	Nauru	na	Uigur	ug
French	fr	Nepali	ne	Ukrainian	uk
Frisian	fy	Norwegian	no	Urdu	ur
Galician	gl	Occitan	oc	Uzbek	uz
Georgian	ka	Oriya	or	Vietnamese	vi
German	de	Pashto, Pushto	ps	Welsh	cy
Greenlandic	kl	Persian	fa	Wolof	wo
Greek	el	Polish	pl	Xhosa	xh
Guamni	gn	Portuguese	pt	Yiddish	yi

continued on next page

Table 21.2
continued

Language	Code	Language	Code	Language	Code
Gujarati	gu	Punjabi	pa	Yoruba	yo
Hausa	ha	Quechua	qu	Zhuang	za
Hebrew	he	Rhaeto-Romance	rm	Zulu	zu

Table 21.3
Two Letter Country Codes from ISO 316

Country	Code	Country	Code	Country	Code
Afghanistan	AF	Germany	DE	Norway	NO
Albania	AL	Ghana	GH	Oman	OM
Algeria	DZ	Gibraltar	GI	Pakistan	PK
American Samoa	AS	Greece	GR	Palau	PW
Andorra	AD	Greenland	GL	Palestinian Territory, Occupied	PS
Angola	AO	Grenada	GD	Panama	PA
Anguilla	AI	Guadeloupe	GP	Papua New Guinea	PG
Antarctica	AQ	Guam	GU	Paraguay	PY
Antigua and Barbuda	AG	Guatemala	GT	Peru	PE
Argentina	AR	Guinea	GN	Philippines	PH
Armenia	AM	Guinea-Bissau	GW	Pitcairn Island	PN
Aruba	AW	Guyana	GY	Poland	PL

continued on next page

Table 21.3
continued

Country	Code	Country	Code	Country	Code
Australia	AU	Haiti	HT	Portugal	PT
Austria	AT	Heard Island and McDonald Islands	HM	Puerto Rico	PR
Azerbaijan	AZ	Holy See (Vatican City State)	VA	Qatar	QA
Bahamas	BS	Honduras	HN	Réunion	RE
Bahrain	BH	Hong Kong	HK	Romania	RO
Bangladesh	BD	Hungary	HU	Russian Federation	RU
Barbados	BB	Iceland	IS	Rwanda	RW
Belarus	BY	India	IN	Saint Helena	SH
Belgium	BE	Indonesia	ID	Saint Kitts and Nevis	KN
Belize	BZ	Iran, Islamic Republic of	IR	Saint Lucia	LC
Benin	BJ	Iraq	IQ	Saint Pierre and Miquelon	PM
Bermuda	BM	Ireland	IE	Saint Vincent and the Grenadines	VC
Bhutan	BT	Israel	IL	Samoa	WS
Bolivia	BO	Italy	IT	San Marino	SM
Bosnia and Herzegovina	BA	Jamaica	JM	Sao Tome and Principe	ST
Botswana	BW	Japan	JP	Saudi Arabia	SA
Bouvet Island	BV	Jordan	JO	Senegal	SN

continued on next page

Table 21.3
continued

Country	Code	Country	Code	Country	Code
Brazil	BR	Kazakstan	KZ	Seychelles	SC
British Indian Ocean Territory	IO	Kenya	KE	Sierra Leone	SL
Brunei Darussalam	BN	Kiribati	KI	Singapore	SG
Bulgaria	BG	Korea, Democratic People's Republic of	KP	Slovakia	SK
Burkina Faso	BF	Korea, Republic of	KR	Slovenia	SI
Burundi	BI	Kuwait	KW	Solomon Islands	SB
Cambodia	KH	Kyrgyzstan	KG	Somalia	SO
Cameroon	CM	Lao People's Democratic Republic	LA	South Africa	ZA
Canada	CA	Latvia	LV	South Georgia and the South Sandwich Islands	GS
Cape Verde	CV	Lebanon	LB	Spain	ES
Cayman Islands	KY	Lesotho	LS	Sri Lanka	LK
Central African Republic	CF	Liberia	LR	Sudan	SD
Chad	TD	Libyan Arab Jamahiriya	LY	Suriname	SR
Chile	CL	Liechtenstein	LI	Svalbard and Jan Mayen	SJ
China	CN	Lithuania	LT	Swaziland	SZ

continued on next page

Table 21.3
continued

Country	Code	Country	Code	Country	Code
Christmas Island	CX	Luxembourg	LU	Sweden	SE
Cocos (Keeling) Islands	CC	Macau	MO	Switzerland	CH
Colombia	CO	Macedonia, The Former Yugoslav Republic of	MK	Syrian Arab Republic	SY
Comoros	KM	Madagascar	MG	Taiwan, Province of China	TW
Congo	CG	Malawi	MW	Tajikstan	TJ
Congo, Democratic Republic of the	CD	Malaysia	MY	Tanzania, United Republic of	TZ
Cook Islands	CK	Maldives	MV	Thailand	TH
Costa Rica	CR	Mali	ML	Togo	TG
Cöte D'Ivoire	CI	Malta	MT	Tokelau	TK
Croatia	HR	Marshall Islands	MH	Tonga	TO
Cuba	CU	Martinique	MQ	Trinidad and Tobago	TT
Cyprus	CY	Mauritania	MR	Tunisia	TN
Czech Republic	CZ	Mauritius	MU	Turkey	TR
Denmark	DK	Mayotte	YT	Turkmenistan	TM
Djibouti	DJ	Mexico	MX	Turks and Caicos Islands	TC
Dominica	DM	Micronesia, Federated States of	FM	Tuvalu	TV

continued on next page

Table 21.3
continued

Country	Code	Country	Code	Country	Code
Dominican Republic	DO	Moldova, Republic of	MD	Uganda	UG
East Timor	TP	Monaco	MC	Ukrane	UA
Ecuador	EC	Mongolia	MN	United Arab Emirates	AE
Egypt	EG	Montserrat	MS	United Kingdom	GB
El Salvador	SV	Morocco	MA	United States	US
Equatorial Guinea	GQ	Mozambique	MZ	United States Minor Outlying Islands	UM
Eritrea	ER	Myanmar	MM	Uruguay	UY
Estonia	EE	Namibia	NA	Uzbekistan	UZ
Ethiopia	ET	Nauru	NR	Vanuatu	VU
Falkland Islands (Malvinas)	FK	Nepal	NP	Venezuela	VE
Faeroe Islands	FO	Netherlands	NL	Vietnam	VN
Fiji	FJ	Netherlands Antilles	AN	Virgin Islands, British	VG
Finland	FI	New Caledonia	NC	Virgin Islands, U.S.	VI
France	FR	New Zealand	NZ	Wallis and Futuna	WF
French Guiana	GF	Nicaragua	NI	Western Sahara	EH
French Polynesia	PF	Niger	NE	Yemen	YE
French Southern Territories	TF	Nigeria	NG	Yugoslavia	YU
Gabon	GA	Niue	NU	Zambia	ZM

continued on next page

Table 21.3
continued

Country	Code	Country	Code	Country	Code
Gambia	GM	Norfolk Island	NF	Zimbabwe	ZW
Georgia	GE	Northern Mariana Islands			MP

CHAPTER 22

The Importance of Documentation

Throughout computing, documentation is often an afterthought, something developers do as they're cleaning up. In many cases, documentation is even seen as a nuisance, something that keeps developers from building the parts of the system that get "real" work done. Unfortunately, most projects have lifespans extending beyond the time their original developers devote to the project. If those original developers—and everyone who follows after them—don't explain themselves beyond the simple, often cryptic declarations that XML 1.0 uses to convey information to processors, then later developers are likely to spend a lot of time shaking their heads and recreating work that was done before. XML's tools for describing both documents and document type definitions are extremely simple, and lack many advanced features, but developers can still make good use of them by sticking to conventions and setting a high value on human-readable documentation.

Documenting DTDs

Document Type Definitions are descriptions of document structures, but highly optimized descriptions that don't provide an enormous amount of information to human readers. Some DTDs, notably simple well-structured DTDs that use verbose element and attribute names, aren't that hard to puzzle out. Once abbreviations and parameter entities creep into a DTD, however, the amount of guessing and cross-referencing that human readers have to endure to figure out what's happening can grow dramatically. To some extent, paying attention to DTD structure, doing things like clustering related definitions, can help with this, but often a good road map with extensive descriptions is both more useful for readers and easier to create.

The only tool that XML 1.0 provides for creating human-readable documentation is the comment. Comments are great in some ways—you can write almost anything you like in a comment without fear of choking a parser—but they're very simple and come with no structure. They cannot appear within declarations (except the document type declaration), making them free-floating. For example:

```
<!ELEMENT SUBTOTAL (#PCDATA)>
<!--This is the amount to charge the customer-->
<!ELEMENT TOTAL (#PCDATA)>
```

Which element declaration is the sandwiched comment describing? If it's describing the SUBTOTAL element, customers will be very happy (no tax, shipping, or handling charges), but the company will be less enthusiastic. Unfortunately, there's nothing in the comment itself to indicate which element it describes. A slightly better approach might look like:

```
<!ELEMENT SUBTOTAL (#PCDATA)>

<!--This is the amount to charge the customer-->
<!ELEMENT TOTAL (#PCDATA)>
```

Unfortunately, given XML's white space normalization rules, parsers aren't required to preserve the extra space and might save the document later as the first version shown. A safer approach would combine comment location and possible prefixes for comments. For example, requiring that comments always appear before the declaration they are describing would solve the problem shown above. In the declarations below, it would be clear that each comment went with the declaration following:

```
<!--Total cost of goods, no tax or Shipping and Handling-->
<!ELEMENT SUBTOTAL (#PCDATA)>
<!--This is the amount to charge the customer-->
<!ELEMENT TOTAL (#PCDATA)>
```

Alternatively, you could prefix the comment with information linking it to the appropriate declaration:

```
<!--EL:SUBTOTAL - Total cost of goods, no tax or Shipping and Handling--
>
<!ELEMENT SUBTOTAL (#PCDATA)>
<!--EL: TOTAL - This is the amount to charge the customer-->
```

```
<!ELEMENT TOTAL (#PCDATA)>
```

or even:

```
<!--EL:SUBTOTAL - Total cost of goods, no tax or Shipping and Handling--
>
<!--EL: TOTAL - This is the amount to charge the customer-->
<!ELEMENT SUBTOTAL (#PCDATA)>
<!ELEMENT TOTAL (#PCDATA)>
```

Both these options let you link comments to declarations, and are probably flexible enough to handle many situations. They don't, however, let you separate different types of comments, and the convention for placement needs to be broadened if developers need a way to describe the entire DTD and not just individual declarations.

Solving these problems isn't very difficult. First, documentation that describes an entire DTD (or a file containing part of a DTD) should appear at the front of the file, before any declarations or processing instructions. Separating those comments from the comments describing the first declaration is easy—use an empty comment (`<!---->`). Different types of comments can be given different prefixes, preferably prefixes that can't be confused with XML names. Starting your prefixes with an "odd" character like @, #, ^, or * will do the trick. Depending on how consistent you are, you may be able to reuse your comments or manage them using software tools that look for different kinds of comments and understand the conventions.

For example, XML Authority (available from **http://www.extensibility.com**) uses a combination of the rules described above. All comments appear before the declarations (or the schema) they describe. Unprefixed comments are *schema notes*, intended for use by other schema designers exploring the DTD. Comments intended for document authors and application developers are *usage notes*, and are prefixed by `#USAGE` to separate them. Version information is stored using a combination of processing instructions (which can let applications know which version of a schema they are using) and comments prefixed by `#CHANGES` that identify how the DTD has changed over time. Even a fairly simple DTD can quickly sprout an enormous amount of documentation, as shown below:

```
<!--The elements in this schema represent paragraphs and smaller units
for use in documents.-->
<!--#USAGE:The paragraph element is for text paragraphs, while the other
elements represent smaller units.-->
<!---->
<!--#CHANGES:05-Oct-99 : Created.-->
<?XA_VERSION_HISTORY DATE = '10/5/99' VERSION = '1.3' NAME = 'Jim
Goodwin' NOTES = 'Added date to paragraph.' ?>

<!--#CHANGES:05-Oct-99 : Created.-->
<?XA_VERSION_HISTORY DATE = '10/5/99' VERSION = '1.2' NAME = 'Jim
```

```
Goodwin' NOTES = 'Added &apos;id&apos; attribute to paragraph element
per JWZ request.' ?>

<!--#CHANGES:04-Oct-99 : Created.-->
<?XA_VERSION_HISTORY DATE = '10/4/99' VERSION = '1.1' NAME = 'Joe
Goodwin' NOTES = 'Added name element to start directory integration.' ?>

<!--#CHANGES:04-Oct-99 : Created.-->
<?XA_DOC_PREFS PROMPT_WHEN_SAVING = 'true' LOG_CHANGES = 'true' ?>

<!--The paragraph element is the highest-level element this schema
module contains.-->
<!--#USAGE:The paragraph element represents a typical text paragraph.-->
<!--#CHANGES:04-Oct-99 : Created.-->
<!--#CHANGES:05-Oct-99 : Changed from: <!ELEMENT paragraph (#PCDATA |
emphasis | citation | note | name )*>
-->
<!ELEMENT paragraph (#PCDATA | emphasis | citation | note | name | date
)*>

<!--This allows developers to identify particular paragraphs and link
using XLink or IDREF.-->
<!--#USAGE:Use the id attribute to assign unique identifiers (within the
document) to your paragraph.-->
<!--#CHANGES:05-Oct-99 : Created.-->
<!ATTLIST paragraph id ID #REQUIRED>

<!--#CHANGES:04-Oct-99 : Created.-->
<!ELEMENT emphasis (#PCDATA )>

<!--#CHANGES:04-Oct-99 : Created.-->
<!ELEMENT citation (#PCDATA )>

<!--#CHANGES:04-Oct-99 : Created.-->
<!ELEMENT note (#PCDATA )>

<!--#CHANGES:04-Oct-99 : Created.-->
<!ELEMENT name (#PCDATA )>

<!--#CHANGES:05-Oct-99 : Created.-->
<!ELEMENT date (#PCDATA )>
```

Is all this information useful? Probably. Some of the comments identifying when elements were created may be superfluous, but they might also help a desperate project manager figure out which developer is breaking the DTD every night. The information on prior versions of declarations could grow as changes are made, requiring occasional manual pruning, but also provides an easy way to roll changes back, and return to a version where things worked as they were supposed to.

Tools have a significant advantage over humans when it comes to creating some of this material. It's easier to keep conventions perfect, and easier to do monotonous tasks like keep track of older versions of declarations. They do tend to go a bit overboard if allowed (most of the automatic notes above can be turned off, however), and the results aren't always easy to read directly. Automatically generated comments may be easier to process into other forms of documentation, however, and provide a way for developers to create some level of documentation without necessarily being aware that they are doing so.

Another area worth considering is the use of markup and other textual conventions within comments. HTML markup can be put into comments—remember, the only limitation on comments is that `-->` can't appear! As long as your HTML doesn't include any comments, you can use it inside XML comments. For example:

```
<!--<ul>
<li>id - The id attribute is an XML ID for the provision of unique
identifiers, usually for reference.</li>
<li>sectionNum - The sectionNum attribute is a string identifying the
section and paragraph number of the current paragraph. This only needs
to be present if you're overriding the calculated value.</li>
</ul>-->
<!ATTLIST paragraph
   id ID #IMPLIED
   sectionNum        CDATA    #IMPLIED>
```

A custom processor could take the contents of comments and turn them into a more complete HTML document describing the DTD, while most processors would just ignore the comment entirely and move through the declarations. Some (older, and technically broken) HTML browsers will conveniently display the HTML if they don't support multi-line comments, but for the most part, your HTML will be hidden until you apply a processor that knows how to display it. You can also use your own custom XML vocabulary within comments.

Documenting Documents

Comments are sometimes used in XML documents as well as in DTDs. Their use in documents is usually a little less crucial, though they can be an important tool to help authors (especially when multiple authors are involved) keep track of the work they're doing and to provide information that shouldn't be part of the parse tree but might be of interest to people. Comments in documents have the same limitations that comments have in DTDs—it's hard to tell what a comment describes—but similar solutions to those used in DTDs are appropriate.

Comments describing a document as a whole may come at the very beginning of the document, after the XML declaration but before the root element. Comments intended to describe the document, rather than the DTD or the internal subset, should probably appear outside the document type declaration. Immediately before the root element is a popular and reasonable location. Comments may also appear after the root element is closed, a convenient location for "to-do" lists and other information about a document in progress. If a document's end is growing, the end is a good place for construction comments.

Comments describing particular content are actually harder to work with in documents than they are in DTDs. Inside a document, comments aren't just entries in a flat list—they can be contained by elements as well. For example, it isn't clear which element the comment below is referring to:

```
<SECTION>
<!--Fix this, will you?-->
<PARAGRAPH>....
```

Is it the SECTION element which needs to be fixed? Or just the paragraph? Although it might be helpful to require writers to specify their meaning more carefully, conventions can also be helpful. Some document authors like to put comments describing an element immediately inside the element, coming before any textual or element content. Others like to put the comment in front of the element being described. As always, the comments cannot appear inside the start- or end-tags for the element.

Naming conventions may be especially useful in team situations, where comments may represent suggestions, commands, or even comments in a literal sense, about a document. Identifying writer and recipient may help smooth communications:

```
<SECTION>
<!--Simon - Fix this, will you? - Julie-->
<PARAGRAPH>....
```

(If you use dashes as separators, remember to avoid two dashes in succession.) Dating comments may also be appropriate, depending on the situation. And, as noted above, you can use markup vocabularies like HTML inside your comments. XML processors will ignore them, but you can build applications that support them.

Documentation Outside of XML 1.0

Although documentation inside XML documents and DTDs is very helpful, it's only a beginning, especially for schemas. Reading a DTD, even a well-commented DTD, can be very difficult without an overview, substantial explanation and examples, and possibly even some pictures. This kind of documentation is commonly included with applications, but it's not always obvious that a mere document (or data) format is worthy of such effort. On the other hand, if you're crafting custom software to support your XML documents, you may be doing this work already. If you hope to make your XML application a standard—something you're submitting to the W3C, the IETF, OASIS, BizTalk.org, or just hoping to share—the documentation process is an important opportunity to convince readers that your visions are worth using.

This documentation can come in a number of forms, all of which are aimed at encouraging users to explore your creations and (perhaps) use them in the way you intended. Paper or HTML documentation is a common standard, with examples and explanation. Standard explanatory documentation is an important approach, but not the only one. A simple style sheet (CSS or XSL, most likely) that helps users read your XML files can win you friends from users trying to decode the structure of your documents. Presenting your document structures visually, in a way users can apply to multiple documents as they learn, is one strategy that can win you users.

Another critical strategy to consider is making software available that handles your markup. Open-source software is especially useful as a tool for including more people. Users can see exactly what's involved, should they want to, and have the advantage of a software foundation they can customize and extend. Depending on the license you choose, and the approach you take, you may be able to build a community of developers around software that supports your XML creations. If the community around your software achieves critical mass and users are contributing happily, your XML format is likely to succeed as well. There are many subtleties involved in making an open-source project work, and it may not be the "magic bullet" for selling your products or even your consulting. For an introduction to some of the possibilities, see *Open Sources, Voices from the Open Source Revolution* (O'Reilly and Associates, 1999—available at **http://www.ora.com/catalog/opensources/book/toc.html**).

Documenting for the Machine—PIs as Comments

Processing instructions (PIs) are much like comments, with similar flexibility. However, unlike comments, all processing instructions and their contents must be reported to the application. The application isn't required to understand anything about them, but it may try, sometimes with bad results. The paragraph DTD example above shows one use of processing instructions to convey comment-like information (a version number) to an application, and PIs are a good way to create comments intended for the application. This use of PIs will be explored further in Chapter 26.

CHAPTER 23

Creating Webs of Documents: XLink

Although many XML documents are self-contained, other XML documents are part of a larger universe of documents, connecting the information they contain with the information in other documents. HTML made hypertext ubiquitous by making it easy, removing most of the constraints that had limited earlier systems. By radically simplifying hypertext connections to forward links between resources that weren't required to know anything about each other, HTML's simple `A` element made hypertext a friendly, easy way to connect information. With the emergence of XML, there are two new problems to solve. First, XML 1.0 itself doesn't identify any linking mechanisms between documents—the only links included are `ID` and `IDREF` attributes. Second, there is an opportunity to build much more powerful and manageable linking systems than the current mechanism provides. XML Linking Language (XLink), together with its supporting XPointer and XPath standards, is attempting to solve both of these problems.

NOTE

Discussion in this chapter is based on versions of these specifications that may not prove stable and the material is subject to change. The XLink discussion is based on the 26 July 1999 Working Draft (http://www.w3.org/1999/07/WD-xlink-19990726), while the XPointer discussion is based on the 9 July 1999 Working

Draft (**http://www.w3.org/1999/07/WD-xptr-19990709**), and the XPath discussion is based on the 8 October 1999 Proposed Recommendation (**http://www.w3.org/TR/1999/PR-xpath-19991008**). An update to this chapter will be available at **http://www.simonstl.com**.

Modeling Relationships

HTML links are very simple. They indicate the presence of *traversal paths* between "here" and a resource specified in the `href` attribute. The behavior of these links is well understood. The contents of these links are highlighted to indicate their presence to users. When a user clicks on the link, the resource specified by the `href` attribute is retrieved. By default, it replaces the content that originally held the link, but (using information in the supporting `target` attribute) may also appear in a new window or a different frame. Clicking on text to reach a destination is a readily-learned interface, and the work required of document authors to implement this interface is minimal, at least at first. Every `A` element-based link in HTML can be described as:

```
here->there
```

The ubiquitous `IMG` element uses its `SRC` attribute in much the same way, though the link is (usually) followed automatically by the Web browser to retrieve the image for insertion into the document. Other HTML linking mechanisms follow a similar pattern.

Other hypertext systems often started at a higher level of abstraction than traversable paths, identifying resources that were related and then generating traversable paths from those relationships. If four resources were somehow related, they could be described as a set:

```
{a, b, c, d}
```

Determining how users or programs could actually move between these resources requires additional information. The simplest cases define connections between none of the resources or all of the resources. If all of the resources are connected, then users can move from each point to all of the others:

```
a-> b, c, d
b-> a, c, d
c-> a, b, d
d-> a, b, c
```

In some cases, one of the resources is the origin point, and all the other resources are only targets:

```
a-> b, c, d
b->
c->
d->
```

Alternately, one of the resources could be a central connector, pointing to all the targets, while those targets only point back to the central connector:

```
a-> b, c, d
b-> a
c-> a
d-> a
```

There are many, many possible combinations of paths between resources, and defining how paths should connect the resources in a set can be difficult. Generally, it requires providing either extra information about the paths between resources or additional descriptions of the resources and rules for processing those descriptions into paths. On the other hand, defining links as resource sets (even when there are only two resources) makes them much more manageable, because they can be centralized in link documents rather than distributed across an ever-growing document base.

The XLink Approach

XLink provides a vocabulary that developers can use to describe both the simple HTML-style links and links based on sets of resources. In its latest draft, XLink moved from an architectural forms approach that permitted developers to use their own vocabularies for describing links to a namespace-based approach that is more recognizable although less flexible. The underlying tools remained largely the same, however, providing two similar sets of descriptions for two very different kinds of links. XLink's "simple links" are much like HTML's links, while XLink's "extended links" support the resource set links described above. In both cases, XLink-aware applications will be able to identify linking information within documents and either process it directly or process it with the aid of style sheets or similar tools. Both versions rely on namespaces to identify their components: the namespace prefix `xlink` maps to the URI **http://www.w3.org/XML/XLink/0.9**, at least for documents based on the Working Draft.

Although XLink's simple links and extended links use similar vocabulary to describe the resources they connect, their underlying processing is very different. In some sense, simple links represent backward compatibility for HTML, while extended links represent motion toward the approach that most hypertext developers were supporting before HTML caught them by surprise and made hypertext a household word. Although the two types of links can be combined in a single document, you'll need to keep track of which kind of link you're using at any given time. As the number of links, especially out-of-line links, grows, tracking down the origin of a particular connection can be difficult. Remembering the distinctions between the two types of links may help you sort out the many paths through your documents, especially as you combine documents of different types.

Simple Links

Simple links connect only two resources, and there is only one connection between them, the "here to there" of HTML. XLink provides two versions of simple links, one an explicit `xlink:simple` element, and the other an attribute-identified version that uses `'xlink:type="simple"'`. The contents of the two versions are similar, though attribute-identified simple links need to repeat the `xlink` namespace prefix on all the attributes that store information. The two approaches allow developers either to keep linking information in separate elements (as HTML does with the `A` element) or to integrate it with existing element types. The properties of a simple link are listed below in Table 23.1.

Table 23.1
The Properties of a Simple Link

Property/ Attribute	Meaning
`href`	**Contains the URI of the target resource.**
`role`	**Describes the "function of the link's content", usually in a form with which automated processors can work.**
`title`	**Provides a human-readable title for the target resource.**
`show`	**Defines how to present the target resource when the link is actuated. Accepts the values** `new`, `parsed`, **and** `replace`. **The** `new` **value presents the resource in a new window, while** `replace` **opens the target resource in the same window or other context as the document that contained the link. The** `parsed` **value indicates that the content of the target resource should be integrated with the linking document.**

continued on next page

Table 23.1
continued

Property/ Attribute	Meaning
actuate	**Defines the context in which the link should be used. If the value is** user**, the link shouldn't be actuated (traversed) until the user clicks on it or does something specific to the link. If the value is** auto**, the link should be actuated when the application feels that the user has "reached" the link. The** A **element in HTML effectively relies on user actuation, while** IMG **is actuated automatically by most browsers.**
inline	**Not actually included in the latest draft, but would specify whether "here" is actually a participant in the link. The current draft discusses inline and out-of-line simple links without providing a mechanism for differentiating them.**

Only the href property is required for a simple link—the rest may help applications process the link as you want, but without a target there really isn't a resource. A simple link might look like:

```
<xlink:simple href="http://www.simonstl.com">Update Site for this
Chapter</xlink:simple>
```

or:

```
<update xlink:type="simple" xlink:href="http://www.simonstl.com">Update
Site for this Chapter</update>
```

To an XLink processor, both links contain the same information, and the text "Update Site for this Chapter" is connected to the resource URI "http://www.simonstl.com". You can supply more information if you like:

```
<xlink:simple href="http://www.simonstl.com" role="update"
title="Chapter Update" show="new" actuate="user">Update Site for this
Chapter</xlink:simple>
```

or:

```
<update xlink:type="simple" xlink:href="http://www.simonstl.com"
xlink:role="update" xlink:title="Chapter Update" xlink:show="new"
xlink:actuate="user">Update Site for this Chapter</update>
```

Both these versions supply the same information, describing the role of this link as "update," and its human-readable title as "Chapter Update." The link should be actuated by the user, and should appear in a new window.

Simple links are used like HTML `A` elements, enclosing usually arbitrary content (though all of the rules for properly nesting XML elements still apply). If you are working in a validating environment, you must declare all the XLink components, both elements and attributes, that you use. This lets your documents get through a validating parser, and also lets you use features like default values for attributes. Remember, however, that your default values may disappear when processed by non-validating parsers. If the links in your document don't show up when opened in a different environment, you probably relied on defaults in the external DTD subset. (Chapter 27 explains this problem in more detail.)

Extended Links

Extended links implement the set of resources model described above, with extra tools for describing connections between resources. Extended links are composed of three parts: a containing element that describes the link as a whole, a set of locators that describe the resources being connected, and an optional set of arcs that provide explicit connections between those resources. The extended link container, the locators, and the arcs can be identified through explicit element names (`xlink:extended`, `xlink:locator`, and `xlink:arc`) or through attribute settings (`xlink:type="extended"`, `xlink:type="locator"`, and `xlink:type="arc"`).

The extended link container stores information about the properties of the link as a whole in its attributes, listed below in Table 23.2. Most of these properties are similar to those used for simple links, but are used to define the larger context of a link that may be used in multiple situations.

Table 23.2
The Properties of an Extended Link

Property/ Attribute	Meaning
`role`	Describes the "function of the link's content" for the entire set of resources, usually in a form with which automated processors can work.

continued on next page

Table 23.2
continued

Property/ Attribute	Meaning
`title`	**Provides a human-readable title for the link as a whole.**
`showdefault`	**Provides a default value for how to present the target resource when the link is actuated. Accepts the values** `new`, `parsed`, **and** `replace`. **The** `new` **value presents the resource in a new window, while** `replace` **opens the target resource in the same window or other context as the document that contained the link. The** `parsed` **value indicates that the content of the target resource should be integrated with the linking document.**
`actuatedefault`	**Provides a default value for the context in which the link should be used. If the value is** `user`, **the link shouldn't be actuated (traversed) until the user clicks on it or does something specific to the link. If the value is** `auto`, **the link should be actuated when the application feels that the user has "reached" the link.**
`inline`	**Again, not actually included in the latest draft, but this would specify whether "here" is actually a participant in the link. The current draft suggests that all extended links are out-of-line.**

Just as with simple links, the `xlink:` prefix must be applied to these property names if the extended link is identified with an `'xlink:type="extended"'` attribute.

The extended link element will contain locators describing particular resources in the set. The properties for locator elements are shown below in Table 23.3.

Table 23.3
The Properties of an Extended Link Locator

Property/ Attribute	Meaning
`href`	**Contains the URI of the target resource.**
`role`	**Describes the resource in a form with which automated processors can work.**
`title`	**Provides a human-readable title for the resource.**
`id`	**An attribute of type ID that is used to identify the locator when used with arcs. Unlike the other properties, there is no need to apply an `xlink` namespace to this attribute.**

With these two components, we can start to build an extended link. The link below connects a set of pictures for a hypertext photo album.

```
<xlink:extended role="russ" title="Links about Russ"
showdefault="replace" actuatedefault="user">
<xlink:locator href="family.xml#russ" title="Russ with Gavin and Judy"
role="picture" id="rgj">
<xlink:locator href="russmeet.xml#russ" title="Russ in a Meeting"
role="picture" id="rmeet"/>
<xlink:locator href="russ.xml#russ" title="Russ with a patient"
role="picture" id="rwp"/>
</xlink:extended>
```

This particular link contains links to album entries, each of which describes a photo, containing pictures about Russ. The `#russ` at the end of the `href` attributes identifies an element in each of the album entry that maps out the space corresponding to Russ. The sample below demonstrates how this might work in an extended link context. Each of the files describing the pictures has areas mapped out with ID attributes in addition to the image and caption information. The files referenced by an extended link aren't required to contain any XLink markup themselves.

```
<?xml version="1.0" encoding="UTF-8"?>
<!DOCTYPE map SYSTEM "map.dtd">
<map>
<image src="3folks.gif" />
<area id="gavin" shape="rect" coords="50,50,150,150" />
<area id="russ" shape="rect" coords="150,50,300,150" />
<area id="russJudy" shape="rect" coords="150,50,400,150" />
<caption>Gavin, Russ, and Judy</caption>
</map>
```

If the application that had access to both of these files supported XLink, users could click on an area containing a picture of Russ, get a menu listing other pictures of Russ, and visit those pictures by selecting them from a menu, as shown below in Figure 23.1. (It might be a pop-up menu, or it might be an entirely different mechanism.) Similarly, they could click on other people's images to get information about other links referring to them.

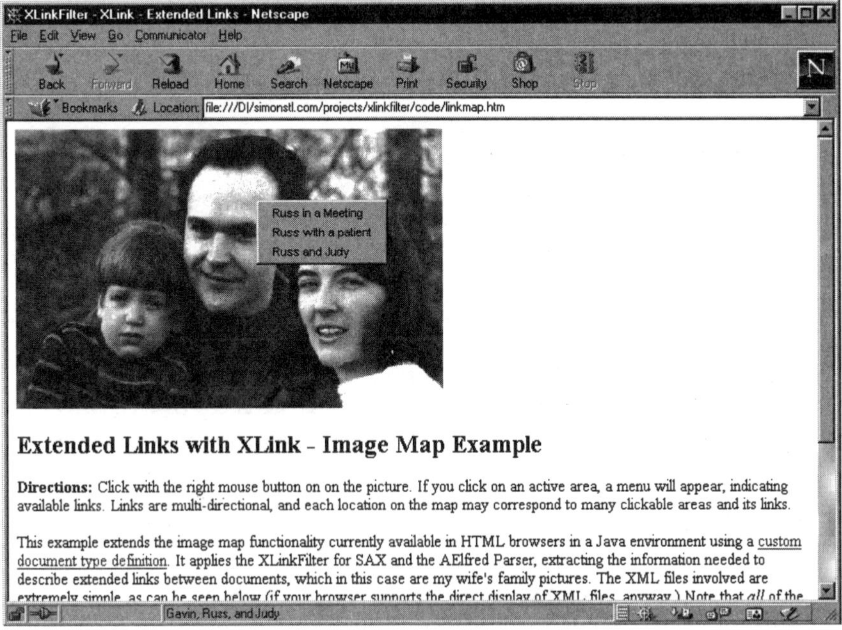

Figure 23.1 Extended links can provide a menu of possibilities

The application above assumed that all the resources connect to each other. This is useful in some situations, but doesn't provide enough information in others, as discussed above in the {a, b, c, d} examples. XLink provides another set of tools to developers who want to describe the traversal paths explicitly without reverting to simple links. Arcs are very simple, using four attributes to define traversal paths, as listed in Table 23.4.

Table 23.4
The Properties of an Arc

Property/ Attribute	Meaning
`from`	**Identifies the origin of the traversal path using a reference to the ID of a locator.**
`to`	**Identifies the target of the traversal path using a reference to the ID of a locator.**
`show`	**Defines how to present the target resource when the link is actuated. Accepts the values** `new`, `parsed`, **and** `replace`. **The** `new` **value presents the resource in a new window, while** `replace` **opens the target resource in the same window or other context as the document that contained the link. The** `parsed` **value indicates that the content of the target resource should be integrated with the linking document.**
`actuate`	**Defines the context in which the link should be used. If the value is** `user`, **the link shouldn't be actuated (traversed) until the user clicks on it or does something specific to the link. If the value is** `auto`, **the link should be actuated when the application feels that the user has "reached" the link.**

Arcs are used in concert with locators to create paths users can follow. If we wanted to specify that the picture shown above could connect to the other two pictures described in the link, but create no link back to the original picture, we could add arcs to the link as shown below:

```
<xlink:extended role="russ" title="Links about Russ"
showdefault="replace" actuatedefault="user">
<xlink:locator href="family.xml#russ" title="Russ with Gavin and Judy"
role="picture" id="rgj">
<xlink:locator href="russmeet.xml#russ" title="Russ in a Meeting"
role="picture" id="rmeet"/>
<xlink:locator href="russ.xml#russ" title="Russ with a patient"
role="picture" id="rwp"/>
<xlink:arc from="rgj" to="rmeet" />
<xlink:arc from="rgj" to="rwp" />
</xlink:extended>
```

In both these arcs, paths are created that lead from the original picture outward, but no paths lead back to the original picture. If we want to allow readers to move from the meeting picture to the patient picture, we can add another arc:

```
<xlink:arc from="rmeet" to="rwp" />
```

This approach lets you create explicit paths between resources, although the number of possible paths grows exponentially with the number of resources.

NOTE
Arcs are a rather controversial addition to XLink and may be modified or dropped—see the online update to this chapter for more information.

Identifying XML Resource Fragments with XPointer and XPath

While the simple ID-based linking used above is adequate for some situations, specifying links outside documents requires a more comprehensive set of tools for identifying parts of documents. ID attributes are useful for identifying entire elements, but there may be times when a portion of a document that isn't necessarily well formed should be part of a link, and there may also be times when you want to link to a document but you're not allowed to add extra ID attributes. XLink's companion standards, XPointer and XPath, provide a vocabulary for describing fragments of XML documents, even fragments that are scattered throughout a document. XPointer is an application of XPath, with extensions, that is specifically for use in URIs and linking. (Extensible Style Language Transformations also use XPath.) XPointer and XPath are growing (and still growing) into rather large standards, so we'll explore only the basics here.

To demonstrate how XPointer works, we'll explore a simple albeit somewhat ridiculous document (`myDoc.xml`), shown below.

```
<myDoc><title>My Document</title><p importance="serious"
author="me">This is my first, and very important, document.</p><giggle
id="hee" /></myDoc>
```

For convenience, we'll refer to the document through the tree structure shown below in Figure 23.2.

The only ID in this document is the one on the `giggle` element, so we'll start with that. The ID-based links used in the documents in previous section are called *bare names*, and are treated as the equivalent to the more formal XPointer id(name). We could refer to element H, the `giggle` element, using either `mydoc.xml#hee` or `mydoc.xml#id(hee)`. These versions are equivalent.

Since we don't have ID attributes on any of the other elements, we'll need to reach them by a different route. XPointer allows you to navigate the document tree using the axes described below in Table 23.5.

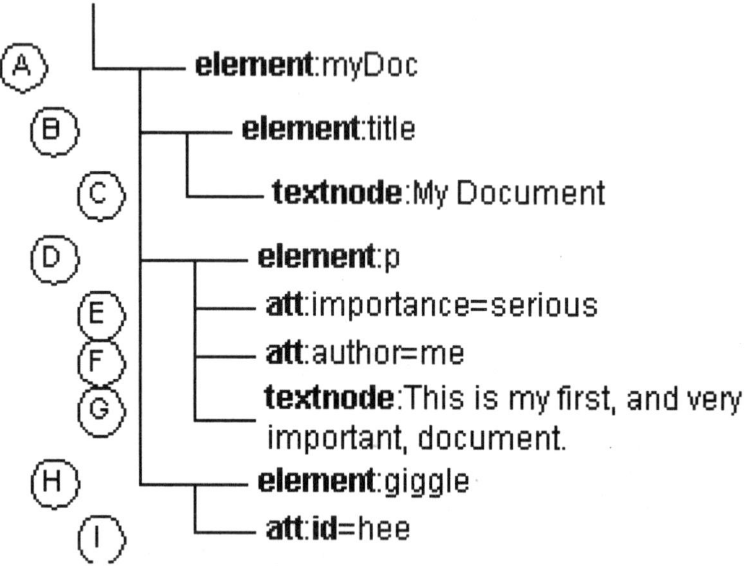

Figure 23.2 The tree structure of the myDoc document

Table 23.5
XPath-derived Axes for XPointer

Axis	Meaning
`child`	Locates nodes that are immediate children of the current node. This includes child elements, processing instructions, comments, and text. (Elements and text are probably the most useful in a linking context. Nodes B, D, and H in the diagram above are children of node A, for example.
`descendant`	Locates nodes that are contained within the current node. All of the nodes from B to D and G to H are descendants of node A. (E, F, and I are attributes and therefore excluded.)
`descendant-or-self`	Like `descendant`, but tests the current node as well. Starting from node A, this would include A to D and G to H.

continued on next page

Table 23.5
continued

Axis	Meaning
`parent`	**Locates nodes that immediately contain the current node. Node A is the parent of nodes B, D, and H.**
`ancestor`	**Locates all nodes that contain the current node. Node G's ancestors are nodes D and A.**
`ancestor-or-self`	**Like `ancestor`, but tests the current node as well. Starting from node G, this would include G, D, and A.**
`preceding-sibling`	**Locates nodes that share a `parent` element and appear before the current node. Starting from node H, nodes D and B would qualify.**
`following-sibling`	**Locates nodes that share a `parent` element and appear after the current node. Starting from node B, nodes D and H would qualify.**
`preceding`	**Locates any nodes before the current node. Starting from node D, nodes C, B, and A would qualify.**
`following`	**Locates any nodes after the current node. Starting from node D, nodes G and H would qualify. (E, F, and I, being attributes, are excluded.)**
`self`	**Locates the current node. Starting from D, only node D would qualify.**
`attribute`	**Locates attributes of the current node. Starting from node D, nodes E and F would qualify.**

XPointers combine lists of these axes with tests and a few additional XPointer-specific components to identify pieces of documents suitable for linking. The first piece of an XPointer may be an absolute location path, listed in Table 23.6. If the first piece is not an absolute location path, root is assumed.

Table 23.6
XPointer's Absolute Location Paths

Path	Meaning
`/ (root)`	**Starts the path at the root element of the document.**
`id()`	**Starts the path at the element whose ID is contained between the parentheses.**
`here()`	**Starts the path at the current element (for use with inline links—it makes it easy to establish relative references within a document).**
`origin()`	**Starts the path wherever the link was actually declared.**

For example, you could refer to node A as `myDoc.xml#/`, or node I as `mydoc.xml#id(hee)`. You could then add further path information using the axes shown above combined with test information, separated by two colons (::). If the test information is just text, it is assumed to contain the name of a node. (Asterisks, *, are wildcards for any name.) For example, to find a child `p` element, you would request `child::p`. XPointer uses a soludus (/) to separate these node tests when they appear in series, and resolves them from left to right. For example, to reach the author attribute of the `p` element above (node F), you might specify:

```
myDoc.xml#child::p/attribute::author
```

You can move up and down the tree if necessary, making it possible to refer to the same node through multiple paths. The two possibilities below both reach node D.

```
myDoc.xml#id(hee)/parent::myDoc/child::p
myDoc.xml#descendant::title/parent::*/descendant::p
```

XPointer also supports namespaces, expanding prefixes as appropriate. If you need to reach textual, comment, or processing instruction nodes, you can use the functions `text()`, `comment()`, or `processing instruction()`. XPointer also provides positional testing, allowing you to choose which of several possible nodes you want to reference.

XPointer adds two critical features to the set provided by XPath that permit references to portions of XML documents that are not well formed. The string axis allows you to perform tasks like linking every reference to a given word within a document, a common task for dictionary-like applications, while the range axis allows you to specify the start and end of a range within a document, letting you specify sections that include multiple or partial nodes. These two features are both in continuing (and sometimes controversial) development.

Extended Link Groups

Once you start describing resources outside the actual document that contains them, you need some way for documents to connect to the links they use. Extended Link Groups allow documents to identify other documents that may contain links relevant to them, allowing multiple documents in a group to share a "hub" document that describes the links between all of them. Sometimes multiple steps are necessary to collect all the links in a document. XLink's Extended Link Groups provides two elements for describing these collections of documents. Unlike the other components of XLink, these elements must be created as elements in the XLink namespace, rather than using the `xlink:type` attribute. Each of the elements has a single attribute.

The documents referred to by the group are listed in `xlink:document` elements, each carrying an `href` attribute identifying the document to be inspected for links. These are enclosed in `xlink:group` elements. The `xlink:group` element has a steps attribute that indicates how far the application should pursue the links found. Apparently the document that includes the `xlink:group` element is included in this count, as the recommended value for exploring the documents referenced by the `xlink:document` elements is 2.

For example, if the photo album described above stored all its links in a single hub document, the documents it described might include the fragment below:

```
<xlink:group steps="2">
<xlink:document href="albumlinks.xml" />
</xlink:group>
```

Limitations

As exciting as XLink is, it has some fairly severe limitations in its current form. Perhaps its most severe limitation is its insistence that all XLink applications use its vocabulary. Although previous drafts allowed developers to map their own attribute names to XLink functionality, those tools have disappeared from the latest draft. This means that integrating XLink with existing vocabularies will be difficult, as the examples shown below are not equivalent:

```
<a href="mydoc.xml#hee">
<a xlink:href="mydoc.xml#hee" xlink:type="simple">
```

Another situation that demonstrates the inflexibility of XLink is the IMG element, which includes both SRC and LONGDESC resource locators as attributes, effectively creating an extended-link situation with no child attributes. Again,

```
<IMG SRC="myGif.gif" LONGDESC="myGifDesc.htm">
```

can't be easily mapped, within the context of XLink, to:

```
<IMG xlink:type="extended">
<SRC xlink:href="myGif.gif" role="src" xlink:type="locator" />
<LONGDESC xlink:href="myGifDesc.htm" role="longdesc"
xlink:type="locator" />
</IMG>
```

On top of the mapping problem, there is no way to assign the behavior needed for these two elements—SRC probably needs an actuate value of auto, while LONGDESC needs an actuate value of user.

XLink is an important start, a possibly ground-breaking move from the W3C. It still has considerable development ahead of it, however, and may yet be eclipsed by other hypertext processing strategies.

PART FOUR

Tools and Features Commonly Misused

CHAPTER 24

Integrating Namespaces with XML 1.0

Although the Namespaces in XML 1.0 recommendation grew out of work that began while XML 1.0 was still in development, the two recommendations don't fit together very smoothly. The critical benefits of namespaces—unique identifiers referenced by variable prefixes—are ignored by XML 1.0 parsers, and can in fact break validating parsers. At the same time, however, the Namespaces in XML recommendation references the validation process as necessary for certain methods of applying namespace declarations. Sorting this out can be complex, and no complete solution has yet appeared—or is even on the horizon.

The Problem of Changing Prefixes

For namespace-aware processors, the prefix is a throwaway, replaced by URI information from the namespace declaration. For validating parsers, the prefix is part of the element or attribute name, and changing it will at least result in errors and may (depending on the parser) actually halt processing of the document entirely. The Namespaces in XML 1.0 recommendation defines a layer of behavior that is separate from XML 1.0 parsing, though still tied to it. Although some describe the namespaces specification as a "layer on top of XML 1.0," the differences in how elements and attributes are identified in XML 1.0 and how those features are identified in Namespaces in XML may not let information get beyond the bottom layer of XML 1.0.

A simple example will help show where XML 1.0 and the Namespaces in XML recommendations collide. Suppose there are two markup languages, the Baseball Markup Language (BML) and the Business Markup Language (BML). The developers of both languages have followed the Namespaces in XML recommendation and created unique namespaces for their documents. Because they'd like to be able to mix in different kinds of markup easily, they included actual prefixes in their DTDs, using the convenient `bml`. Baseball Markup Language uses a vocabulary that looks like:

```
<bml:position>2B</bml:position> <!--Second base-->
<bml:RBIs>32</bml:RBIs><!--Runs batted in-->
<bml:ERA>1.74</bml:ERA><!--Earned Run Average-->
```

Business markup language uses a vocabulary like:

```
<bml:salary currency="USD">60,000</bml:salary>
<bml:term unit="years">4</bml:term>
```

Because the designers of Business Markup Language knew that their language would be used in concert with other vocabularies to define job contracts for different industries, they left a space open for the terms particular to given industries, using `ANY` in their DTD to provide the needed extensibility. This way, developers could combine other DTDs with Business Markup Language with a minimum of difficulty.

For most cases, this works very well. Mixing and matching most namespaces is easily done by including multiple DTDs in the document type declarations and letting the applications process the information however they like. One day, however, a sports agent is drawing up a contract for a baseball player, and needs to integrate information about bonuses based on performance with a contract marked up in Business Markup Language. Baseball Markup Language has all the necessary ingredients, so the agent selects Baseball Markup Language as an extra piece and starts work. The agent makes some calls, writes the document up, and saves it. Two days later the agent gets a very strange call from the contract processing department, complaining that whatever the agent wrote is giving their applications huge problems. They can look at the information through a browser, with style sheets working just fine, and their validator says that the document is fine. The application, however, spits it out.

What the agent doesn't know is that the document has a namespace conflict. The document includes a section that looks like:

```
<bml:performance-rules>
<bml:minimum>
<bml:RBIs>50</bml:RBIs>
```

```
</bml:minimum>
<bml:maximum>
<bml:errors>10</bml:errors>
</bml:maximum>
<bml:reward currency="USD" frequency="annual">500,000</bml:reward>
</bml:performance-rules>
```

All this validates fine, because `bml:minimum` and `bml:maximum` were defined as `ANY` in the DTD, and the Baseball Markup Language DTD has also been included. Unfortunately, it's not clear what namespace `bml:RBIs` and `bml:errors` belong to. The designers of the original DTD assumed that these would be enclosed in other Baseball Markup Language elements and the `bml` prefix would be mapped to the Baseball Markup Language URI. Instead, the prefix is mapped to Business Markup Language, and the Business processor can't figure out what RBIs and errors are.

The easy way out of this problem, which also makes the document easier to read, is the approach recommended by the Namespaces recommendation. The `bml` prefix is nothing but a pointer to a URI. Replace `bml` with `bbml` in all cases where Baseball Markup Language is in use, and let `bbml` refer to the appropriate URI for Baseball Markup Language, while `bml` continues to refer to the URI for Business Markup Language.

The document then looks like:

```
<bml:performance-rules>
<bml:minimum>
<bbml:RBIs>50</bbml:RBIs>
</bml:minimum>
<bml:maximum>
<bbml:errors>10</bbml:errors>
</bml:maximum>
<bml:reward currency="USD" frequency="annual">500,000</bml:reward>
</bml:performance-rules>
```

This gets the document through the contract processor, and everything seems fine until the document is sent to document storage. The agent then gets a call that the document isn't valid and none of the Baseball Markup Language is getting through the validating parser they use on the front end of their storage facility.

Because validating XML 1.0 parsers only understand prefixes as part of element and attribute names, they can't cope with the change that was made above to get Baseball Markup Language through a namespace-aware processor. Early drafts of the namespaces specification included a mechanism (a processing instruction) that could have been used to inform XML parsers of namespace mappings, but it disappeared in later drafts. Reluctance to change XML 1.0 has kept DTD validation from graduating to the namespace awareness that is a key part of the W3C's strategy for managing vocabularies.

Defaulting (and Declaring) Namespace Declarations

There's a special irony in the Namespaces recommendation when it discusses the use of defaulted attribute declarations for namespaces. Rather that inserting an attribute into every single document, a namespace declaration can be expressed as a default attribute on appropriate elements, typically elements that might be root elements. For example, XPDL, an XML format for describing XML document types, defines a default namespace in its root element:

```
<!ELEMENT xpd (class?, content?, styles?, profile?, extension?)>
<!ATTLIST xpd
    xmlns CDATA "http://purl.oclc.org/NET/xpdl/" >
```

This approach gets around having to include the namespace declaration in every single document that uses it. For example, without the declaration above, `xpd` elements would all have to start with:

```
<xpd xmlns="http://purl.oclc.org/NET/xpdl/">
```

Because non-validating parsers may never read the attribute list declaration that defaults the namespace, the Namespaces recommendation warns that this is only safe when using a validating parser. However, validating parsers are going to have problems like those noted above—and may not even be able to find the right element to supply a default for when the element name changes. On top of that, the declarations that create XML namespaces include the prefix as part of the attribute name. If you want to change the prefix that corresponds to a namespace, you need to include an additional declaration for that namespace. Validating parsers won't let that new declaration—an attribute with a new, unrecognized name—through without an error either.

Disappearing Prefixes

Because prefixes are considered mere connectors to URIs in the namespaces specification, a number of tools throw away the original prefixes, making it difficult to get back to the original document. Although editing software should keep track of prefixes, some applications (including XSL transformations) may not. The Canonical XML working draft (**http://www.w3.org/TR/xml-c14n**) takes this approach, replacing all namespace prefixes with the standardized names `n1`, `n2`, and so on. Once a processor has done this to a document, validation against an XML 1.0 DTD is going to be impossible, unless it happened to use `n1`, `n2`, etc. as prefixes.

Validating Qualified Names

All this would probably be easier if there were a mechanism for connecting namespace URIs to prefixes within DTDs as well as within documents. A processing instruction that included a prefix and a URI as pseudo-attributes could conceivably provide this information in a form that validating parsers could then use to interpret documents. Alternatively, if namespaces were declared using defaulted attributes, those defaults would contain the information the parser needed to figure out the connections between namespaces and URIs. There is no sign, however, of any activity on this front with regard to DTDs, although the schemas described in Chapter 29 will support this level of functionality.

There are a number of strategies you can use to avoid these problems. The simplest, of course, is to ignore either namespaces or validation, and treat them as tools for two different categories of documents. Alternatively, you can provide default namespace declarations on every element type. This means an enormous number of duplicated XML attribute list declarations and possibly additional overhead during processing, but it might be an acceptable approach if you have other attributes that you're already assigning to every element. This practice is common with ID attributes, and adding a namespace might not be so difficult, as shown below:

```
<!ENTITY % attsForAll "
   id ID #IMPLIED
   xmlns CDATA        #FIXED 'http://www.example.com/namespace/'
">
<!ATTLIST element1
   %attsForAll;>
<!ATTLIST element2
   %attsForAll;
   myAttribute CDATA "default">
<!ATTLIST element3
   %attsForAll;>
```

This applies a namespace declaration to all the attributes along with an ID attribute, simplifying the process of mixing these elements with elements from other DTDs and namespaces. Combining elements from multiple DTDs is easier if the elements in all the DTDs to be combined use a similar strategy, something that isn't always easy to enforce if you're working with a DTD you don't control. Whatever strategy you choose, be sure to document it. The name of the parameter entity shown above doesn't indicate that it contains namespaces, and developers won't necessarily know where to look for the defaulted declarations.

An Argument for Well-Formedness

In their current form, namespaces may seem broken. However, they can be used to powerful effect in documents where structural validation is not a concern. If you treat namespace URIs as indicators of the origin of a document, rather than as descriptions of a document type, you can build processors that look for patterns in well-formed documents, with or without a DTD or schema. Expectations are connected to the URI of the namespace, not the information in the document type declaration. If the incompatibilities of namespaces and validation seem like a liability, it may be possible to do without one or the other, and choosing namespaces over validation is certainly an option. If you go this route, remember to make all your namespace declarations explicitly within documents (or at least in the internal subset)—non-validating parsers may not notice namespace declarations made through defaulted attributes at all, thus foiling your processing strategy.

CHAPTER 25

Describing Document Types Precisely

An important part of the appeal of XML is the ability to send documents over networks easily, using Web infrastructures much like those used to send HTML. Unfortunately, while HTML was (more or less) uniform, and any HTML could (again, more or less) be processed by an HTML processor, XML is both more and less exchangeable. Any XML processor can read any XML document; however, knowing what to do with it takes a bit more information. A key part of the Web infrastructure, MIME content-types, is getting an update to handle XML, although only the first phase of that work is complete. Namespaces and document type declarations both provide descriptions of XML documents, although they appear inside documents. These layers of tools are often conflicting, and don't actually contain very much information at present. Developers will find themselves developing their own solutions for a little while at least, while more generic answers percolate.

The Hazards of Self-Identifying Documents (DTDs and Namespaces)

XML 1.0 was designed with a foundation understanding that documents would contain all the information (or references to information) needed to get them through an XML processor. Although applications would have to bring their own information regarding the meaning of an XML document's content (is TITLE the title of a book or the title—Mr., Ms., Mrs., M., Lord, etc.—of a person?), the document itself would provide the information needed to get it through a validating processor, if appropriate. This has several advantages:

- It allows parsers to take a single input, possibly retrieve additional material, and return a single output.
- It ensures that the same XML document will return the same information in any validating parser.
- It avoids versioning conflicts—documents using different versions of document structures can just reference the appropriate version of DTD.
- It permits authors to use the internal subset to add extra information about document structure and content.

The model fits various documents that are expected to be exchanged all over the Internet quite well. By being "self-contained," XML document processing can be initiated by sending a single document, from which all other processing flows. This allows the use of standard Web protocols, notably HTTP, for XML document transport, and avoids certain potentially complex content negotiation.

Although all those features are useful, applications are still left with a difficult question every time they receive a document. The document passes validation and has a root element of the type they were expecting. But is it what they actually wanted? How can they tell if the document referenced the right version of the DTD, or if some perverse user (or cracker, perhaps) hasn't fed them a document with a completely different structure created through the internal subset? Some parsers make this information available to applications, but many others don't, and the application is stuck. Relying on validation alone is no way to guarantee that a document contains even the structures, never mind the content, that it is supposed to.

Note

Applications could keep a DTD that describes the content they are looking for, and then apply it to incoming documents as a sanity check before or after they pass validation on their own. As of this writing, no XML parser provides this functionality, but there have been several discussions of this kind of "validator" service that may still lead to products. In the meantime, DTD validation is stuck in the context of document parsing and is not available as a separate service.

Because of this uncertainty, applications are still forced to check incoming document structures and content themselves, and to be prepared for code that doesn't meet their standards. Robust applications should not rely solely on the information provided by documents to protect them from wide variations in document content. "Trust but verify" is a good rule for such situations.

Namespaces provide another tool for identifying document content, once again within the body of the document. Even apart from their conflicts with validation, discussed in the previous chapter, namespaces are of limited use to applications trying to determine the content in a document. Namespace URIs provide only unique identifiers, *not* necessarily references to schemas, DTDs, or other resources describing document content. Namespace URIs can be very useful within a program for passing information to appropriate application code, but they provide no assurance that information conforms to a particular format. They assert that elements and attributes belong to a given namespace, but say nothing about any relationship between those structures.

This viewpoint, which appears in the Namespaces in XML recommendation and in several hundred postings on the XML-dev mailing lists, may not last forever, or may change with the advent of the XML Packaging proposals described below. The main public (and extremely heated) discussions of the role of namespaces in XML took place on the XML-dev list in January 1999 with the release of the recommendation (**http://www.lists.ic.ac.uk/hypermail/xml-dev/xml-dev-Jan-1999/index.html**) and in September 1999 (**http://www.lists.ic.ac.uk/hypermail/xml-dev/xml-dev-Sep-1999/index.html**) with new controversy over their role in XHTML, the reformulation of HTML as an XML application. In the latter discussion, Tim Berners-Lee, Director of the W3C, stated "in no official capacity" (at **http://www.lists.ic.ac.uk/hypermail/xml-dev/xml-dev-Sep-1999/1253.html**) that:

> I think that the essential thing for me is the availability of the definitive schema (the resource identified by the namespace URI) for making definitive pronouncements by the language publisher....

This may not signal an official change in the W3C's perspective, but it certainly opens up new questions about the role of namespaces in document type identification.

MIME Types and Content Negotiation

One of the key infrastructures that has made the Web easy to use is MIME content types. MIME stands for Multipurpose Internet Mail Extensions, although the "multipurpose" has in many ways eclipsed the "mail." MIME is defined in four RFCs, 2045 through 2048, maintained by the Internet Engineering Task Force (IETF—**http://www.ietf.org**). Work on MIME and its supporting standards is in the domain of the IETF, not the W3C.

MIME content type identifiers use a two-level scheme for identifying content. The first part of the identifier provides general information about the resource—that is text, image, model, audio, or application. The "application" type is a general space for everything not included in another type. While text may sound appropriate to XML, it comes with some historical baggage that may make it difficult to exchange XML in certain character encodings as text, so application is generally a safer choice. The second part of the identifier provides specific information about the content type. Although `image` is useful information, `image/gif` or `image/jpeg` gives an application the information actually needed to display GIF or JPEG information, allowing it to pass off processing of that information to an appropriate handler. (For some MIME types and programs, the handler is code within a program, while in other cases MIME types are used to hand off programming to "helper applications" or to alert the user that the application has no idea what to do with content of a particular MIME type and ask for help.)

RFC 2376 is the current standard for identifying XML documents using MIME content-type identifiers, although a revision (mostly extension) process is beginning. RFC 2376 (**http://www.ietf.org/rfc/rfc2376.txt**) created two new MIME content type identifiers, `text/xml` and `application/xml`, and provides extensive explanations of how they should be combined with other parameters, primarily the charset parameter for identifying character encodings. These two MIME content identifiers give developers a standardized way to exchange XML documents, providing a basic level of support for directing XML documents to XML processors. (The revision process has also proposed `application/xml-dtd` for external DTD subsets, but this is not yet accepted.)

Knowing that a document is XML helps applications route incoming XML documents to XML parsers, but does very little to route them to the appropriate application processing after they have been parsed. In fact, applications have no way of knowing if they even can do anything more than parse the information in an XML document until they have retrieved it and parsed. For some applications—browsers, for instance—this approach is acceptable. Users may just want to save the file when it appears on a screen, or view it through a style sheet specified within the document. For other applications, it can be a nuisance. Graphics programs that support import of Scalable Vector Graphics (SVG) have no way to know which XML documents actually contain graphics. Automated processors handling batches of documents have no way to separate the documents they want from the ones they don't want without going through a trial-and-error process that puts extra load on systems and networks.

One solution for these applications is to create their own MIME types, separate from `application/xml` or `text/xml`—like `image/svg`. The identifier image/svg will help applications find the SVG needles in the XML haystacks, avoiding the trial-and-error approach brought on by `application/xml`. Unfortunately, solutions like these come at a cost. The burden of the trial-and-error approach is now passed to developers of generic XML tools, from search engines to linking managers, that need to maintain lists of which formats are XML and which are not. If it weren't for the exploding number of XML document types, this probably wouldn't be a problem, but XML's infinite vocabularies may have a significant impact on the number of XML-based MIME types.

The Internet-Draft proposing revisions to RFC 2376 (**draft-murata-xml-00.txt**, available from directories listed at **http://www.ietf.org/shadow.html**) addresses this problem by creating a suffix for MIME content type identifiers that are used for XML-based content. Instead of just `image/svg`, `image/svg-xml` would be used, for example. Both graphics processors that only want SVG files and XML processors that will accept any XML format can determine from that MIME content type identifier that these documents contain information they can use. This revision is not yet accepted, and may still prove controversial, but it does offer one solution to the problem. Perhaps best of all, this solution is compatible with existing protocols that rely on MIME types, like HTTP. (The author of this book is one of the co-authors of the Internet-Draft.)

Another option for describing XML documents would use some combination of a content type identifier for XML documents and a negotiation process that lets requesting applications discover general information about the contents of a document. That information might include the root element of a document and any namespaces included in it. If an XHTML document included both MathML and SVG fragments, the program serving the document could inform the requesting application that the document requested contained these three namespaces. If the requesting application didn't know how to process them, it could either halt the transfer or find a different means of processing the information, perhaps by asking the user. Content negotiation may require modification of existing protocols that don't support this level of communication, but it definitely provides a deeper description of the information being exchanged. (In some circumstances, a server could even change the format of the information to accommodate particular application needs, rather than merely reporting on the format. XML's transformation potential makes this process possible on a large scale.)

Building Better Packages

Document Type Definitions only describe a small amount of what might be considered a document type. A reasonably complete description of a document type might include more information on document content, presentation information (style sheets), human-readable documentation, minimum standards for "complete" processing, security information, optimization information, and information about the document type's relationship to other data sources. Phase III of the W3C's XML Activity is starting work on an "XML Packaging" facility that may include some or all of this information, but in the meantime developers may need both to prepare information for use in packaging and possibly send some documents with packaging information.

One approach, created by the author of this book, is XML Processing Description Language, or XPDL. (Draft specifications are available at **http://purl.oclc.org/NET/xpdl.**) XML Processing Descriptions, or XPDs, include information describing how XML documents should be processed, connecting document types to particular schemas (including DTDs), entity and notation lists, style sheets, and documentation. The XPD for XPDL itself includes a number of these features, as shown below:

```
<?xml version="1.0"?>
<xpd version="wd092999" xmlns="http://purl.oclc.org/NET/xpdl/">

<class classID="http://purl.oclc.org/NET/xpdl/v1"
    MIMEtype="application/x-xpdl"
    className="XPD"
    version="1.0">
<owner href="http://www.simonstl.com/">Simon St.Laurent,
initial editor</owner>
<description href="http://purl.oclc.org/NET/xpdl">XML Processing
Description Language (XPDL)
</description>
</class>

<content>
<constraints href="http://www.simonstl.com/projects/xpdl/xpdl1.dtd"
type="dtd" required="no" internal="no" root="xpd"/>
<attributes href="http://www.simonstl.com/projects/xpdl/xpdl1.dtd"
type="dtd" required="yes" internal="no"/>
<entities href="http://www.simonstl.com/projects/xpdl/xpdl1.dtd"
type="dtd" required="no" internal="no"/>
<notations href="http://www.simonstl.com/projects/xpdl/xpdl1.dtd"
type="dtd" required="no" internal="no"/>
</content>

<styles>
<style href="http://www.simonstl.com/projects/xpdl/xpdl1.css"
type="text/css" title="XPDL Default Style Sheet" />
</styles>

<profile fragmentIdentifier="XPointer"
    linking="XLink"
    namespaces="yes" />

<extension />

</xpd>
```

The root element (`xpd`) contains information about what version of XPDL is used for this package, allowing applications to support multiple versions or reject versions they don't understand. The default namespace is also declared, giving the document a base namespace. (Extensions may declare their own namespaces in the extension element, but otherwise the entire document uses only a single namespace.)

The `class` element provides information about this class of documents—a MIME type identifier it might be used with, a name and version for this class, and information about the document class' creator and documentation. Both a short description and a link to a more formal description are provided—there's no point in making processors that aren't concerned with documentation wade through kilobytes of extra material, but enough information to get a person started is encouraged.

The `content` element allows developers to specify constraints, attribute defaults, entities, and notations separately. All of this information will be taken into account during processing by an XPDL-aware processor, and used in place of the document type declaration of documents. (The internal subset may still be used, if permitted by the `internal` attribute.) An `all` element may be used in place of the `constraints`, `attributes`, `entities`, and `notations` elements, and multiple elements may be used to bring in multiple resources. The resource type is specified in the element referencing it, allowing a single package to mix DTDs and schemas.

The next two elements move into information beyond that typically provided by an XML DTD. The `style` element allows developers to provide a default style sheet, or lists of style sheets, that may be appropriate for viewing the document. These don't prohibit designers from specifying style sheets for individual documents; instead, they provide a baseline style sheet that could be used in the absence of other style information. The `profile` element allows document type developers to specify what linking and fragment conventions they are using. Some XML document types, like SVG and Synchronized Multimedia Integration Language (SMIL, also from the W3C) don't support the full range of XPointer fragment identifiers or XLink links, and some types may move beyond them entirely. The `profile` element lets applications call in special tools, if these are appropriate. Finally, the namespaces attribute of the `profile` element lets developers identify whether documents use namespaces or not. If the value of this is no, applications should treat any prefix before a colon as part of the element name rather than replacing it with a URI.

The last element in the XPD, `extension`, is probably the most important, because there are many aspects of document processing that could be associated with a document type but aren't yet listed in the XPD. Among these are:

- Security—Should documents of this type be encrypted or receive special handling?
- Transformations—Are there predefined pathways to other document types?
- Relations to Other Resources—Does this document class "belong" to a particular database?

- Legal—Are there legal considerations for processing these documents?
- Optimization—Are there acceptable ways for reducing the size of these documents?
- Analysis—Are there generic rules that will help an application understand the content of these documents?

XPDL is unlikely to be widely adopted in its current form, and there are in fact no processors that currently support it. XPDL may, however, be useful as a starting point for creating machine-readable document types.

Connecting those document types to documents is another issue that will have to be addressed. Chapter 15 noted the existence of directories at the IETF corresponding to MIME content types and pointing readers to the official definitions of those types, typically human-readable RFCs. (See **http://www.isi.edu/in-notes/iana/assignments/media-types/text/html** for an example.) A similar system could be used to connect XPDs to particular MIME content-type identifiers. Alternately, notation and namespace URIs could be used to refer to packages. This would provide a layer of indirection between the schema and the documents, as well as a place to store more information about the document type without piling everything into the schema.

Tip
Watch http://www.w3.org/XML/ for developments in XML packaging.

CHAPTER 26

Processing Instructions: Working Outside Content

Processing instructions, or PIs as they're commonly abbreviated, have an unfortunate reputation. They are seen as highly abusable, even dangerous, an odd holdover that threatens the strict rules for document structure and invites the conflation of procedural code and declarative content. Like notations and unparsed entities, processing instructions depend on applications for interpretation, and very few PIs have been created with the intention of working across different varieties of XML. Despite this reputation, processing instructions have the potential to add entirely new dimensions to XML processing, opening up possibilities beyond providing applications with static content. Using PIs for these purposes, however, requires an understanding of the reasons behind their poor reputation and ways to avoid those problems.

Abusing Comments

Before we discuss processing instruction abuse, we'll explore various "abuses" of comments that are similar to problems with processing instructions, and investigate why comments and processing instructions have been given different marching orders. Both comments and processing instructions can appear anywhere in the document structure; neither comments nor processing instructions need to be declared in any way.

Applications are not required to do anything at all with the contents of either comments or processing instructions, unless they have some reason to be interested. In one widely used SGML-based environment where processing instructions were not available (HTML), comment abuse became a common part of respected practices for markup. This happened partly because of the rapid (and uncontrolled) pace of HTML's early development, and partly because there were no other recognized mechanisms for creating "safe" disappearing extensions.

The first "abuse" involved hiding scripts from older browsers that didn't know how to process scripts. A JavaScript module that was supposed to display a ticker in the status bar of a browser didn't look as good as the first screen of content across the top of a Web page. Although newer browsers (Netscape browsers, initially) could handle JavaScript and process SCRIPT elements properly, older browsers often ignored the SCRIPT element and treating its contents as regular document content. A convention for getting around this problem soon emerged, taking advantage of the way Netscape browsers looked for scripts and the safely disappearing nature of comments. By putting all the JavaScript code inside a comment inside the SCRIPT element, the script would work on script-aware browsers (because Microsoft Internet Explorer also picked up this convention) and disappear entirely on browsers that didn't understand how to interpret the scripts. For example, the HTML document below would generate a small document on browsers that understood scripts, and a mostly empty page on browsers that didn't understand scripts.

```
<HTML>
<HEAD><TITLE>Generating Content - Or Not</TITLE></HEAD>
<BODY>
<SCRIPT LANGUAGE="JavaScript"><!--
document.writeln("<H1>Generated Content</H1>");
var todaysDate=new Date();
var message="<P>Welcome to " + (todaysDate.getMonth()+1) + "/" +
todaysDate.getDate() + "/" + todaysDate.getYear() + "!</P>";
document.writeln(message);
//-->
</SCRIPT>
<!-- // is used to hide the HTML comment closing from JavaScript-->
</BODY>
</HTML>
```

This worked, as shown below in Figure 26.1, because the browser would ignore the comments within the scripting element. This rule was a common enough convention to become a part of the HTML specification—see **http://www.w3.org/TR/html40/interact/scripts.html#h-18.3.2** for details. Nonetheless, it seems to flaunt the basic understanding of what XML comments are for, though those rules don't apply to HTML. (Whether this convention survives into XHTML remains to be seen.)

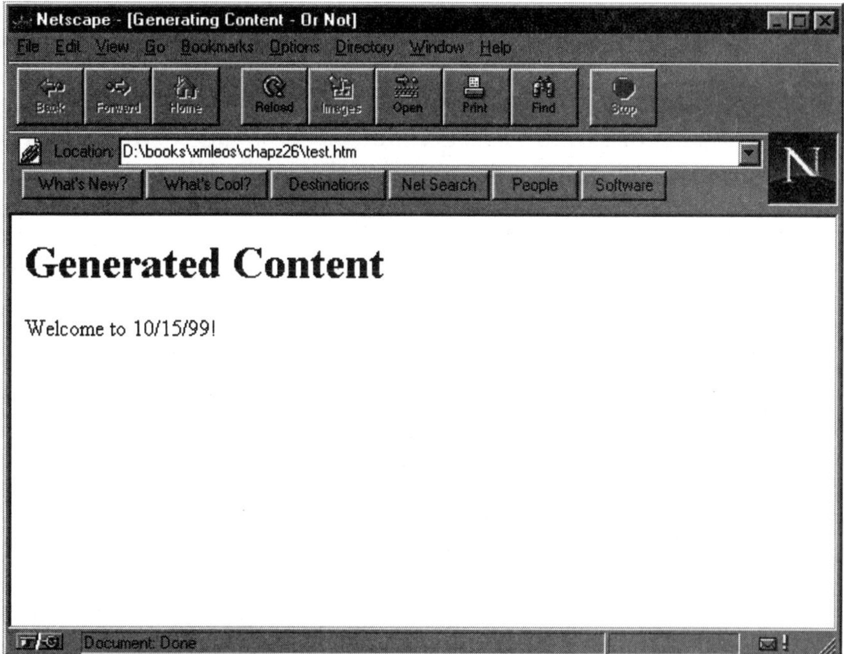

Figure 26.1 Script-aware browsers can work around comments

Another commonly used technique, this time on the server, is server-side includes, or SSIs. Server-side includes are instructions that lurk within comments, instructing Web servers to insert other files. If the file is read by a browser without the server's making the inclusions, the worst thing that can happen is that information will be missing. Although server-side includes require Web servers to read documents as they send them, sometimes increasing server load significantly, they are a useful enough tool that Web developers often use them despite the extra processing cost. Among other things, they let developers reference generated content from inside static content, and they also use local (to the server) file references, letting developers include information that might not be directly accessible from outside the Web server. For example:

```
<HTML>
<HEAD><TITLE>SSI</TITLE></HEAD>
<BODY>
<H1>Today's News</H1>
<!--#INCLUDE FILE "todaysNews.html"-->
<P>Copyright (c) 1999, Today's News Inc.</P>
</BODY>
</HTML>
```

This file, when requested, would be shipped out to browsers with the contents of the file "todaysNews.html" in place of the INCLUDE comment. If the server stopped processing SSIs, or if a user opened the file from the file system instead of through the server, nothing would appear where the INCLUDE comment was—like all comments, it would be stripped out.

Calling these conventions "abuses" is probably overkill, certainly from the perspective of the more flexible world of HTML. From an XML perspective, however, they use comments where processing instructions are more appropriate. The division of labor between comments and processing instructions is fairly simple: Section 2.6 states that "Processing instructions allow documents to contain instructions for applications," and XML processors are required to pass this information to applications. Section 2.5 doesn't explicitly state that comments are for human consumption, but XML processors are not required to pass comments on to the application, limiting their usefulness. Although it is unlikely that processing instructions will replace comments in the applications described above—the conventions are too well entrenched—PIs would probably be much more appropriate a tool than comments.

The "abuses of processing instructions" described below could also be done using comments, although at risk of the processors, not passing the information to the application. Both processing instructions and comments have the significant advantage of being able to appear anywhere in the parse tree without prior declaration. In order not to demonstrate the same types of "abuses" twice, the abuses shown below will be performed using the more appropriate tool for passing information to applications, processing instructions.

Abusing Processing Instructions

Because processing instructions can appear anywhere in the document tree (in content, anyway—they can't appear within start- or end-tags), and because they don't need to be declared in advance, PIs offer document authors a way to build trees outside the basic document structure. For example, XML doesn't allow overlapping elements. The case below is illegal.

```
<element1><element2></element1></element2>
```

element1 is not allowed to contain the start-tag, but not the end-tag, of element2, and similarly, element2 is not allowed to contain the end-tag, but not the start-tag, of element1. However, because processing instructions don't have to fit in the document tree the same way as elements, the case below is legal.

```
<element1><?PI1 start?></element1><?PI1 end?>
```

From the perspective of an XML parser, `element1` contains the processing instruction `PI1 start`, and the processing instruction `PI1 end` follows the end of the element. The parser won't see any connection between the processing instructions—only people and perhaps applications will do that. Although the exact usage above is fairly unlikely, there are at least two cases where such overlapping tree approaches to PIs may seem useful: formatting and identifying locations for linking. Formatting that crosses element boundaries isn't unusual in HTML, for example:

```
<p><b>This is bold. <i>This is bold italic.</b> This is italic.</i></p>
```

This code should produce (in HTML browsers, anyway):

This is bold. *This is bold italic.* *This is italic.*

In XML, however, it just produces an error. Application developers could circumvent this by supporting code that looks like:

```
<p><?b?>This is bold. <?i?>This is bold italic.<?b /?> This is
italic.<?i /?></p>
```

This is perfectly legal XML, but the application sees another tree separate from that specified by the element structure. A simpler and cleaner solution might look like:

```
<p><b>This is bold. <i>This is bold italic.</i></b><i>This is
italic.</i></p>
```

It takes about the same amount of effort and is clearer to applications that don't understand what the processing instructions are supposed to do.

Another case where stepping outside the element tree is useful is markup for linking. In poetry, for example, sentiments often cross lines, as in the poem below. Processing instructions are used to mark the beginnings and ends of links discussing the content of the poem. Some of those links are within element boundaries, and others cross the boundaries:

```
<poem author="anon">
<stanza>
<line><?affection start?>Love<?affection end?> me not for <?virtues
start?>comely grace, </line>
<line>For my pleasing eye or face<?virtues end?>, </line>
<line>Nor for any <?virtues start?>outward part<?virtues end?>, </line>
<line>No, nor for <?virtues start?>my constant heart<?virtues end?>,-
</line>
   <line><?disaster start?>For those may fail, or turn to ill</line>
   <line>So thou and I shall sever;<?disaster end?> </line>
<line>Keep therefore a true woman's eye, </line>
<line>And <?affection start?>love me still<?affection end?> but not know
why-</line>
```

```
    <line>So hast thou the same reason still</line>
    <line>To <?affection start?>doat upon me ever<?affection end?>!
</line>
</stanza>
</poem>
```

Literary structures are often difficult to represent within the strictures of an element tree. Similar problems emerge in many kinds of documents. For these cases, however, the XML family offers a different set of tools for indicating those connections. XLink, XPointer, and XPath, discussed in Chapter 23, are designed to allow document authors to create links without disrupting the basic markup of the poem. Links may be non-contiguous, cross element boundaries, reference attribute values, or do all kinds of things that aren't locked into the basic tree structure, but these links build on the tree structure rather than "pollute" it with extra markup aimed at subverting it.

There isn't any way to bar the usage shown above, and most applications will just ignore all the extra PIs they don't understand anyway. The problem isn't really that PIs are violating the structure; rather, it is that there is usually a better way to solve the problem. That "better way" may not always be obvious, unfortunately, but it's usually worth looking for.

Using Processing Instructions

Processing instructions do have their uses, however, and in some cases they are in fact the best solution to a given problem, at least within certain requirements. For example, the W3C Recommendation "Associating Style Sheets with XML Documents Version 1.0" (**http://www.w3.org/TR/xml-stylesheet/**) comes with a big warning in the "Status of this Document Section":

> The use of XML processing instructions in this specification should not be taken as a precedent. The W3C does not anticipate recommending the use of processing instructions in any future specification.

It is fairly clear that the W3C is not happy about processing instructions, and would like to find a better solution. However, the Rationale provides a clear picture of why processing instructions are actually useful:

> There was an urgent requirement for a specification for style sheet linking that could be completed in time for the next release from major browser vendors. Only by choosing a simple mechanism closely based on a proven existing mechanism could the specification be completed in time to meet this requirement.

Use of a processing instruction avoids polluting the main document structure with application specific processing information. However disliked processing instructions may be, they provide an extremely convenient way to supply certain kinds of information to document processors without requiring XML documents to change their structure.

Processing instructions may be used to supply information at several levels of a document. In some cases, like the style sheet association processing instruction created by the W3C, the processing instruction defines information that is used for processing the entire document. In other cases, the information only applies to a portion of the document, typically either the portion following the processing instruction or the element containing the processing instruction. (In use, processing instructions seem to precede the information to which they apply, but there are no hard and fast rules—applications may interpret them however they like.)

Processing instructions may be used to associate external resources with a document, in which case they often use a structure that looks much like an HTML or XLink link:

```
<?include href="targetdoc.xml"?>
```

An application that understood this `include` processing instruction might treat it as something like the server-side includes described above, retrieve the resource referenced by the href attribute, and add it to the document tree. Other linking behaviors are also possible. The W3C's `xml-stylesheet` processing instruction, for instance, references external resources in order that applications may apply them as style sheets, not include them as content:

```
<?xml-stylesheet href="memostyle.css" type="text/css"?>
```

or

```
<?xml-stylesheet href="memostyle.xsl" type="text/xsl"?>
```

The `xml-stylesheet` processing instruction even provides support for multiple stylesheets, allowing developers to cascade style sheets or create menus of style sheets from which users can choose:

```
<?xml-stylesheet href="memostyle.css" type="text/css" title="Basic
CSS"?>
<?xml-stylesheet href="memostyle.xsl" type="text/xsl" alternate="yes"
title="Basic XSL"?>
<?xml-stylesheet href="memosmstyle.css" type="text/css" alternate="yes"
title="Tiny CSS"?>
<?xml-stylesheet href="memosmstyle.xsl" type="text/xsl" alternate="yes"
title="Tiny XSL"?>
<?xml-stylesheet href="memolgstyle.css" type="text/css" alternate="yes"
title="Large CSS"?>
```

```
<?xml-stylesheet href="memolgstyle.xsl" type="text/xsl" alternate="yes"
title="Large XSL"?>
```

Applications supporting this processing instruction have to support not only a target and a set of pseudo-attributes, but also a set of rules for handling multiple instances of the same processing instruction.

Creating Generalized Processing Instructions

You may find processing instructions useful in a particular document project, but there may also be times when, as demonstrated by the W3C in the above example, you want to create a processing instruction that is useful in multiple document contexts. After exploring existing options and making sure that a processing instruction is capable of supporting your needs, you'll need to document the processing instruction you're creating, create software to test that processing instruction, and possibly assign an identifying URI to the processing instruction target using a notation.

For example, there is no generic way to include scripts (like JavaScript, VBScript, Tcl, or Python) in XML files. Although some formats (notably XHTML) provide explicit spaces for scripts within documents, there is no generic mechanism for doing so. Processing instructions seem a reasonably natural fit for scripts, especially because the XML working group used a ?> to terminate the processing instruction rather than the much more frequently encountered (in scripts, anyway) > symbol. Processing instructions' status outside the regular document structure is good fit for scripts, which typically modify document content or present it in a different way without necessarily being a part of it. A set of conventions that use processing instructions to include scripting information in XML documents will provide significant functionality without requiring developers to modify their DTDs.

The PI target seems a useful way to identify the scripting language, as demonstrated in Chapter 15, so creating targets that reflect the language of the scripting language being used might be appropriate:

```
<?ECMAScript script ?>
<?TclScript script ?>
<?PerlScript script ?>
<?PythonScript script ?>
```

When applications encountered these processing instructions, they could then pass the content of the PI to a script processor of the appropriate type. Alternately, to include scripts of various languages using an approach with attributes, you could use:

```
<?Script href="myScript.js" language="ECMAScript"?>
```

Applications could retrieve the file indicated by the href pseudo-attribute and pass them to a processor appropriate to the language identified by the language pseudo-attribute's value. The notation declarations described in Chapter 15 can provide developers with some independence from the particular naming conventions you choose. For example, ECMAScript is commonly referred to as JavaScript (by Netscape) and JScript (by Microsoft). You could alias all of these to the same URI by creating similar notations:

```
<!NOTATION ECMAScript SYSTEM "http://www.ecma.ch/stand/ECMA-262.htm">
<!NOTATION JavaScript SYSTEM "http://www.ecma.ch/stand/ECMA-262.htm">
<!NOTATION JScript SYSTEM "http://www.ecma.ch/stand/ECMA-262.htm">
```

These three processing instructions might then be considered identical by an application mapping PI targets to notations:

```
<?ECMAScript {document.write("Hello, World!");}?>
<?JavaScript {document.write("Hello, World!");}?>
<?JScript {document.write("Hello, World!");}?>
```

Making processing instructions work across multiple applications is mostly a matter of finding an approach that works well and convincing other developers to use it. The W3C has a unique advantage in being the keeper of the XML standard, but there are other ways to make your generic processing instructions well known, from posting them on Web sites and mailing lists to shipping products that include them. As long as your processing instructions are open to all comers, you may have a chance of making them widely used.

The Need for an Application Framework

All processing instructions work at the whim of the application that receives them. Some applications may process them according to the desires of their creator, others may ignore them but preserve them, and yet others may discard them entirely. Processing instructions are difficult to use reliably outside the application for which they were originally designed, and there is currently very little infrastructure available to support interoperability of various processing instruction schemes. The processing instruction described by the W3C for associating style sheets with documents may well be the last PI to receive such official blessing and to receive support across a variety of applications.

Those who dislike processing instructions (typically because of the abuses they can be used for) may not be unhappy to see them go, but developers who find them useful may need to keep them around for a long time to come. Processing instructions can cause problems with interchange—document structures are typically well understood, but there are no mechanisms within DTDs (beyond the simple information optionally provided by notations) for describing what processing instructions do or how they should be treated. Making PIs work effectively in distributed environments, where participants all support the basic structures but don't necessarily provide application-level support for things like processing instructions, can be very difficult.

If you want your processing instruction to work in environments outside those over which you have immediate control, you're going to need to document and demonstrate your processing instruction's intended behavior, often in multiple working environments. Because there are very few frameworks for describing what a processing instruction should do or could do (the Document Object Model doesn't really speak to such issues), you may need to develop a description of a layer between the XML processor and the parser, a framework in which your processing instructions can operate. No general framework is presently available, but perhaps one will emerge from the many varieties of XML processing.

CHAPTER 27

Troubles with Non-validating Parsers

One of XML's most important improvements over its SGML predecessor has some unfortunate side effects that can lead to quietly disappearing information. By creating separate categories for well-formed and valid documents, and providing for corresponding non-validating and validating parsers, XML 1.0 created enormous and extremely useful flexibility. Well-formed documents make it much easier to get started in XML, without requiring the learning curve and extra processing of validation. Unfortunately, the XML 1.0 recommendation allows non-validating parsers some extra privileges that go beyond ignoring validity constraints, and these privileges can wreak havoc with document processing.

The Problem

Non-validating parsers are not required to retrieve resources outside the body of the actual document they are parsing. They don't have to retrieve the external subset of the DTD, external parameter entities, or external general entities. They do have to process all the declarations in the DTD (including the external DTD subset and the contents of external parameter entities *if* the parser actually read them), but they don't have to check the document structure against those declarations. This allows non-validating parsers to support some DTD functionality (notably defaulted attributes and entity declarations) if they read the declarations. Reading external declarations was made optional because of concerns about browsers' "hanging" while waiting for an external resource to be processed—the creators of the XML 1.0 specification were more concerned in this case about performance than consistency.

References to this behavior appear several times in the specification (Section 4.4 describes entity processing), but the main statement describing the rules for non-validating parsers appears at the end of Section 5.1:

> Non-validating parsers are required to check only the document entity, including the entire internal DTD subset, for well-formedness.

Non-validating parsers are responsible for processing and applying all the declarations they encounter, up to the first reference to an external parameter entity that they haven't retrieved. (*If* they read the external DTD subset, the same rules apply.) This means that the internal subset is a "safe" place for attribute defaulting and entity declarations, and also means that the developers of non-validating parsers are still responsible for writing code to handle a lot of situations that aren't typically encountered in well-formed documents.

The implications of this design decision are spelled out in greater detail in Section 5.2, which notes that the results generated by non-validating parsers are far less predictable than those from validating parsers, that some well-formedness constraints may not in fact be caught by non-validating parsers, and that defaulted attributes and entities may not be processed. (Attribute normalization may not be done correctly either.) The last paragraph announces that:

> For maximum reliability in interoperating between different XML processors, applications which use non-validating processors should not rely on any behaviors not required of such processors.

This makes many frequently used tools for simplifying XML documents unreliable in a non-validating environment. XML's tiny number of built-in entities (especially compared to the list for HTML 4.0) has driven many developers to create HTML entity lists. Although developers could cut and paste to include the entities they need in the internal subset of documents, it's a lot simpler to simply reference a list. If the list doesn't get included, a lot of entity references are going to remain unexpanded. That may be acceptable in some situations, but isn't likely to work well in the kinds of Web browsing situations for which this exemption was granted.

The other set of applications for which this may cause problems is hypertext linking applications that use the W3C's own XLink mechanisms (described in Chapter 23) or namespace applications. XLink relies for the most part on attributes to identify links and link types, and use of defaulted (or even fixed) values for attributes in an external DTD can make creating XLink documents much simpler and the documents considerably less verbose. Unfortunately, these hypertext links will probably disappear if a non-validating parser processes the document—the attributes won't default, and the application won't see the links. In the end, neither will users, transforming XML hypertexts back into a series of static documents. Similarly, namespace declarations made in defaulted attributes will disappear, leaving prefixes (or even the default) hanging without a corresponding URI. These disappearances can have a significant impact on applications that plan to use information stored in default attributes, from architectural forms processors to style sheets to interchange systems.

Solution 1: The Standalone Declaration

At first glance, XML 1.0 appears to have a solution to this problem built right into the XML declaration at the start of the document. The standalone declaration accepts clear values—"yes" and "no"—that specify whether the document references external resources. The impact of this declaration, however, is limited in a way that prevents it from solving the problem of lost external resources. The only value for the standalone declaration that has meaning is "yes." If the value of the standalone declaration is "yes," then XML processors are required to report errors when external resources are referenced. This can be useful if your documents are all supposed to be complete, perhaps Canonical XML (as described in the section below), allowing your applications to note that something slipped through a processor that probably shouldn't have.

Unfortunately, using a value of "no" or omitting the standalone declaration has no effect on processing. Non-validating parsers won't report the errors noted above, but they won't retrieve external resources needed to fix the problem either. XML documents are "self-describing," but the description provided by the standalone declaration won't be used by parsers to seek out additional descriptions.

Solution 2: Controlling Your Applications

Although there are non-validating parsers that do read external DTD subsets and entity references, you can only count on applications to use those parsers if you have control over the behavior of all the applications that may process your documents. If a document that relies on external resources is passed along a chain of processors written by different organizations, and even one of those processors drops the external resources, the final recipient isn't likely to see any of those resources unless they were pushed into the document by a special-purpose processor. In the example below, for example, a default value is set for a security attribute that might be important.

```
<!ATTLIST document
   security (high | low | none)       "high">
```

In Figure 27.1 below, a non-validating parser accepts this document and processes it without the DTD. It then passes the information (not the document reference) to a repository. Later, when another application gets the document, it doesn't seen any sign of a security attribute.

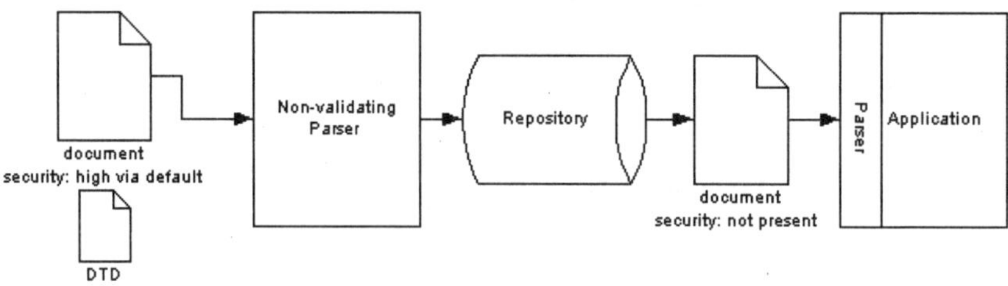

Figure 27.1 Losing a default attribute value on the way to the repository

This, of course, is bad design—it might be better to make the security attribute `#REQUIRED` rather than provide a default value. Authors using editing software aware of the DTD would then be forced to explicitly provide a value. Well-written code might also note the absence of the security attribute in later iterations and announce an error. However, if document and application designers expect that things will work using the DTD as expected, problems like this may well creep in.

If your projects require the use of non-validating parsers and also might require features like defaulted attributes and external entities, you may be able to squeak through by using a single parser consistently. Microstar's Java Aelfred parser for XML (**http://www.microstar.com/aelfred.html**), for instance, is a non-validating parser that will retrieve external declarations and entities. Some parsers, like recent versions of IBM's XML4J parser (**http://www.alphaworks.ibm.com/tech/xml4j**), will let application developers configure whether or not external resources of various kinds are retrieved. If you have control over the application environment, and not just over the document format, you may be able to ignore these problems by using tools that don't raise them.

Unfortunately, even if you think you have control over the application, XML documents have a tendency to spread beyond the bounds of a particular application. Sometimes this is deliberate, part of an information-sharing agreement or even posting on the Web, while at other times it is the result of developers' writing new applications for old documents or the transfer of a document set from one group or organization to another. If you can ensure that such transfers won't happen, you may be secure in your control over the application. Unfortunately, the very processability of XML, one of its best features, makes it hard to retain such control. XML documents are easy to process and easy to write custom applications around. You never really know when someone will put together a custom tool that helps get the job done but may use a parser that loses information.

The W3C has a proposal in development that will help if your application needs to exchange documents without fear of losing this information: Canonical XML (**http://www.w3.org/TR/xml-c14n**). Canonical XML describes a format that can be used for transferring complete representations of documents, with all attributes already defaulted and normalized, all entities already included, and all namespaces processed to a simpler form (throwing away the prefixes used in the original document). All DTD information is discarded after it has been used to complete the document, along with notations, comments, and CDATA sections. All text is represented using the UTF-8 encoding, and all character references are standardized. Although Canonical XML's purpose is to reduce documents to the simplest possible form for comparison, it also provides a "safe" format that can be sent to non-validating XML processors without concerns for their support of external resources. You'll still need to control all processing up to the point where your XML is canonicalized, but after that happens, you can let anyone process the XML with any non-validating processor. (On the other hand, canonical XML, stripped of its DTD, is no longer valid and won't go through validating processors.)

Solution 3: Document and Double-Check

It's not always satisfactory, but sometimes this problem can be solved in documentation. Comments within documents can warn of dire consequences if external resources aren't loaded, although more typically those comments will appear in the very external resources that won't necessarily be loaded. Specifications that describe DTDs and their usage should always make clear the impact of processing a document with a non-validating parser, and describe the severity (from not important to catastrophic) the consequences of not loading external resources. Developers building applications on your specifications will then have a warning and should be able to choose parsers accordingly. This doesn't always work—people don't always read specifications—but it should help, and can't hurt.

Solution 4: Don't Use the Features

Most of the problems involved in the interactions between non-validating parsers and external resources can easily be avoided by not using the features. If you don't ever use external DTD subsets or external entities, you'll never lose information. In some situations, this makes sense. Simple well-formed documents that don't have DTDs are probably not going to need to use external resources, and you can warn people to use only a subset of XML's functionality. Forbidding the use of DOCTYPE declarations pretty much takes care of this subsetting. You could alternatively require that attribute declarations not provide default values, or that all DTDs appear in the internal subset, but the simpler version is often a lot easier to use and explain.

Unfortunately, these "simple XML" documents aren't ever going to be able to go through a validating parser, unless your application does some fancy tricks like generating DTDs to fit every document that comes along. Although valid documents can go through non-validating parsers without errors (though not necessarily without problems), well-formed documents are going to generate an enormous number of errors as they go through validating parsers—if parsers even let processing complete. Once you've taken this approach you've gone off the map as far as validating parsers are concerned.

Reconciling the many possibilities of XML 1.0 documents and the different types of parsers allowed by the XML 1.0 specification is unfortunately difficult. Because valid documents may appear quite different when processed by certain types of non-validating parsers while merely well-formed documents won't pass through most validating parsers (admittedly, the spec states that they should be processed, just with a lot of errors), developers are stuck with some ugly choices for feature selection.

The Future? Layers of Processing?

These inconveniences and strictures may disappear with new generations of specifications and processors. The W3C's XML Schemas proposal is written without concern for the type of XML document it is applied to, making it possible to think of XML Schemas as a layer that operates on the results generated by an XML 1.0 parser without concern for the nature of that parser. A schemas processor could check those results against its constraints and supply information from the schema, unhindered by the rules governing XML 1.0 processing. (On the other hand, this specification is new, undergoing significant change, and could develop the same kinds of complexity that the XML 1.0 recommendation has.)

Another possibility is a set of packaging tools supporting XML. The XML Working Group announced work on this project as part of Phase III of the XML Activity (see **http://www.w3.org/XML/Activity.html**). Whether or not that packaging will support improved handling of XML 1.0 DTDs is not clear—the XML Working Group could conceivably choose to support only the upcoming schemas' work with its packaging. For an unofficial model of what packaging might look like, designed specifically to address the problems of XML 1.0 DTD processing, you can explore

XML Processing Description Language (XPDL—**http://purl.oclc.org/NET/xpdl**), a project mine. My essay "Toward a Layered Model for XML" (**http://www.simonstl.com/articles/layering/layered.htm**), although it doesn't conform to the monolithic processing approach described by the XML 1.0 recommendation, also provides suggestions for how to handle these issues. More configurable parsers (notably the IBM XML4J parser) have been appearing, and these new features may make it simpler to fix problems when they occur. It will probably still require modifying some code, but it may be as easy as changing a preferences file (perhaps even an XML-based preferences file).

CHAPTER 28

XML Processing Architectures: Trees and Streams

Most XML processing is done following one of two natural-sounding models. Streams flow, and processors read off the flow of a document as they parse it. Trees are sturdy structures in which branches have other branches which may also have branches or may have leaves. Tree-based processors build a model based on the document structure and content that follows a tree-like model, where elements form most of the branches and their contents form either additional branches or leaves. Neither of these approaches has a definite advantage over the over—both of them are useful in particular situations. When you choose XML parsers, however, you will probably have to choose which architecture is more appropriate to the needs of your application. Some parsers support both modes, while others support only one, and there are many tools for converting between the two modes.

NOTE

This chapter is an introduction to the basic models of XML processing, not an in-depth tutorial describing the programming tools and APIs used to implement them. For a detailed look at stream-based parsers, see *Building XML Applications*, by Simon St.Laurent and Ethan Cerami (McGraw-Hill, 1999). For a detailed look at work with a tree-based parser, see *XML and Java: Developing Web Applications*, by Hiroshi Maruyama, Kent Tamura, and Naohiko Uramoto (Addison-Wesley, 1999.)

Reading Event Streams

Stream-based parsers (sometimes called *event-based parsers*) read off the contents of a document as they move from its beginning to its end. They start with the XML declaration, move through the prolog, report the body of the document to the application, and end with any comments or processing instructions that appear at the end of the root element. These parsers report varying amounts of information to the application. Some can report all the declarations that appear in the document type declaration, while others report nothing but the minimum required by the XML 1.0 recommendation—element and attribute content, plus processing instructions. That doesn't mean that they ignore all the rest of the material—they may, in fact, use the DTD content to complete the document (with entities and defaulted attributes) or even validate it.

The most important thing about stream-based parsers is that they only keep track of the bare minimum amount of information needed to support the parse. They may have an internal representation of the DTD, or at least the parts they've read, they have some idea where they are in the document tree (a simple stack will do for non-validating parsers, while validating parsers keep a more complete picture), and they know fundamental things like the character encoding used for the document. They don't, however, build a complete picture of the document's structure. (They may not even load the entire document into memory at once.) They move forward through the document, reporting what they find and checking it against well-formedness and perhaps validity constraints. If the application wants to build structures based on the information the parser is producing, it can, but that structure building is not the task of a stream-based parser.

This lightweight profile makes pure stream-based parsers very efficient, and even tiny. Because they don't need to keep track of an entire document, they can be used to process enormous documents. (A 3.3-megabyte XML version of the Old Testament is a popular test file, but reports occasionally appear of developers working with files in the multiple gigabyte range.) Freed from the memory and code overhead of retaining what they've read, stream-based parsers can read an extremely wide range of documents, although in many cases the burden of building the structures is merely passed to the application. For applications that care only about small portions of documents, however, this tradeoff is worthwhile.

The most commonly used API (application programming interface) for event stream-based parsers is the Java-based Simple API for XML (SAX). Documentation is available at **http://www.megginson.com/SAX/**. (Updated information on the next version of SAX is available at **http://www.megginson.com/SAX/SAX2/**.) The SAX API is widely used for Java parsers, and widely imitated in other environments, including Python, Perl, and C++. To demonstrate how a sample stream session might work, we'll take a very simple XML document and follow the SAX events a parser might produce reading it.

The sample document has four elements, some attributes for those elements, and a bit of textual content.

```
<myDoc><title>My Document</title><p importance="serious"
author="me">This is my first, and very important, document.
</p><giggle /></myDoc>
```

The SAX parser, after configuration, will first call the `startDocument()` method of the application's document handler. Next, the SAX parser will call the `startElement()` method, passing the string `myDoc` for the name argument and an empty attribute list, since `myDoc` has no attributes. After that, the SAX parser will again call `startElement()`, passing it the string "title" for the name argument and another empty attribute list. To handle the text `My Document`, the parser will call the document handler's `characters()` method. Most likely, it will call it once and pass the entire string `My Document` as an array of characters, but it may break up the text and pass it through repeated calls to `characters()` if appropriate. After it finishes passing the text, the SAX parser calls the document handler's `endElement()` method, passing it the string `title` to indicate that the end tag for the title element has been reached.

The `p` element will be passed to the application by calling `startElement()` again, with the string `paragraph` as the first argument and an attribute list object (which contains the attributes as a list of name/value pairs) as the second object. The application thus gets attributes when the start tag is read. The text "This is my first, and very important, document." will be sent to the application through the `characters()` method described above. Afterward, a call to `endElement()` with the argument `p` will indicate that the `p` element's end tag has been reached. The empty element `giggle` generates two events: a call to `startElement()` and a call to `endElement()` immediately following, with no calls to `characters()` in between. Finally, the `endElement()` method is called with the argument `myDoc`, to indicate the root element's closing, and the `endDocument()` method may be called as well.

Although the parser is sending the application a representation of the XML document consisting of a string of fragments, with no context except the previous method calls from the parser, this approach makes it very easy to attach an XML parser to an application and let that application build its own data structures. The application gets reassurance from the parser that the information is actually XML, but isn't required to build its internal structures around the XML document structures. If the application needs the context information, it can keep the information it feels appropriate, and discard information it doesn't need. Neither the parser nor the application is obliged to keep around any more information than required, thereby reducing overhead significantly.

One "feature" of stream-based parsing is worth noting: it pushes the rules set forth in the XML 1.0 recommendation for well-formedness violations. Parsers aren't supposed to pass information to the application (apart from errors) "in the normal way" in the event of a well-formedness violation. Because the application already has information up to the point of the error, it may be up to the application to flush its structures of potentially corrupt information. Making sure that your applications are capable of such rollback is an important aspect of writing software that uses stream-based parsers.

Writing (and Modifying) Event Streams

It isn't especially common to write to event streams, except when parsing documents, but the SAX API and similar approaches make it possible to represent all kinds of information within an application as a set of structures that can be parsed like an XML document. A database engine could, for example, accept queries and respond to the request with a series of SAX events, making that database engine look like an XML parser although the database format has nothing to do with XML. These techniques can be used to make all kinds of information look like XML, though it will be up to the application generating the events to make sure that the events are appropriate, that an `endElement()` method appears for every `startElement()`, and so forth. Although you may not cause disasters by failing to create "well-formed streams," some applications may misbehave.

Stream processing also opens up another set of possibilities: filters. Filters accept SAX events from a parser (or another filter), perform some processing on them, and then pass them on to the application (or, again, another filter). Developers can create stacks of filters that extract particular information, block out information, transform information, or add new information. Filters of different kinds can be used to create different application structures or to process a variety of document types. John Cowan's ParserFilter class (available at **http://www.ccil.org/~cowan/XML/**) is a foundation for building such filters in Java, while MDSAX (available at **http://www.jxml.com/mdsax/index.html**) is a set of tools that apply those filters to create application structures from XML documents.

Reading Trees

Tree-based parsers require much less oversight than stream-based parsers, accepting the name of a file to parse and returning at the end of the parsing process with a complete snapshot of the file that was just parsed. A top-level document object contains nodes, which then represent the parts of an XML document. These nodes may contain other nodes following the same rules that exist within XML documents: element nodes may contain attribute nodes, text nodes, comment nodes, processing instructions nodes. The node representing the root element of the document contains all the element and text nodes, although other information (like comments and processing instructions) may appear before or after that node.

Typically, tree-based parsers return a standardized picture of the XML document that can be accessed and manipulated through the Document Object Model (DOM) API developed by the W3C (see **http://www.w3.org/TR/REC-DOM-Level-1/**). DOM Level 1 represents only the document content, while DOM Level 2 represents additional information, including some DTD information, style information, and event handlers. The DOM was originally created to address the incompatibilities among Dynamic HTML implementations, notably from Microsoft and Netscape, but has continued to grow as a key tool for working with XML. The DOM doesn't specify anything about the underlying structure of the tree, requiring only that it be a hierarchically organized set of nodes that make XML and HTML documents accessible through a standardized API. That API is defined for Java, JavaScript, and CORBA IDLs. Most tree-based Java parsers implement the Core DOM API, although more pieces of the DOM are regularly being implemented across parsers, especially as DOM Level 2 reaches maturity.

For applications that need to work closely with the structures of an XML document, this prebuilt application object representation of a document is fine. The same information and the same structures that appeared in the XML document will be present in the DOM representation, and most DOM models provide methods for saving the tree representation back to an XML file. The DOM represents a processed version of the XML document, not the original version, but provides easy access to all the information that document represents. Although the DOM provides a standard set of tools for "walking the tree" and navigating among nodes, parser developers have added to the DOM with their own tools for reaching particular nodes quickly, helping applications find information rapidly.

The tree-based model fits the containment approach of XML very well. Rather than reading off tags, the tree-based model uses start- and end-tags to mark the boundaries of named objects. Attributes are represented as nodes contained within their elements, and the elements, text, comments, and processing instructions that appear within elements are treated as a list of contained items. If we look at the document used for the stream-based parser above through a tree-based view, we'll see something similar, but quite different. First, there is the document:

```
<myDoc><title>My Document</title><p importance="serious"
author="me">This is my first, and very important, document.
</p><giggle /></myDoc>
```

Next, there is the tree representation of that document.

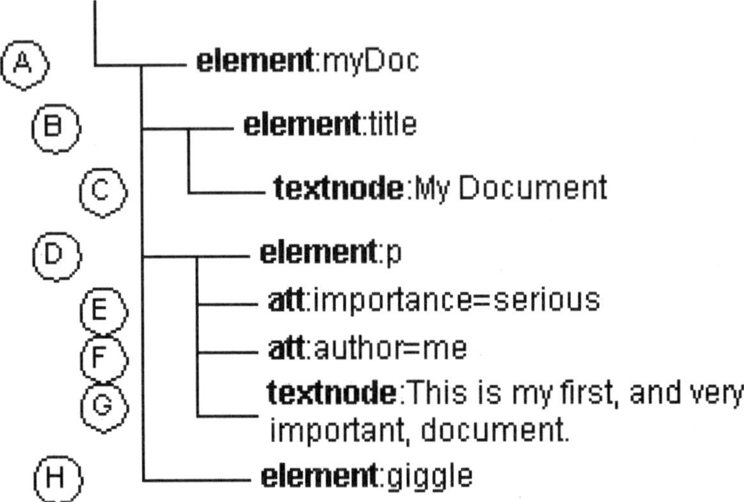

Figure 28.1 A tree-based representation of a document

The elements are no longer start- and end-tags—instead, they are nodes contained by the overall document. The `myDoc` element (A) is the root element, containing all the other elements. The `title` element (B) only contains a text node (C) holding the string "My Document." The `p` element (D) is next, and contains three nodes. The attributes "`importance`" (E) and "`author`" (F) are stored with their values in attribute nodes, while the text node (G) contains the text "This is my first, and very important, document." Finally, the empty element "`giggle`" (H) contains no other nodes, as it has neither textual content nor attributes.

The DOM API provides applications with tools for navigating among these nodes, allowing them to request information like "the first child element of the root element node." (Other proposals from the W3C, like XPath and XPointer, take this approach to a more abstract level.) As long as they stick to the methods provided by the W3C DOM, applications should be able to take different XML parsers, feed them the same documents, and read and manipulate those documents the same way. DOM trees also have the significant advantage that applications can begin processing the information they contain after the parser is finished, avoiding the complexities of rolling back changes already made to an application's internal structures. With a set of tools like this, applications can maintain a greater distance from the details of XML parsing and simplify their internal code, though at some cost—DOM processors, because they have to maintain a tree, consume considerably more memory and other resources.

Writing Trees

Although DOM trees are commonly seen as the output of a parser, they can be used to go the other direction as well. Most tree-based parsers provide a means of writing the DOM tree back out to a file, as well as methods for creating new (blank) DOM trees that applications can use to create elements and other XML document components. If you're more comfortable letting a component write out your XML documents instead of having to custom craft code yourself, a DOM parser can be a fine tool for exporting your application data structures to XML as well as importing information from XML. You'll need to create code that writes your information into a DOM tree, adding nodes of various types, but that may be cleaner than creating I/O code that writes text to a file directly. (You may lose some functionality, like support for DTD declarations, however.)

This same functionality allows you to create applications that masquerade as XML parsers, much like the SAX interface tricks described above. A component that builds a DOM tree can pass it to another component, and the recipient has no way of knowing that the tree was generated internally and not as the result of a parse. Using DOM trees lets you ignore the problems of mismatched beginnings and ends for elements—the containment will always be perfect, provided that you stick to the API provided. If you want to represent database recordsets as DOM trees to pass them to a particular type of application that accepts DOM trees, you can do it, without ever serializing your information back to XML.

Although the DOM doesn't have filters, it isn't too difficult to create components that accept a tree as an argument and return another tree (or modify the original tree) as the result. This approach makes it easy to build DOM-based transformation engines and processing. Like SAX filters, these components can modify, extract, suppress, supplement, or transform the original tree. Provided that they stick to the W3C's APIs (and don't take advantage of parser-specific calls), these components should be able to operate on trees created by any DOM-compliant parser.

Choosing

It may seem that stream-based parsers are always going to be the right choice when the application needs tight control and large documents are a looming possibility, or that tree-based parsers are always going to be the right choice when you want to keep your application out of the parsing business yet still have access to all the content of an XML document. There are a lot more variables involved, however, and choosing the right parsing model (not to mention the right parser) can involve a large number of factors.

If performance and size are critical, there are a number of small stream-based parsers, like Aelfred from Microstar (**http://www.microstar.com**) and expat and XP from James Clark (**http://www.jclark.com/xml**), that offer speed and a tiny footprint. These smaller parsers typically provide no support for tree building, leaving such work to the application. Larger parsers, like the XML4J parser from IBM (**http://www.alphaWorks.ibm.com**) and the ProjectX parser from Sun Microsystems (**http://java.sun.com**) offer both stream- and tree-based parsing, letting you substitute a heavy hitter if and when it's appropriate, but no tree-based parser can compete with the small size of purely stream-based (and non-validating) parsers. Use of the SAX interface is common across Java parsers, making it easy to switch parsers when you find it necessary.

Many tree-based parsers are available, with most providing a DOM-based interface. Almost all these parsers provide extensions beyond the W3C's basic API. To some extent this is because features are missing from the W3C's spec (like methods for opening and saving documents), and to some extent these features provide more efficient approaches to navigating through trees. The more you use these features, however, the more tightly bound to that parser you'll find yourself. Selecting a tree-based parser is often a matter of balancing performance, resource consumption (which is much greater than for stream-based parsers), and features. The DOM API provides you with some foundations, and can help you move from parser to parser if necessary, but it ensures that applications using the DOM are going to be fairly large creatures with sizable footprints.

To some extent, you may find yourself locked into one or the other of these approaches. If your requirements later change, it can be difficult to reorient your application to the other approach. Fortunately, there are tools available for converting event streams into trees (like the Docuverse DOM, available from **http://www.docuverse.com/**) and for converting trees into event streams (like John Cowan's DOM Parser, available at **http://www.ccil.org/~cowan/XML/**). The XMLSoftware.com Web site can help you find more of these kinds of parser-oriented tools, providing you with the flexibility you need to keep the trade-offs from costing too much.

CHAPTER 29

Waiting for the Future: XML Schemas and Data Typing

Although XML 1.0 provides some very flexible tools for describing document structures, those tools haven't satisfied certain important groups of users. Even before XML 1.0 became a W3C Recommendation, Microsoft, DataChannel, and Inso had submitted a proposal for a different set of tools describing document and data structures, called XML-Data. Over the next year, three more proposals—SOX, DCD, and DDML—were submitted, and the W3C set up its own working group to create a standard tool for describing the contents of XML documents using XML-based schemas. XML Schemas are currently under development, with many issues yet to be resolved. They hold out significant promise, however, and seem to be the upgrade path the W3C plans for XML validation beyond XML 1.0.

NOTE

Discussion in this chapter is based on versions of the schema specifications that may not prove stable and the material is subject to change. The XML Schema structures discussion is based on the 24 September 1999 Working Draft (http://www.w3.org/TR/1999/WD-xmlschema-1-19990924), while the XML Schema datatypes discussion is based on another Working Draft released the same day (http://www.w3.org/TR/1999/WD-xmlschema-2-19990924). An update to this chapter will be available at http://www.simonstl.com.

The Problems

We've spent most of this book discussing DTDs and what a good job they can do describing your data and letting you model information. What is so wrong with DTDs that they need to be replaced by an entirely new standard, one that promises to be even more complex? There are several key issues driving schema development:

- Quirky DTD syntax—DTD syntax isn't very much like the rest of XML, and is processed as a list rather than a hierarchy. An external DTD isn't actually a validatable XML document. For developers who want to store and process schemas with the rest of their XML information, and be able to reference their schemas using the same tools as XML documents, the current DTD syntax is a nuisance.
- Limited data types—XML DTDs do a fine job of describing hierarchically structured text. They don't, however, understand integers, floating-point numbers, currency, dates, or any of the many other kinds of information most computing systems handle. Although the conventions discussed in Chapter 11 can solve many of these problems, they are only conventions, not part of the XML 1.0 recommendation.
- Documentation—Comments are not an especially powerful tool for documenting structures. XML-based schemas can provide more sophisticated vocabularies that better reference particular declarations.
- Requiring complete descriptions—Valid documents are only valid if every single element and attribute type used is declared somewhere in the DTD.
- History of obscurity—Although XML definitely simplified SGML to a much smaller set of tools, some of those tools (notations, unparsed entities, etc.) still had reputations as arcane, and the minimal explanations provided by the XML 1.0 recommendation didn't do much to help that.
- W3C neglect—Whether it is to keep XML 1.0 as stable as possible to encourage new users, or because DTD syntax was seen as a dead end, the W3C has shown almost no signs of interest in supporting DTD syntax with extensions or hooks from new standards like XPath. The lack of integration between namespaces and DTDs has already created problems for DTDs, and there are no public statements regarding the future of DTDs.

Schemas definitely have momentum within the W3C, but it may be a long while before they are stable, much less ready for use. The current working draft is a mix of revisions and sections that are out of date, and it isn't clear how many of its features will make it into a W3C recommendation. The Schemas Working Group has an enormous number of activities within the W3C that need support, including cooperation with a very different schema project, that for Resource Description Framework (RDF). A joint statement issued by members of the RDF Schemas Working Group and the XML Schemas Working Group, the "Cambridge Communique" (**http://www.w3.org/TR/schema-arch**), suggests that there is considerable work yet to be done.

While the work on XML Schemas proceeds, many developers are moving ahead with information modeling using existing tools. DTDs are one option, but XML-Data and SOX (the Schema for Object-Oriented XML—**http://www.w3.org/TR/NOTE-SOX**) are two others receiving commercial use. XML-Data is presently the foundation for Microsoft's BizTalk schema repository initiative (**http://www.biztalk.org**) and figures prominently in several of its other projects.

Examples

For an example, we'll explore the billing DTD used as an example in Chapter 11, and present it in several different formats: the original DTD, an XML-Data representation of that DTD, a SOX representation of that DTD, and a representation using the latest draft from the XML Schemas working group.

The original billing DTD represents information contained in a fairly simple bill for bulk commodities, and uses the data-typing conventions discussed in Chapter 11:

```
<!ELEMENT bill        (refNum , addressee , shipments , total )>
<!ATTLIST bill        dateSent CDATA   #REQUIRED
   paid  CDATA        #IMPLIED
   a-dtype   NMTOKENS 'dateSent date
   paid  boolean' >
<!ELEMENT refNum      (#PCDATA )>
<!ATTLIST refNum      e-dtype NMTOKEN  #FIXED 'int' >

<!ELEMENT addressee  (CustomerName , CustomerAddress , CustomerAddress2
, City , StateProvince , PostalCode , Country )>

<!ELEMENT shipments  (shipDate , material , tons , priceTon )>

<!ELEMENT total       (#PCDATA )>
<!ATTLIST total       e-dtype NMTOKEN  #FIXED 'fixed.14.4' >

<!ELEMENT shipDate    (#PCDATA )>
<!ATTLIST shipDate    e-dtype NMTOKEN  #FIXED 'date' >

<!ELEMENT tons        (#PCDATA )>
<!ATTLIST tons        e-dtype NMTOKEN  #FIXED 'decimal' >

<!ELEMENT priceTon    (#PCDATA )>
<!ATTLIST priceTon    e-dtype NMTOKEN  #FIXED 'fixed.14.4' >

<!ELEMENT material    (#PCDATA )>
```

```
<!ELEMENT CustomerName       (#PCDATA )>
<!ELEMENT CustomerAddress    (#PCDATA )>
<!ELEMENT CustomerAddress2   (#PCDATA )>
<!ELEMENT City       (#PCDATA )>
<!ELEMENT StateProvince      (#PCDATA )>
<!ELEMENT PostalCode (#PCDATA )>
<!ELEMENT Country    (#PCDATA )>
```

This DTD uses some extra attribute declarations to indicate data type, but is otherwise a fairly conventional description of a document structure. The same document structure, described in XML-Data, looks like:

```
<?xml version ="1.0"?>
<!--Generated by XML Authority.
   Conforms to XML Data subset for IE 5-->
<Schema name="bill.xdr"
    xmlns="urn:schemas-microsoft-com:xml-data"
    xmlns:dt="urn:schemas-microsoft-com:datatypes"
    xmlns:xa="www.extensibility.com/schemas/xdr/metaprops.xdr">
   <ElementType name="bill" content="eltOnly" order="seq"
                model="closed">
   <AttributeType name="dateSent" dt:type="date" required="yes"/>
   <AttributeType name="paid" dt:type="boolean"/>
   <attribute type="dateSent"/>
   <attribute type="paid"/>
   <element type="refNum"/>
   <element type="addressee"/>
   <element type="shipments"/>
   <element type="total"/>
   </ElementType>

   <ElementType name="refNum" content="textOnly" dt:type="int"
                model="closed"/>
   <ElementType name="addressee" content="eltOnly" order="seq"
                model="closed">
   <element type="CustomerName"/>
   <element type="CustomerAddress"/>
   <element type="CustomerAddress2"/>
   <element type="City"/>
   <element type="StateProvince"/>
   <element type="PostalCode"/>
   <element type="Country"/>
   </ElementType>

   <ElementType name="shipments" content="eltOnly" order="seq"
                model="closed">
   <element type="shipDate"/>
   <element type="material"/>
   <element type="tons"/>
   <element type="priceTon"/>
   </ElementType>

   <ElementType name="total" content="textOnly" dt:type="fixed.14.4"
                model="closed"/>
   <ElementType name="CustomerName" content="textOnly" model="closed"/>
   <ElementType name="CustomerAddress" content="textOnly"
                model="closed"/>
   <ElementType name="CustomerAddress2" content="textOnly"
```

```
                model="closed"/>
   <ElementType name="City" content="textOnly" model="closed"/>
   <ElementType name="StateProvince" content="textOnly" model="closed"/>
   <ElementType name="PostalCode" content="textOnly" model="closed"/>
   <ElementType name="Country" content="textOnly" model="closed"/>
   <ElementType name="shipDate" content="textOnly" dt:type="date"
                model="closed"/>
   <ElementType name="tons" content="textOnly" dt:type="decimal"
                model="closed"/>
   <ElementType name="priceTon" content="textOnly" dt:type="fixed.14.4"
                model="closed"/>
   <ElementType name="material" content="textOnly" model="closed"/>
</Schema>
```

The first notable difference is that this information is stored as a well-formed XML document, not a list of declarations. Namespaces are used to differentiate the core XML-Data declarations from declarations (`dt:type`) that use a separate list of data types. Attribute types are defined separately from their assignment to elements, making it possible to reuse them later without having to redefine their content. Overall, descriptions are much more verbose than is possible in compact grammar used for DTDs. (Also note the presence of the model attribute, which will be discussed later.)

Converting to an XML document model, even a verbose one, doesn't automatically answer all questions, however. There are lots of possible schema structures, reflecting different perspectives on how best to structure this information. SOX, for example, uses a very different document structure to represent the same information.

```
<?xml version ="1.0"?>
<!DOCTYPE schema SYSTEM "urn:x-
commerceone:document:com:commerceone:xdk:xml:schema.dtd$1.0">
<!--Generated by XML Authority.
   Conforms to Conforms to Commerce One SOX 2.0-->
<schema uri="bill.sox" soxlang-version="V0.2.2">
   <elementtype name="bill">
   <model>
   <sequence>
   <element type="refNum"/>
   <element type="addressee"/>
   <element type="shipments"/>
   <element type="total"/>
   </sequence>
   </model>
   <attdef name="dateSent" datatype="date">
   <required/>
   </attdef>
   <attdef name="paid" datatype="boolean"/>
   </elementtype>

   <attdef name="dateSent" datatype="date">
   <required/>
   </attdef>

   <attdef name="paid" datatype="boolean"/>
   <elementtype name="refNum">
```

```
<model>
<string datatype="int"/>
</model>
</elementtype>

<elementtype name="addressee">
<model>
<sequence>
<element type="CustomerName"/>
<element type="CustomerAddress"/>
<element type="CustomerAddress2"/>
<element type="City"/>
<element type="StateProvince"/>
<element type="PostalCode"/>
<element type="Country"/>
</sequence>
</model>
</elementtype>

<elementtype name="shipments">
<model>
<sequence>
<element type="shipDate"/>
<element type="material"/>
<element type="tons"/>
<element type="priceTon"/>
</sequence>
</model>
</elementtype>

<elementtype name="total">
<model>
<string datatype="number"/>
</model>
</elementtype>

<elementtype name="CustomerName">
<model>
<string/>
</model>
</elementtype>

<elementtype name="CustomerAddress">
<model>
<string/>
</model>
</elementtype>

<elementtype name="CustomerAddress2">
<model>
<string/>
</model>
</elementtype>

<elementtype name="City">
<model>
<string/>
</model>
</elementtype>
```

```
    <elementtype name="StateProvince">
    <model>
    <string/>
    </model>
    </elementtype>

    <elementtype name="PostalCode">
    <model>
    <string/>
    </model>
    </elementtype>

    <elementtype name="Country">
    <model>
    <string/>
    </model>
    </elementtype>

    <elementtype name="shipDate">
    <model>
    <string datatype="date"/>
    </model>
    </elementtype>

    <elementtype name="tons">
    <model>
    <string datatype="number"/>
    </model>
    </elementtype>

    <elementtype name="priceTon">
    <model>
    <string datatype="number"/>
    </model>
    </elementtype>

    <elementtype name="material">
    <model>
    <string/>
    </model>
    </elementtype>

</schema>
```

Again, the schema is represented by an XML document. (Note the use of the `URN` in the DOCTYPE declaration. Although this is technically legal, most validating parsers will have no idea how to handle it. Non-validating parsers, at least those which don't retrieve external resources, should be fine. The SOX notation, of which this example only shows a small portion, relies on child elements rather than attributes for much of the information that XML-Data represented with attributes. Attribute type definitions appear inside the declarations for element types, but without the separate type declaration and application to the element used by XML-Data. Both element content models and string or data character models are represented using the `model` element. Data types for elements are represented here, as they were in the extended DTD shown originally, as strings that have extra constraints. SOX also provides a variety of other intrinsic datatypes that may be refined using similar mechanisms, like binary, boolean, scalar, date, and char. The two attributes for the `bill` element use these. SOX doesn't use namespaces internally—everything in the schema is simply SOX information.

In the representation based on the latest version of the XML Schema working draft, we have yet another set of structures to consider:

```
<?xml version ="1.0"?>
<schema name="bill.xsd"
    xmlns="http://www.w3.org/1999/09/23-xmlschema/structures/
           structures.xsd">
   <element name="bill" type="billType" />

   <archetype name="billType">
   <element name="refNum" type="integer"/>
   <element name="addressee"/>
   <element name="shipments"/>
   <element name="total"/>
   <attribute name="dateSent" datatype="date" required="true" />
   <attribute name="paid" datatype="boolean" />
   </archetype>

   <element name="addressee" type="addresseeType" />

   <archetype name="addresseeType">
   <element name="CustomerName" type="string" />
   <element name="CustomerAddress" type="string" />
   <element name="CustomerAddress2" type="string" />
   <element name="City"/>
   <element name="StateProvince" type="string" />
   <element name="PostalCode" type="string"/>
   <element name="Country" type="string"/>
   </archetype>

   <element name="shipments" type="shipmentType" />

   <archetype>
   <element name="shipDate" type="date"/>
   <element name="material" type="string"/>
   <element name="tons" type="decimal" />
   <element name="priceTon" type="decimal"/>   </archetype>
</schema>
```

NOTE
Given the rate of change on the XML Schema specification, the example above may be obsolete by the time this book reaches stores. Check the update site (http://www.simonstl.com) for the latest information.

XML Schema provides a more compact and perhaps more extensible form than its predecessors. Elements are declared to be of types, which may be atomic data types (including user-defined datatypes) or *archetypes*, which allow the description of more sophisticated content models, including attributes. This makes it easy to create multiple element types with the same content model and attributes.

Advanced Features

This example focused on the most stable aspects of the various schema formats, but all of the formats provide capabilities that move beyond the DTD model of lists of descriptions. XML Schema's move to the archetype approach for content description, if it holds, is a significant departure from the content model approach used by most other schema designs, and a large leap away from DTDs. "Open" and "closed" content models, noted above for XML-Data and also possible in XML Schemas, provide rules for processing elements that haven't been declared elsewhere, instead of simply banning them permanently. Archetype "refinement," still a controversial development, allows schema developers to mix and match different types of declarations. XML Schema's typing features go beyond archetypes, providing tools schema designers can use to define their own data types with regular expressions. Multi-part data types (currencies with indicators like $, dates, even CSS rules) can be specified with these data typing tools.

The W3C's Schema working draft also provides support for the attribute defaulting and entity and notation support (called information set contributions), providing a superset of the services available in XML 1.0. Parameter entities disappear, their role taken over by general entities within the schema document (heck, it's an XML document) and archetypes. XML Schemas will come with a documentation mechanism and probably an extension mechanism, but those tools are still under development.

Planning the Transition

Unless you have extremely pressing needs (or are a compulsive early adopter), leaping to schemas may not be an appropriate move, at least not yet. Tools are available for processing XML-Data and SOX schemas, and some very preliminary tools are appearing for the W3C's XML Schemas, but it may be a while before schemas become the standard for XML processing. This doesn't mean that you should ignore schema developments, by any means—it means that you should plan for a future that involves schemas while using tools appropriate to your current needs. If you are working in a document-centric field with minimal need for data typing, vanilla XML 1.0 DTDs may meet your needs. The data typing extensions described in Chapter 11 give DTDs additional capabilities for data handling, though you may want to try SOX or XML-Data.

Whatever tools you use to define document structures (if in fact you do so), you should be able to convert to the final draft of XML Schemas without too much difficulty. Already, tools like XML Authority (**http://www.extensibility.com**) can import and export the same schema information in different formats, letting you move among schema grammars while still maintaining the same view of the document structure. As XML Schema moves closer to completion, expect to see a large number of conversion tools appear. Converting a DTD to a simple XML Schema is not very difficult, although making that schema take advantage of all XML Schema's features may involve another round of effort. While it isn't clear that DTDs or schemas are here to stay in their current forms, their commonality of purpose ensures that paths between them won't be hard to create.

NOTE

For a very different approach to schemas, see Rick Jelliffe's Schematron (http://www.ascc.net/xml/resource/schematron/schematron.html). Schematron tests assertions about patterns rather than describing constraints, using tools like XSLT or the Omnimark set of markup processing tools. Schematron is designed to be used in conjunction with other schema languages, and not as a replacement.

PART FIVE

An Approach to Style

CHAPTER 30

Seeking Consistency

There is rarely only a single model for a given set of information, but it also rarely pays to use all the models possible. Even within a given model, it is usually worthwhile to represent similar kinds of information using similar approaches, designing the overall framework out of relatively similar components. Consistency can help developers implement tools for working with your XML documents, simplify overall maintenance, keep teams working on different aspects of a project from conflicting, and even help automate some aspects of XML document modeling. Balancing a consistent approach with the flexibility often needed to model some semblance of reality can be a difficult task, but consistency is usually a goal worth striving for.

NOTE
This chapter describes techniques for creating very conventional document structures. The techniques discussed here may not always be appropriate for use in more radical strategies like those discussed in Chapter 35.

Consistent Criteria

Although data are frequently irregular, unless you are modeling information that has already been homogenized, the way you model information needs to have some level of regularity. Choosing whether to use elements or attributes, for instance, is something that you could do at random, but it probably makes sense to apply a similar set of rules to all the cases you address in a given solution. Most people wouldn't make those decisions at random, but different teams working on different parts of a project may make those decisions in very different ways, and structures that look as though they'd been created randomly, or perhaps by a designer deliberately attempting to make things difficult, sometimes result.

Although it may seem arbitrary to create rules describing things like which pieces of information deserve representation as elements and which deserve to be treated as attributes, having a set of rules, even one created arbitrarily, may be better than letting people make decisions in ways which aren't arbitrary but aren't consistent, either. Even individual designers sometimes fluctuate in their opinions about data modeling over the course of a project, and having to keep up with extra changes puts extra stress on the people designing supporting tools for the document structures. Style sheets are easier to write if they can be attached to a single model that determines style choice—when some styles are applied based on element names and others are applied based on attribute values, the complexity of the style sheet can grow exponentially. (If the element name and the attribute value actually represent the same thing, the problem can seem especially perverse.) Application designers face the same problems, but often in a world where search-and-replace isn't as simple.

XML does have some advantages that can help you dig yourself out from these situations if you encounter them. You can transform information so that it all fits a single model using the tools described in Chapter 18, *if* the models you have are compatible enough. If the information in two document formats is similar but the way that information was broken down is too different for the creation of automatic conversions, you may have to resort to more costly (and very tedious) human intervention. It won't always come to this, especially if designers make certain that their structures contain the information in the smallest useful form, but this danger lurks when projects grow large and communications wear thin. XML provides a lot flexibility, perhaps too much flexibility at times. If you want to avoid tangled webs of XML, you'll do well to talk about design principles at the start of a project rather than at its conclusion.

Consistent Communications

Even if you have broad rules for defining markup structures, and feel confident that your team, your users, and your management share common goals (admittedly, an unusual circumstance), you need to support these rules by keeping communications channels open. Some of this is basic project management practice, and some of it reflects needs particular to XML document design and practice. A large number of information technology projects count on experts to gather information from users, and then retreat to dark chambers to create solutions to the problems they encountered in the field. Although users are periodically consulted about the look of the project, they are rarely encouraged to discuss issues like data formats and structures.

For some XML projects, this traditional approach will probably work well, or at least as well as it has for other aspects of computing. It may doom other projects to failure, in large part because of the kinds of promises XML makes. The largest benefit of XML is its ability to be used in interchange applications, where users working with standardized tools can share a common view of information and then process it according to their own needs. Many XML projects are about sharing information across the boundaries that normally separate computing systems and organizations, even across the boundaries that typically separate competitors. Collecting input and retreating to contemplate an ideal design is probably not a good strategy for a project that needs to be sold to its users, some of whom may question how good an idea sharing information is in the first place. XML is capable of carrying many kinds of information, but there are very few cases where XML is the absolute best or only choice.

Involving users throughout the development process—whether formally, through industry consortia or even committees, or informally, with regular phone calls and emails to stay in touch with possible changing needs—is an important step toward making users feel that these data structures are their own. The processability of XML makes it a threat in many ways, to people's jobs and organizational structures. Empire-builders who insist on shrouding their projects in secrecy are likely to be unhappy about putting their information into systems where others, even their managers, can take out a file and throw it into a spreadsheet for a quick analysis. People whose jobs revolve around converting information from one format to another may be threatened by the ease with which XML-based information can be reused. Involving these people in the project may be difficult, but it can both improve your project (the most important part) and make it more difficult for those who dislike the potential impact of your project to claim they were never consulted (the sad and painful political aspect).

Even within a project, communications is important. Some of this work is simple documentation, using comments effectively, and sending out warnings to other developers with dependencies on declarations that change. On any large project, the criteria originally set forth for information modeling are likely to be challenged by particular circumstances and needs. Rather than taking a best-guess approach and hoping it doesn't cause problems, discussing the challenges with a larger group may result in a cleaner, better-justified solution, or even clarify or (very occasionally) change the criteria used for modeling. Effective communications within a group, especially communications that get recorded, can make life much easier for whoever must do the documentation.

Developers working on one-person projects may not think communications nearly as important—enough developers already talk to themselves, after all—but communications can be just as important on small projects as on large ones. Documenting the reasons you made a decision can make it easier to address both that decision and later decisions as you move through a project. Although some people do have "personal" vocabularies they use only on their own work, most XML is meant to be shared at some stage. The notes you write to yourself can help others figure out what you meant when they try to apply your work to their problems.

Consistent Conventions

A clear set of conventions can make reading documents and DTDs much simpler and reduce the need for repetitive documentation. Chapters 19, 20, and 22 have already discussed conventions for modules, extensions, and documentation, but the general case for establishing conventions early in a project is strong. A consistent set of rules for naming the parts of your structures is a promise to both users and other developers that they won't have to work too hard to figure what a given component is supposed to represent. Even if other users and developers aren't working directly on your DTDs, they will certainly encounter the names of elements and attributes, and straightforward naming conventions can simplify their work.

In some cases, tools can simplify the use of conventions. Conventions often mean extra typing for those who prefer to create their documents and DTDs "the old-fashioned way," by hand (including this author). It may not always seem worth the effort to indicate whether a comment is intended for users creating documents based on a DTD or for the developers helping build that DTD. Without tools that both simplify the creation of such directed comments and process the comments into documentation, it may in fact not be worth the effort. Given the promise of a simpler documentation process, however, lots of developers may be willing to put in the effort. (Having both written documentation and contributed information to those writing documentation, I can testify that the process is painful and best avoided.)

It's also important to make sure that the conventions you use during the development of a document structure aren't focused on the development process to the exclusion of the document's eventual use. While it might be useful to see elements named `devGroupTyrell:title` and `devGroupDeckard:title` during the development of a document structure, most users of that structure will be happier to see `book:title` and `person:title` instead. XML Namespaces can be useful for supporting multiple needs like this—as long as "devGroupTyrell" and "book" refer to the same URI, they can be exchanged easily. (Chapter 24 points out limitations with this, but these kinds of prefix changes can usually be accommodated with a very simple search-and-replace.)

Consistent Decision-Making

You have criteria, communications, and conventions. The foundations are strong. What could cause problems now? All that consistency may be wasted if the decision-making backing it up isn't consistent. Projects change hands, developers change projects, and sometimes people just go on vacation. 100% consistency is probably a thoroughly unrealistic goal, even for one-person projects. In the end, the consistency of a project all comes down to a series of decisions made by people over the course of that project, influenced by changing requirements, varying priorities, deadline pressure, and sometimes the weather or too much coffee.

Maintaining consistency under these circumstances is still possible. In large part, it means taking time with decisions to avoid sudden changes of course in the middle of a project. Often this means examining what has already been done, by exploring documentation that was created along the way. If changes to the criteria being used to design document structures are needed, this may mean rebuilding prior work to bring it into conformance with the new rules. Examining decisions that affect a portion of a project in the light of the rest of the project may help both the decision-making and the revision process.

Consistent Application Design

As convenient as it is to label people's decision-making as inconsistent and computing processes as highly consistent, there are times when inconsistencies among tools can cause as much or more chaos than the very human information-modeling process. Although XML may look consistent on the surface, there are a number of dangers lurking beneath its rules for processing documents. Chapter 24 described the difficulties of integrating the Namespaces in XML recommendation with the XML 1.0 recommendation, and Chapter 27 noted the potential for information loss created by XML 1.0's granting extra privileges to non-validating parsers. These inconsistencies are also created by humans, but they require extra attention to make sure that your applications behave consistently.

There are no standards yet for describing the "profiles" of XML that particular documents need for their processing, but these may yet emerge from the W3C's packaging work, discussed in Chapter 25. In the meantime, developers of XML documents need to do their own profiling, describing the processing requirements of the document types they create. If handling a given document type correctly requires that attribute defaults from an external DTD be applied, this should be made clear early in the documentation for application developers. Similarly, the DTD's use of namespaces, if any, also needs to be explained. Any work done outside the bounds of ordinary DTD development, like the data typing conventions described in Chapter 11, should also be explained. Developers who aren't informed that data type information is available may not explore the DTD and use simpler processing that won't make use of the work. Although documentation isn't a perfect solution to this kind of inconsistency, it's the best solution available today.

CHAPTER 31

Building on Past Works

Although "reinventing the wheel" is a popular pastime for many developers, XML offers opportunities for reusing information and structures that may reduce the need to start fresh for every project or every change in requirements. Although XML is a relatively new technology, its roots go back much farther, and many SGML and other tools can be used with XML when appropriate. Even within your own projects, which may seem too young to really have a history, there are often opportunities to take advantage of data modeling done for other formats. XML is a new technology, and the temptation to start with a clean slate may be strong, but it's usually worth looking around to see what previous work you can include in your own.

History Can Be Useful

XML is a newcomer to computing, but its predecessor, SGML, has been in development and in use for almost 30 years. Although SGML's legacy is sometimes questioned, the SGML community's experience has produced a large number of tools worth exploring, and many of those tools are still in active development. XML can be used with many existing SGML parsers and applications, some of which were the early test beds for XML processing. (See James Clark's "Comparison of SGML and XML" at

http://www.w3.org/TR/NOTE-sgml-xml-971215 for details on the relationship and using XML in SGML tools.) The W3C doesn't seem to be planning future expansion of XML to make it more like SGML, but SGML has a number of supporting standards that are well worth exploring.

HyTime, the Hypermedia/Time-base Structuring Language, ISO/IEC 10744, is a standard describing hypertext and multimedia applications of SGML. HyTime defined a wide range of tools that went well beyond the domain of simple hypertext. Many of those tools, HyTime's supporters suggest, are being reinvented or reapplied to XML in smaller chunks. The architectural forms processing described in Chapters 11 and 18 comes from HyTime, as does a lot of the thought behind XLink, discussed in Chapter 23, and some of the considerations in the next generation of schemas, discussed in Chapter 29. Groves, a data model that can be used across multiple formats, is another key piece of HyTime that is reemerging in XML processing. HyTime's main drawback is that it is enormous, but you may be able to find pieces appropriate to your problems. More information on HyTime is available at **http://www.hytime.org**. Another standard from SGML that is still in use, under development, and easily applied to XML is DSSSL, the Document Style and Semantics Specification Language. DSSSL provides a lot of the foundations for XSL processing, and may be a tool you can apply to particular projects. The OpenJade project (**http://www.netfolder.com/DSSSL/**) is the main standard bearer for DSSSL software development.

SGML isn't the only "historical" standard worth exploring, either. An important part of XML's appeal is that it plays well with existing standards. A wide range of such standards, from ISO 8601 (which describes date formats) to the IETF's MIME content-types, can be used either within XML documents or to describe and transport XML documents. To some extent, you'll be integrating XML with your existing infrastructures, but some of these tools may be worth exploring whether or not you use them in your current application structures.

Remodeling or Demolition and Rebuilding?

Whether you're modifying someone else's vision or updating your own, determining how closely you'll follow what came before sets the rules for the work to come. Some projects require only minor additions, a thin veneer on top of a previous model or some extra space to hold additional information. Other projects require tearing down the previous version, taking from it the few structures appropriate to your new plans, and rebuilding almost from scratch. Although scratch-building can bring its own gratification, in many cases simple remodeling can save considerable time while preserving compatibility with the tools used to process and mange the prior version. Unless you're rebuilding a project with known gigantic flaws, or trying to convert an application-specific vocabulary to a more generic one, preservation may be a better idea than demolition.

Providing an Upward (and Downward) Path: Transformations

Whatever approach you take to modifying an older version of a document structure, you can simplify the transition by supplementing your new version with code (programs or style sheets) that transforms information in the old format to the new format, and possibly by supplying a backward transformation as well. In situations where a document format is in wide use, especially when that use is across multiple organizations, a simple roll-out of new formats and software isn't likely. Instead, version conflicts between documents and software will linger, causing problems until the new document format is accepted or rejected. Supplying transformation tools makes it easier to mix old and new software, keeping older systems on life-support while exploring and building on the new features.

A clear versioning strategy can make your transformation development easier. Including version information in DTDs and documents (often through a default attribute on the root element) makes it easier for transformation tools to determine which set of rules to apply, and makes it easier to supply packages of transformations for those times when more than two versions of a given format are in use. To some extent, the XML Packaging work getting started at the W3C may provide assistance for this project, but for now you should treat versioning and transformations as part of a documentation strategy, with hooks to that documentation (a simple version ID will suffice) in your documents.

Preserving Compatibility

Creating new document formats that will work with applications designed for the old format isn't always easy, even in a relatively light remodeling job. Three general types of projects often cause problems: replacement, extension, and reduction. Any time you completely replace a structure, incompatibility is probably a necessary and unavoidable cost. Extensions and reductions, however, can sometimes be done within existing frameworks without breaking applications. The application structures can have as much impact on this process as the document structures, so examining your applications early in the process is probably a good idea.

Some applications handle "extra" information in documents easily—they ignore it, or make it accessible to users in a very simple form. Extra attributes are often completely ignored because applications just don't look for them when processing event streams or trees. Applications that take XML documents only as input won't cause problems in this kind of situations, though they may of course need extension if you want them to support the added functionality. Applications that import XML documents to internal application structures and then write those structures back out as XML documents may have problems, however, especially if they do so by writing out a whole new document structure. If an application uses a DOM tree internally and updates that tree to represent changes as the application makes them, document structures outside the application's understanding will usually be preserved (unless, of course, the application overwrites a section that contains the extra information). Adding extensions to document structures in this way without breaking applications or having applications break the documents may be possible, but requires consultation with the builders and maintainers of the applications.

Reducing a document structure by creating a subset generally creates less complex problems, though applications designed to export their structures in the larger format may overwrite files again. The main problems in reductions are determining which information applications consider critical to their processing. Some applications, especially those that process documents, are extremely forgiving of different levels of markup. (If you take out all the formatting and structuring information in the body of an HTML document, it's still an HTML document, for instance.) Data-oriented applications that have to map information from XML document structures to fixed structures like those found in many database tables may not be as forgiving. A missing element could cause an entire set of updates to be lost. (If the developers didn't provide robust error handling, this could happen silently, or with a violent crash.) Although subsetting is usually easier to support than extensions, making a document structure simpler can create as many difficulties as making it more complex.

Thinking Ahead

Retrofitting current needs on to an older document structure can be an unpleasant task, especially if either the document structures or the application structures weren't designed with future updates in mind. Even if you don't think anyone is ever going to want to modify your "perfect" design, thinking ahead may be worth the small amount of extra effort it costs. Your applications will be better able to cope with different situations, and your document structure may enjoy a much longer life-span than it would have otherwise. The developers who follow you (even if they happen to *be* you) will have a much easier time changing your document structures if you plan ahead for change.

The techniques for creating extensible DTDs discussed in Chapter 20 are appropriate to all kinds of document structure design. Document type definitions don't offer the open models that will likely be available in the next generation of schemata, but leaving spaces in DTDs, using `ANY` or leaving elements undeclared. Storing extra information in attributes, which requires fewer changes to the document structure, is sometimes a useful option, though it may not be capable of supporting structured information. By leaving room to grow from the start, you can reduce the burden on later developers.

Application designers building processing tools for particular document structures should make sure to provide support for information outside the usual framework. "Extra" information may seem as though it has less importance than the normal flow of data, but in many cases that "extra" information is a signal that a particular document is in fact especially important. Applications that read XML documents and rewrite them back in the same format should take precautions to avoid losing information between the reading and rewriting process. (This doesn't apply to transformation applications in general, although data preservation could be important there as well.) Similarly, applications that expect to receive information in a certain structure should be prepared to report in some form—a log file, an e-mail, paging a system administrator—when those expectations aren't met. Applications that crash when presented information in a different form or that fail silently are menaces to developers trying to improve document structures. Planning ahead, and communicating these needs to everyone involved with a document format, can simplify future work even when you don't know what direction it will take.

CHAPTER 32

Maximizing Information Quantity and Quality

XML seems to offer it all—structured, labeled, easily exchanged information. It may not be the most efficient format for exchanging or storing information (it is, after all, a text-based format), but XML has just about every other advantage going for it. XML provides flexibility, processability, and easily documented formats. Developers just need to take advantage of these tools, right? Well, almost. The tools XML provides are only a foundation—the information modeling is left as an exercise for the developer, and this exercise will largely determine whether your XML projects succeed or fail.

Including and Excluding Information

Choosing which information your document format will include is the first step in information modeling. One document type per type of information seems like a good rule, but deciding which information belongs in a set is not always as simple as a requirements document might make it look. XML 1.0's requirement that valid documents include declarations for every element and attribute type used makes it especially important that you decide early on which pieces of information actually belong in your documents. You can leave possibilities open by keeping room for extensions (as discussed in Chapter 20), but relying on extensions has its limitations. You have to define at least a core set of information that is critical and set boundaries that separate other information (which you may be leaving to extenders of your DTD) from the core.

In some cases, your information set is already built. If you're creating a DTD based on a database schema or on a legacy format, the core is usually defined. Modeled information that someone else has already modeled is usually easier than starting from scratch. Even if you aren't happy about the particular way the information was modeled, converting it to XML is often an opportunity to modify the approach without changing the actual data set.

In other cases, you're starting at the beginning, collecting requirements from different users (or, sometimes, making them up yourself.) If you can collect different perspectives on a project, and figure out the minimum core required to support all the participants, you've got a start. Once you have a core, you can present that and collect reactions to evaluate how much additional material you need to support to accommodate particular needs. This part of information modeling may be a formal process done through a large-scale consortium with hundreds of members collecting internal input and presenting it to the group, or it could be a friendly set of meetings over coffee and doughnuts. The most important thing in this phase of document structure development is typically communications, making sure that you haven't missed a critical set of deeply felt needs. Converting those needs to an information set and determining how to represent that information is difficult, but projects without initial boundaries may grow into monsters of enormous and unmanageable proportions. It may be easiest to provide a lot of information in a useful form over the long term by starting with a smaller core set of information and extending that core with additional modules in a controlled way.

Choosing Conventions

In some sense, the very document structures you create are conventions, and "choosing conventions" could be used to describe the entire information modeling process. In a more limited sense, choosing conventions means making sure that the labels you use in your document structures are intelligible to readers not involved in the design process, and that the basic structures you choose are followed throughout. Chapter 30 has already discussed reasons for making conventions consistent, so this section will focus on making conventions useful.

Labels aren't of much use to people and applications that can't understand them. If the label doesn't provide much information, or provides too little information, users may have to throw away the value the label was supposed to describe. (Labels that contain too much information can also be unwieldy.) This point has been raised repeatedly in computing, where labels are often the bridge between the internal representations used by the computer and tools people use to manipulate them, but you still occasionally see real working documents (not just examples describing structures) that look like:

```
<document attribute1="top-secret">
<element1>Critical Information</element1>
<element2><element3>October</element3><element4>31</element4> is
<element5>Halloween</element5>. <element6 attribute1="PBB">We</element6>
are concerned that <element7 attribute1="Pluto">aliens</element7> will
use this holiday to subvert <element8 attribute1="US">our
government</element8> using the cover provided by millions of
trick-or-treaters.</element2>
</document>
```

This intriguing fragment is well-formed XML, and could even have a DTD describing the format and providing more information about what exactly these elements and attributes mean. Given enough of these documents and some spare time, readers could probably figure out that `element1` is a headline, `element2` is a paragraph, `element3` is a month, the `document` element's `attribute1` has something to do with security levels, and so on. You could even build applications and style sheets that operate on these documents, relying on these very simple labels to identify content types.

On the other hand, the document below makes the same document a lot easier for those not versed in information analysis to understand.

```
<warning security="top-secret">
<title>Critical Information</title>
<paragraph><month>October</month><day>31</day> is
<holiday>Halloween</holiday>. <organization acronym="PBB">We
</organization> are concerned that <enemy home="Pluto">aliens</enemy>
will use this holiday to subvert <government acronym="US">our
government</government> using the cover provided by millions of
trick-or-treaters.</paragraph>
</warning>
```

More sophisticated labels and structures are of course possible, but meaningful labels have contributed a lot more information to the document and made it easier to create applications and style sheets appropriate to its content. Even if you adopt the radically flexible approach discussed in Chapter 35, intelligible labels can provide important hints to both processors and people. Labels, and the conventions used to create them, should add to the overall semantic content of a document.

Working Toward Multiple Purposes

The "levels" of markup discussed in Chapter 17 describe a spectrum of possibilities for information modeling, from approaches that focus on describing data to approaches that focus on the use of those data in a particular application. Although an application-specific approach may be useful in many cases, and application-specific vocabularies are undoubtedly a necessary part of the XML family, they often have more limitations than vocabularies that describe data at a higher, more generic, level. If there is a significant chance that the information you are modeling will need to be processed in multiple contexts, you'll need to create a model that balances the needs of those contexts.

That may mean moving to a higher level of abstraction. Instead of describing a menu in a platform-specific or even language-specific way, describe it as a list, identifying the items a user will interact with and describing those items' functionality with simple descriptions rather than tying them to specific function calls that may hold no meaning for other systems. Instead of using the four-letter labels for data from a legacy database system, expand those labels to meaningful descriptions and provide tools for converting that labeled information to and from the database entries. When interchange is important, as described in the next chapter, multiple usage contexts are even more likely, and support for them is critical to the success of your vocabularies.

Choosing a level of abstraction for describing your content can follow a process much like that described above for setting the boundaries of your information set. Survey users to determine the ways in which the information will be used. Explore in particular how those users will be viewing the information, and what capabilities they have for processing different types of labels. Make sure that the level of abstraction you support doesn't favor one group's needs over the rest, and that you choose labels and structures that users can integrate with their applications with no more than a single (hopefully simple) transformation.

Document Your Meanings

As noted in Chapter 22, the labels used for XML document components provide only a certain amount of information. The label `TITLE` is ambiguous, and may even remain ambiguous despite supporting context information. Most languages have significant levels of ambiguity, and the usual tendency toward short labels for XML markup compounds this problem. Even if you aren't concerned about hammering down meanings so precisely that there is no room for error, supporting your labels with an extra layer of description can help other users work with your information. (This applies to both rigorously structured information that requires a DTD and validation and loosely structured information that may not bother with formal structural descriptions.) If you plan to share your information with anyone else, be sure to document the meanings of your labels. It may not resolve all ambiguity or help you avoid writing a more complete set of documentation, but it does make processing your XML easier for everyone, yourself included.

CHAPTER 33

Designing for Large-Scale Interchange

Interchange is what XML is all about—creating standardized formats that use a similar grammar to express different kinds of information so that applications of all kinds can read them. XML makes this dream achievable, building a foundation on which programs on all kinds of different platforms written in all kinds of different languages can build common understanding and share information. Although XML opens the doors to a new world of interchange possibilities, it doesn't automatically enable interchange. Building XML document structures that can be shared by large numbers of users, organizations, and applications requires combining all the work discussed in the context of general XML development with the needs of a large and often divided set of consumers and potential consumers. Creating standards for use in interchange requires your best information modeling skills, your best work in convention creations, your clearest documentation, and the ability to listen to and moderate users of all kinds. Developing interchange standards can be a process as political as it is technical.

Collecting Input

All of the suggestions described in previous chapters for analyzing requirements apply to interchange design, although they may prove more difficult to implement. Collecting input from large numbers of users in multiple organizations, not all of whom may care about your project, can be extremely difficult. It may well take a team of people to make all the necessary contacts, and the members of that team may have different perspectives on the project as well. Simple surveys are rarely enough to collect the materials needed to create a successful interchange format. You may discover along the way that interchange in one area is dependent on interchange in another, and have to expand the scope of your research, or you may find that new users who weren't originally included in your sampling pop up with new ideas and plans for using your structures.

There are a number of ways you can control this chaos without simply shutting out those people whose requirements you're attempting to meet. Sometimes existing interchange standards can provide a stable foundation for your new XML project, and you can leverage the work that's already been done in creating them. Sometimes you can find instances of small-scale interchange, as between two members of a potentially larger community, and model those processes to create an initial test platform. Most interchange standards are intended to pipe information between existing application structures, and you may be able to explore the intended inputs and outputs of these systems so that you can create mappings from your format to the existing structures. Describing your project as a connection mechanism between various systems, rather than expecting it to be the system in itself, can also help you explain the tools you're creating to the keepers of existing systems, and help you focus on the flow of information rather than the demands of particular users.

Managing Expectations

XML has both benefited and suffered from an outlandish amount of hype. Foundation standards rarely receive this kind of press, and XML's generic approach has made it seem like everything to everyone, capable of fulfilling all the needs presented to it. Although XML is maturing into a useful tool for representing a wide variety of information types, it isn't yet the cure-all that many people wish it were. Like Java in the early days, the tools are basic and require plenty of hard work to get good results. As more XML tools reach the market, and as organizations get a better grasp of what "XML development" really looks like, these expectations will probably become more realistic, both because of the tempering they get from experience and because of steady improvement in XML's capabilities.

The implications of this for particular projects are both good and bad. You can take advantage of the hype to get people interested in your project, selling them on the marquee value of XML and the promises it makes for universal interchange. Developers and managers may see it (in 2000, anyway) as a good way to enhance their resume and learn a new technology. On the other hand, you may have to keep people who've read a little bit about XML's promise from thinking that XML will magically solve the problems. XML solves many of the problems, but those that remain are important enough to sink a project that isn't well thought out.

Focus on Meaning

Abstractions are critical in standards designed for interchange, in part because they provide an important area in which different participants can compromise. Using Windows-specific or Java-specific vocabularies on a project that involves interchange between users of both platforms isn't likely to go over well with everyone. Fortunately, these platforms have a lot in common, even if they call things by different names and structure them somewhat differently. To get beyond the religious wars you'll face if you try to force application-specific vocabularies on a project meant for multiple applications, focus on commonalties rather than emphasizing specifics. Describe the data, and not the way it is represented in a particular document presentation, database table, or application structure.

If you can get the participants in a project to agree on names for things—not always easy, but an important first step—you can then use that common vocabulary to plan out structures using those names and more precise descriptions of the contents labeled by those names. Initial agreements may not always hold up and sometimes a compromise provides the worst of both worlds, but finding a common vocabulary, even a fudged vocabulary, can keep a project from getting stuck in the particular visions of its varying participants. If you can keep this process amicable, you may have helped your participants learn to compromise with each other.

XML does provide a significant advantage useful for building compromises and resolving disputes: a strong set of tools for transforming information among formats. Although the promise of an easy transformation to a particularly insistent participant's chosen structures may not be enough to get you through all the conflicts, it can help. Demonstrating such transformations, and actively supporting them, can sometimes sway an otherwise discontented person or organization.

Testing, Testing, Testing

As you hammer out names and especially structures, you'll need to make sure those structures will mesh with the inputs and outputs of the communications process. Although this testing process is common to pretty much all XML vocabulary development, interchange applications often require more and deeper testing than XML vocabularies designed for a single controlled environment. Depending on the nature of your project, you may have enthusiastic participants waiting to get their hands on your specification, or thousands of potential users who have never heard of your project, its requirements, its results, or you.

In either case, you'll need to provide test versions of your document structures and a set of documents that can be used to test conformance in various systems. Conformance testing is rarely the most exciting part of a project, but your users will have no way of knowing how well the system works without extensive processing of a large set of documents. The size of the set of test documents varies widely depending on the size and complexity of the document structures, but it should always include both documents that are supposed to work and documents that aren't supposed to work. Assuming that everyone will send documents that conform to the standard precisely is usually a very bad idea, so testing failures and their impact on receiving applications is critical. Testing the tools that generate XML in your format is similarly important, and you may have to build some kind of validating application that checks generated documents against all the strictures of your specification (not just those in the DTD) to ensure that programmers built the generators correctly.

The testing process typically generates two kinds of results. Some require changes in the XML generators or receivers, while others suggest that the specification needs to be changed. In some cases the specification needs to be clarified to removed dangerous ambiguities, while in others it needs to be loosened to support a wider range of possibilities. Fine-tuning document structures is difficult to do without real-world implementation, and you should always expect the fine-tuning process to take longer than it seems it should.

Communicating Outside XML

Making an XML interchange project work requires a lot of labor that goes well outside the technical responsibilities of DTD design and information modeling. Interchange projects are useless if the people who have to work with them can't figure them out. A perfect data structure that reflects the needs of all participants without too much lost to compromise is a beautiful thing, but a good explanation of what is contained in that structure is needed to make the structure useful. There are many opportunities throughout the design process to create descriptions of your structures and their use, at every phase from requirements to testing. Testing can be a particularly important phase for this kind of communication, as it provides an opportunity to find out how well people can work with your structures as well as how well the structures work.

Politics may not be for everyone, and in an ideal technical world the computers might well communicate without needing constant human intervention. Unfortunately, politics grows in importance as projects and their number of potential users grow in size. Some developers try to avoid politics by keeping design groups small and focused, while others try to maintain more open processes to make sure that the political issues of ownership and inclusion are kept to a minimum. Choosing an appropriate communications strategy will depend on the nature of the project and of the participants. Creating technically good standards is one aspect of a project; creating standards that people want to use is another, often more difficult, aspect.

CHAPTER 34

XML and Data Integration

XML 1.0, wonderful though it is, is primarily a document-oriented format. Its clean structures and relatively simple integration with various kinds of applications have spurred its use in a wide variety of data-intensive applications. Although the basic structures of XML—nested named containers—are a good fit for these applications, the rudimentary vocabulary XML provides for describing the contents of those containers isn't adequate for many of the tasks data applications would like to be able to hand off to an XML processor and forget about. Tools like the data typing conventions described in Chapter 11 and the schema developments discussed in Chapter 29 can help data-oriented developers make good use of XML, but creating complete solutions will take some effort and time.

Documents as Data

XML 1.0 doesn't provide a description of its documents as an "information set," although the ongoing work on an XML Infoset is striving toward that goal. The various tools for processing XML documents, like the SAX and DOM APIs discussed in Chapter 28, use somewhat different (albeit convertible) presentations of document information. The XML 1.0 recommendation's decision to allow non-validating parsers to report a view of a document different (lacking external resources) from what a validating parser reports, and the possibility of namespaces, complicates the data modeling situation even further.

Despite these problems, it isn't very difficult to treat an XML document as a set of labeled data and extract information from that document based on its label and its position in the document tree. By choosing a particular parsing model (validating or non-validating, with or without namespaces) and sticking to it, applications can get a consistent presentation of information, absorb it into their internal structures, and possibly store those internal structures back in XML documents if necessary. Although XML documents are designed to be capable of holding complex, often arbitrary, document structures, applications that want to use them to store data of pretty much any kind can use them for that purpose.

Data as Documents

Storing data in linear XML documents has advantages and disadvantages. The main advantage, as noted repeatedly in this book, is that it's easy to send, store, and process XML documents. However, XML is *not* the ideal format to store information that needs to be retrieved rapidly or randomly. Finding a particular piece of information in an XML document requires starting at the beginning of the document and reading through all the bytes encountered up to at least the point at which the information is found (and possibly the end, if all matches are to be found.) XML can do an excellent job of representing structures like relational database tables and software objects, but it can't provide access to the information it stores in nearly as rapid a manner. For small data sets (like a set of preferences for a particular program) this may be acceptable, but large data sets will be stored in ever longer documents that are difficult to process efficiently.

These disadvantages don't always matter—there are important cases where an application would need to read through every item in a data set to find or present the information it needs. Databases are set up to help applications find the fragments of information they need more rapidly, organizing that information to support speedy retrieval of that information. When information is exchanged between two databases however, or when tables are backed up to a text file and retrieved, the entire data set is going to be explored. In other data-intensive cases like the preferences file described above, the document will be parsed when the application starts and all further operations will be performed on the parsed version of the document, which can be optimized like any other application structure.

As long as a collection of data represents a set of information that can be treated as a unit (or, in some cases, that needs to be treated as a unit), XML documents can be an appropriate format for representing that information. If databases need to move or back up sets of information, they can export it to XML and import back to the native database format when appropriate. If an applications needs access to a complete set of information, it can parse an XML document containing those data and work with the data internally after the parse. XML is only a format used to store information outside the application, for storage or interchange.

Extending XML to Support Data

XML has several important use-cases for data storage, as noted above. Unfortunately, it has very limited mechanisms for describing the data. The few data types provided by XML don't map very well to the needs of most data-intensive applications, requiring those applications to perform validation beyond that provided by XML parsers. Although this can be done, and is done, it would significantly ease the use of XML for data to have validation processes that can handle data type checking as well as the structural checking provided by current XML 1.0 parsers.

There are two possibilities currently open to application developers, both of which still require processing after the initial XML 1.0 parse. The first approach uses the data typing mechanisms described in Chapter 11 or similar mechanisms to provide extra information about content along with the labels and structures returned by the XML parser. Implementing this requires either a filter that sits between a parser and an application and inspects the data, or a tool for checking a given tree structure and reporting on its conformance to the data type information provided. The other possibility moves beyond the DTD entirely, shifting to the schemas discussed in Chapter 29. These schemas can provide both structural and content information for use in data processing, and certain support features (like inheritance) that mesh well with existing application architectures. Again, developers will still need to apply the schema processor as a layer that operates after XML 1.0 parsing is complete, but they may be able to perform more kinds of conformance checking and support features like namespaces.

Middleware Solutions

XML has become a popular tool in the middleware application space. Middleware tools provide a variety of services supporting network interactions, and are commonly used to convert or filter information from one format to another. The ease of processing, filtering, and transforming XML makes it a natural fit for products in this development space. Middleware tools can use XML, often invisibly after the initial setup, to connect different systems. They can work at varying levels of abstraction, hiding complexity behind a simplified interface.

In one situation, a database application that needs to request a table from a different database asks a middleware component to retrieve that table for it; using XML, that middleware component contacts a middleware component for the other database, and makes the request. The middleware that receives the request changes it into a form appropriate to the database holding the table, gets the table, and sends it as XML to the original middleware making the request. That piece of middleware interprets the XML and passes it to the original database application in a form that it can understand, perhaps a SQL query. This particular process is shown below in Figure 34.1.

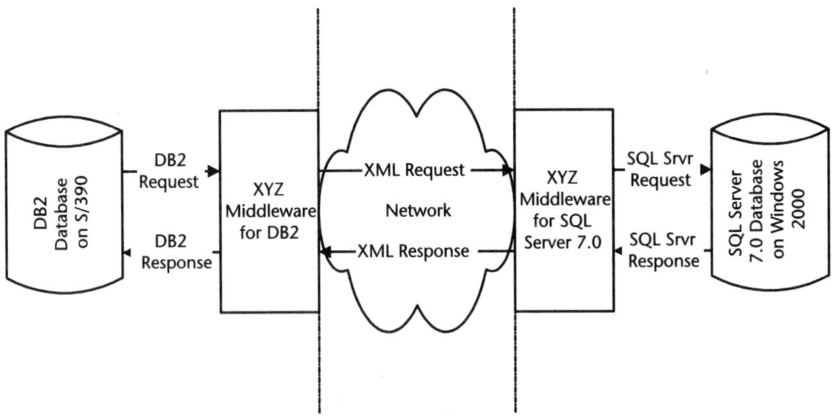

Figure 34.1 Using middleware to ease communication between databases of different types

Using this approach, the database developers on both ends only need to know how to communicate with the middleware. It doesn't matter what kind of database lurks behind the middleware on the other end of the network—the middleware will take care of all mismatches as it converts the requests and responses to and from XML. Similar approaches can be used with a wide variety of applications, between clients and servers as well as between databases.

Moving Forward

A common question about using XML for data exchange is "Is it ready?" If you're waiting for a complete, integrated, and stable set of tools for describing data structures and content the answer is no (in October 1999, anyway). For many purposes, however, the tools available today are up to the task. You can start modeling document structures and datatypes using DTDs and the conventions described in Chapter 11, or you can start using the XML Schemas under development at the W3C and elsewhere in experimental tools. Although these tools may be a bit rough for large-scale deployment, they may be adequate to meet the needs of early adopters, and should be convertible to more "official" solutions when those solutions arrive. (XML Schemas, like other XML documents, are easily transformed to conform to new rules. XML DTDs aren't XML documents, but they are similarly easy to convert.) If you're ready to start modeling your information in XML, XML has the tools you need to do it, although there will be some fine-tuning along the way as the tools mature.

CHAPTER 35

Maximizing Flexibility: Radical Extensibility

After all the discussion elsewhere in this book about creating consistent document structures that are easily processed in standardized ways, and similar undercurrents in most discussions of XML, you might think that creating standard vocabularies is really what XML is all about. Although that is an important part of what XML is for, it is hardly the only possibility. XML provides a foundation grammar for structuring and labeling information, and you don't need to create "official" or "standardized" vocabularies to use XML. It takes a very different set of priorities to go this route, and a somewhat different set of tools, but it is possible. XML's basic structures are strong enough tools for helping applications comprehend the meaning of a document that standardization across organizations and processes may not be necessary the way it has been in the past, and standardization may in fact prevent users from taking full advantage of XML's potential.

Don't Count on Consistency

The threat is that when a company introduces a new document type, no one else will understand it. XML makes it easy for everyone to have their own markup languages. We might therefore see an end to

> the idyllic situation that has prevailed thus far on the Web—the predominance of HTML, which has helped all of us share documents easily. Can it be that, a decade into the Web's existence, XML will give us a freedom that forcibly leads us back toward myriad incompatible languages? This is indeed a serious possibility, but one that has been anticipated.
>
> —Tim Berners-Lee, Director of the W3C, in *Weaving the Web*, page 161.

This fear of anarchy, of recreating the Tower of Babel, has haunted XML throughout its existence. Although SGML provided some form of safety net, requiring all documents to have DTDs, XML's provisions for well-formedness open the doors to creating new vocabularies on the fly without so much as pondering an overall structure. Anyone who wants to can create documents in any vocabulary, without bothering with a DOCTYPE declaration. The only foundation XML demands is well-formedness, adherence to a basic set of rules regarding the type and placement of markup that ensure a neatly named hierarchical structure. Consistency in structures, if it is desired, has to be created and enforced by a separate set of processes.

The floodgate that Tim Berners-Lee goes on to propose is XML Namespaces. Apparent he expects that these identifiers will connect to schemas or further information about the document type as described in Chapter 25. Namespaces are, in fact, a powerful tool for managing this anarchy, but they may encourage it rather than contain it, allowing it to work more smoothly than it might have otherwise. Because namespaces, according to the Namespaces in XML recommendation, are merely identifiers, they can be used to enforce both consistency on a large scale—standards built with schemas by industry consortia and smaller organizations—and on a very small scale—the kinds of informal conventions that govern how most people talk, for instance. Namespaces make it just as easy to identify personal vocabularies as it is to identify standardized vocabularies.

Standardized vocabularies demand that their users conform to those vocabularies, while personal vocabularies require only that writers and readers understand them. Standardized vocabularies are often expressed formally, as DTDs or schemas, and the temptation to hammer down single "true" interpretations often leads to long development processes. Personal vocabularies are rarely expressed formally, and have far more in common with natural languages even in cases where they are expressed using a formal grammar like XML. Personal vocabularies are changeable, requiring only an informal network of contacts to explain modifications that readers can't understand.

Why has there been so much emphasis on standardization and consistency in XML if personal vocabularies offer so much flexibility? In some part, at least, the fear of anarchy still presides in large parts of the computing environment. Various technologies that focused on flexibility rather than predictability have faced resistance throughout the history of computing. The packet-based switching that provides the backbone for the Internet was initially scoffed at by engineers with years of experience in circuit switching who didn't believe that the flexible rules for fragmenting and directing information could possibly compete with the simplicity and availability of a complete circuit connecting two points directly. Similarly, HTML's loose rules for describing hypertext links, and the many possibilities they opened for broken links, disturbed hypertext theorists who preferred more controllable closed systems with centralized link management.

Standardization has also been a critical aspect of getting information into and out of computers, converting the blizzard of information in the "real world" to a readily understood stream of information stored on computer systems. Information modeling is in large part a process of converting information from the varied forms that people see to a simplified form that computers can manage and understand easily. Creating unique identifiers, assigning structures, and reducing ambiguity have been critical tools for simplifying information into forms that computers with limited memory and processing power are capable of working with at the speeds we humans demand. If computers could handle natural languages more easily, many of these issues would be moot, and XML itself might disappear. As it stands, XML can provide a key set of tools so that users can move closer to personal vocabularies without making all the demands required by natural language processing.

Machine Reading

XML provides a solid set of structures that computers can learn (more likely, be taught) to recognize. Labels and structures together provide recognizable information that computers can use to convert information from the material they are fed into their own internal structures for additional processing. The easiest applications to write are those built to handle a single set of labels and structures, but these aren't very useful when forced to cope with a different set of structures. XML DTDs provided a limited range of flexibility, with features like optional and repeatable content models, but that limited range isn't very difficult to write into single-minded applications.

Building more flexible systems means planning pathways from input to internal structures (and often from those internal structures to output) that can be modified to accommodate different circumstances. In some cases, the application itself may be able to create new and different pathways, and in other cases human intervention may be required to create those pathways. Either case requires application developers to trust potentially unreliable algorithms or users. Building this trust is harder, in many ways, than building the applications. Having spent years pulling information processing away from unreliable human factors, and given the reputation of algorithms for understanding irregular information, many application developers may face cultural barriers to this approach that are greater than the technological barriers. On the other hand, people doing real jobs in the real world are often assigned responsibility, and corrected when and if something goes wrong—why should this be any different? (It's all right to be nervous about this.)

Plan for Change

Unlike standardized vocabularies, where extensions are often treated as ignorable and changing versions can incur enormous costs, systems that rely on personal vocabularies have to be prepared to support variations. Variations, as Walter Perry pointed out in his editorial at XML Developer Days '99 (**http://metalab.unc.edu/bosak/conf/xmldev99/perry/1.htm**), often indicate that something critically important is happening outside the ordinary transactions that computers can handle easily. When something changes, it doesn't necessarily mean that a document is "wrong" and should be quietly rejected—instead, it may mean that document represents something new and different that needs to be addressed. Some of that work can be handled by automated processors, and some of it may mean that human intervention is needed to teach the application how to handle a new situation. Working with unconstrained vocabularies means that you need to be ready to handle exceptions on a regular basis, and to treat exceptions as a normal part of processing rather than a specialized error-handling behavior.

Model Jobs, Not Data

Personal (or, more likely, role-based) vocabularies allow people to create descriptions of the information they work with that fit their perception of the information. Shipping clerks have a different perspective on information than do accountants, while customers and CEOs have their own perspectives. As long as a consistent description of the parts of the transaction needed by each user is available, there is no need for a shipping clerk to see credit card information, or for a CEO to read through 1,500 orders for different types of widgets to understand the sales figures for a given day.

A workflow approach, where different senders use different vocabularies, can reduce some of these problems. Namespaces can help identify these vocabularies, as shown below, or users can keep track of the origins of messages to interpret their vocabularies. A customer placing an order for goods could send an initial request that read like:

```
<order xmlns="mailto:joe@consumer.com" vendor="example.com">
<customer>
<name>Joe Consumer</name>
<address1>123 Doe Lane</address1>
<city>Myville</city> <state>CA</state> <zip>94111</zip>
</customer>
<goods>
<shoes size="8" style="XYZ" quantity="2" unitPrice="$19.95"/>
<shirt collar="16" sleeve="32" style="BDLS" color="blue" unit-
Price="$27.00"/>
</goods>
<shipping delivery="overnight"/>
<payment type="Credit card" number="1234 4567 8910 1234" exp="08/99" />
</order>
```

If an automated processor receiving this order couldn't figure out needed information—does the credit card bill to Joe's address?—it could always send a reply to Joe asking him to provide additional information, and keep that information around for future reference in case Joe placed an additional order at a later date. By storing information about previous transactions, a processor could build maps for converting assorted formats, even hundreds of formats, to its internal format.

The warehouse might get a message from that processor that looks like:

```
<order xmlns="http://example.com/orders/warehouse" id="1999092012482">
<ship-to>
<name>Joe Consumer</name>
<address1>123 Doe Lane</address1>
<city>Myville</city> <state>CA</state> <zip>94111</zip>
</ship-to>
<goods>
<item aisle="10" shelf="8XY" quantity="2"/>
<item aisle="15" shelf="7AC" quantity="1" />
</goods>
<shipping delivery="FedExPM"/>
</order>
```

The warehouse would retrieve the shirts and shoes, package them, and ship them. The purchasing department for the company could be informed of the change in inventory with a message like:

```
<inventory xmlns="http://example.com/warehouse" id="1999092012482">
<item aisle="10" shelf="8XY" adjust="-2" />
<item aisle="15" shelf="7AC" adjust="-1" />
</inventory>
```

The warehouse might also might send a message to accounting that looked like:

```
<order xmlns="http://example.com/warehouse" id="1999092012482">
<shipped status="complete" date="19990921" />
</order>
```

Accounting could combine this with the message from the orders department, shown below, and bill Joe's credit card.

```
<order xmlns=" http://example.com/warehouse/receivable" >
<bill-to>
<name>Joe Consumer</name>
<address1>123 Doe Lane</address1>
<city>Myville</city> <state>CA</state> <zip>94111</zip>
</bill-to>
<total>$91.34</total>
<payment type="Credit card" number="1234 4567 8910 1234" exp="08/99" />
</order>
```

Once accounts receivable had done that, they could create similar messages that informed the accounting department of the transaction to create more general information that reflected the company's financial standards.

This can grow into much more sizable webs of information flow, using various mechanisms to describe information. A centrally administered database could still be an important part of this system, or information could be stored in local storage for particular users, depending on the model the company felt was more cost-effective. Creating these pathways requires development effort, but once they've been established, the vocabularies used to describe a transaction can be specific to particular pathways. No "grand view" describing the entire transaction is necessary.

Build Up Your Toolset

Creating these pathways means using tools that can accept and transmit XML information in a very flexible way. Transformation is a critical piece of this puzzle, even if vocabularies remain fairly stable for long periods of time. Expressing those transformations in ways easy for humans to understand without a familiarity with transformation vocabularies remains a difficult project, one that may have to wait for developers to create a workable interface. Breaking down transactions into pathways requires workflow analysis, which may itself be difficult, but supporting multiple vocabularies along those pathways means giving users the tools to create and manage vocabularies instead of creating everything for them in a fixed application. The tools currently available for creating and editing XML documents aren't well suited to this kind of approach, so it may require creating your own tools or participating in the creation of such tools.

Moving Toward an Adaptable Web

Although the tools that would let users express their needs in their own vocabularies and interpret messages sent by other users are currently primitive, this model may be appropriate for circumstances that demand more flexibility than can be extracted from relatively slow-moving collaborative design processes. Design practices that focus on the creation of single vocabularies are appropriate to certain circumstances, but can't address every need. By treating schemas as tools for describing structures rather than tools for making structures conform, developers can create systems that adapt to changing circumstances rather than ones that address a particular set of requirements laid down at the beginning of the design process.

Anarchic vocabularies are unmanageable if you don't have the right tools, are afraid of your users, and aren't used to thinking of transformation as a regular part of life. If formal vocabularies feel like straitjackets, limiting your possibilities while restraining you from injuring yourself, moving to a less constrained approach may let you take full advantage of XML's extensibility. It won't be the easiest route, at least at present, and it will require changing your perspective on many fundamental computing issues, but it may prove an effective way to create systems that users can manage themselves. Finding the right balance between anarchy and restraint is difficult and often controversial. Both approaches can incur real costs—the price of training and trusting users and the price of making upgrades to inflexible systems as needs change. Developers should explore both options before settling on a particular approach.

Index

Note: Boldface numbers indicate illustrations.

F

O

P

T

Z

ABOUT THE AUTHOR

Simon St.Laurent is a web developer, network administrator, and XML troubleshooter. He has authored several books, including *XML: A Primer*, *Building XML Applications*, *Cookies*, and *Inside XML DTDs: Scientific and Technical*.